ELIZABETH MANNING HAWTHORNE

ELIZABETH MANNING HAWTHORNE

A Life in Letters

Edited and with an Introduction by
CECILE ANNE DE ROCHER

THE UNIVERSITY OF ALABAMA PRESS

Tuscaloosa

Designer: Michele Myatt Quinn
Typeface: AGaramond and Voluta Script

∞

The paper on which this book is printed meets the minimum
requirements of American National Standard for Information
Sciences-Permanence of Paper for Printed Library Materials,
ANSI Z39.48-1984.

Library of Congress Cataloging-in-Publication Data

Hawthorne, Elizabeth Manning, 1802–1883.
  [Correspondence. Selections]
  Elizabeth Manning Hawthorne : a life in letters / edited and with
an introduction by Cecile Anne de Rocher.
      p. cm.
  Includes bibliographical references and index.
  ISBN-13: 978-0-8173-1498-9 (alk. paper)
  ISBN-10: 0-8173-1498-9 (alk. paper)
  1. Hawthorne, Elizabeth Manning, 1802–1883—Correspondence.
2. Authors, American—19th century—Family relationships.
3. Hawthorne, Nathaniel, 1804–1864—Correspondence. 4. Authors,
American—19th century—Correspondence. 5. Hawthorne,
Nathaniel, 1804–1864—Family. 6. Salem (Mass.)—Social life and
customs. 7. Hawthorne family. I. De Rocher, Cecile Anne. II. Title.
  PS1881.A42 2006
  813'.3—dc22

                                                    2005019253

Contents

Acknowledgments

I would like to express my gratitude to those who helped make this book.

The staffs at the following libraries have given me access to their manuscripts: the Hawthorne-Longfellow Library at Bowdoin College; the Phillips Library at the Peabody-Essex Museum; the New York Public Library; the Huntington Library; the Beinecke Library at Yale University; the Bancroft Library at the University of California–Berkeley; and the Boston Public Library. I especially thank curators Richard H. F. Lindemann, Roberta Zonghi, Irene Axelrod, and Pat Willis.

Many people at Georgia State University made my research possible. The university, the College of Arts and Sciences, and the Department of English, with their grants and assistantship, lent much institutional and financial support, as did the administrative acumen of Marta Hess and Tammy Mills. I thank Reiner Smolinski, Robert Sattelmeyer, and Jan Gabler-Hover for giving me courage in seeking publication.

At my new home institution, Dalton State College, I have enjoyed the support of my colleagues in the Division of Humanities and of the staff at the Derrell C. Roberts Library.

I have had the pleasure to work with Daniel Waterman, humanities acquisitions editor at the University of Alabama Press.

Margaret B. Moore, herself an Elizabeth Hawthorne scholar, has lent me personal support and with her book *The Salem World of Nathaniel Hawthorne* has enabled me to enrich my own work.

Finally, I thank my family and friends: my mother and father, academicians themselves, who never asked what madness I had undertaken and never hesitated to write checks; my brothers, who understand long projects; and Jillian Terry and Jason Whitt, departmental elves, cheerful presences, and motivators.

Chronology

1801	Nathaniel Hathorne and Elizabeth Clarke Manning marry*
1802	Elizabeth Manning Hawthorne born in Salem, Massachusetts
1804	Nathaniel Hawthorne born
1808	Maria Louisa Hawthorne born
	Elder Nathaniel Hathorne dies
	Elizabeth Clarke Manning Hathorne moves to the Manning home in Salem
1817	Priscilla Manning and John Dike marry
1821	Nathaniel Hawthorne enrolls at Bowdoin College in Brunswick, Maine
1825	Nathaniel Hawthorne graduates and returns to the Manning home
1836	Nathaniel Hawthorne and Elizabeth Manning Hawthorne edit *American Magazine of Useful and Entertaining Knowledge* and write *Peter Parley's Universal History*
1842	Nathaniel Hawthorne and Sophia Peabody marry
1844	Una Hawthorne born
1846	Julian Hawthorne born
1849	Elizabeth Clarke Manning Hawthorne dies
1850	Elizabeth Manning Hawthorne moves to Montserrat, north of Salem
1851	Rose Hawthorne born
1852	Maria Louisa Hawthorne dies
1864	Nathaniel Hawthorne dies
1865	Richard C. Manning and Elizabeth Yeaton Gould marry
1867	Richard C. Manning Jr. born
1868	Hawthorne family moves to Dresden, Germany
1869	Samuel Cole dies
	Rebecca Dodge Burnham Manning of North Salem dies
1870	Julian Hawthorne and Mary Albertina Amelung marry

* Before the young Nathaniel changed it, the name was originally spelled "Hathorne." The newer, more familiar spelling, "Hawthorne," has been used throughout the text, except here in the chronology and in the early letters.

1871   Sophia Peabody Hawthorne dies
       John Dike dies
       Rose Hawthorne and George Parsons Lathrop marry
1873   Priscilla Manning Dike dies
1876   Harriet Cole dies
1877   Una Hawthorne dies
1883   Elizabeth Manning Hawthorne dies in Beverly, Massachusetts
1894   Elizabeth Palmer Peabody dies
1926   Rose Hawthorne dies
1934   Julian Hawthorne dies

Preface

Most people have never heard of Elizabeth Hawthorne. Readers with an interest in her brother, Nathaniel, hear of her as a dark, lovely figure, the analog for Hester Prynne in *The Scarlet Letter,* and know of the three little Hawthorne children who went to live with their mother's family after their father's death at sea. These same readers know of the closeness between Nathaniel and his older sister; of Elizabeth's intelligence; of her informal, deep learning; and of her solitary ways. But Elizabeth deserves closer study in her own right, not as the sister of an important novelist, but as the author of a huge corpus of letters that spans seven decades in young America's fascinating nineteenth century. Although Elizabeth's letters were meant only to correspond with her family, they also serve to capture happenings in Salem, in New England, in the nation, and on the international scene. Many of these letters survive, recording events in the Hawthorne-Manning family, episodes of the Civil War, and the literature and issues of the day, all seen in present tense and on a personal scale. Few works that are so extensive, so insightful, and so well written exist, and only now has an edition of Elizabeth Manning Hawthorne's letters seen publication.

Many readers underestimate the difficulty in reconstructing any human life from text. However common and important an exercise, to make a psyche into a consumable product imposes an ulterior structure on its subject and does it a well-intentioned violence. Researching the life and work of a nineteenth-century woman who has been rarely examined and frequently overlooked presents a particular set of difficulties. If she is the sister of the young Republic's foremost romancer, what little information about her exists may be presented largely in relation to him and his development, his oeuvre, and his legacy. If her body of written work is a large set of widely scattered, edited, excised, sometimes fragmentary letters that span most of her lifetime, they must be reunited, dated, and annotated so that they furnish a departure point for biographic study. Such is the case with Elizabeth Manning Hawthorne, and this study of her life was made with such obstacles looming. These difficulties, though, while they may frustrate attempts at biography and leave room for much unsubstantiable conjecture, also create a method for gathering and evaluating material with which to write about Elizabeth Hawthorne's own life and work.

In the early stages of this project, gleaning biographical material from works written on Nathaniel Hawthorne sufficed, as nearly all biographies include Elizabeth's life dates, her role in her brother's courtship of Sophia Peabody, variable accounts of her contribution to her brother's hack work, and her eventual withdrawal to Beverly, Massachusetts, where she died at the age of eighty. Indeed, this biographical project provides an opportunity to reexamine and reevaluate materials that scholars have long used, and perhaps misused, to study the Hawthorne family. Very few articles, none recent, and no books treat Elizabeth Hawthorne as their central subject, although most biographies or genealogical studies have provided some information on her in the course of illuminating her brother's life.

Among the most famous such biographies is Julian Hawthorne's two-volume work *Nathaniel Hawthorne and His Wife,* first published in 1884. Written partly from Julian's own memoirs and supplemented with edited, selected letters and anecdotes from those who were close to his father, the book is the work of an insider, an interested party. And although the work contains useful information, and indeed has served Hawthorne scholars for over one hundred years, readers must question its value as a source of unbiased information. Vernon Loggins fills his *The Hawthornes: The Story of Seven Generations of an American Family,* published in 1951, with vibrant, colorful vignettes of family life. Narrated as if by a participant, or at least a sharp observer, the work incorporates novelistic techniques into a study situating Nathaniel Hawthorne in a family chronology that begins with the Massachusetts Bay Colony and ends in the early twentieth century. However, while it is a pleasure to read, Loggins's book does not make sources clear or retrievable. His acknowledgment page mentions the Essex Institute, now the Peabody-Essex Museum, and the bibliographic information lists several titles that are relevant to Elizabeth Hawthorne, but leaves specific pieces of information uncited. Of course Loggins, writing in the 1940s, operated under different research and documentation conventions than writers of today, but in keeping his citations general he necessarily casts doubt on the rigor of his biographic method and the accuracy of his source materials. Those who are familiar with the Hawthorne materials housed in various manuscript collections will recognize certain details that Loggins provides, but may wonder how he knows the minds of such anonymous or long-dead figures as Elizabeth's prospective suitors, who apparently "found her cold, hard, and painfully proud" (230). Perhaps most disturbing is Loggins's bibliographic note: "In collecting details for the portraits of Hawthorne and his mother and sisters I depended [in part] on . . . *Hawthorne's First Diary,* ed. Samuel T. Pickard (Boston, 1897). Though this little book was withdrawn from circulation when the editor discovered that it was not wholly authentic, I drew from it details which *fit into the pattern* of what is definitely known concerning Hawthorne's boyhood" (348, emphasis added).

Some of what Loggins elected to use, then, may be fictitious but plausible, and although Pickard writes very little about Elizabeth and nothing except what appears in Nathaniel's own correspondence, his work also shifts suspicion onto Loggins. Some of Loggins's descriptions of Elizabeth, reproduced here to represent a maximal number of sources and angles, also function to call attention to the unfortunate paucity of reliable, specific information about her.

A fairly recent Hawthorne biography, Edwin Haviland Miller's "*Salem Is My Dwelling Place": A Life of Nathaniel Hawthorne* (1991), is also a product of its author's own times. Carefully documented and displaying a skepticism and psychological method to which contemporary readers have become accustomed, this biography delves into Nathaniel Hawthorne's mind and diagnoses the patient as chronically depressed, neurotic, and a latent homosexual. These views on the romancer, widely held and not groundless, may represent the vogue in biography, but they focus on Nathaniel, not Elizabeth. Like most Hawthorne biographers, Brenda Wineapple, author of the masterful *Hawthorne: A Life* (2003), portrays Elizabeth as a shadowy, tangential figure.

Philip Young, who argues that incestuous themes in Nathaniel Hawthorne's work suggest his unusual relationship with Elizabeth, describes events of the Hawthorne children's lives that he considers significant to his hypothesis, but *Hawthorne's Secret: An Untold Tale* (1984), although useful for her characterization, is by no means a chronicle of Elizabeth's life. Gloria Erlich's *Family Themes and Hawthorne's Fiction: The Tenacious Web* (1984) also includes much information, but treats Nathaniel's writing, not Elizabeth's. Another recent book, Margaret B. Moore's *The Salem World of Nathaniel Hawthorne* (1998), studies the romancer's hometown. Four articles have proved useful in illuminating Elizabeth's character and writing: Manning Hawthorne's "Aunt Ebe" (1947), Raymona E. Hull's "'Aunt Ebe'" (1978), Jane Stanbrough's entry in Lina Mainiero and Langdon Lynne Faust's *American Women Writers* (1980), and Margaret B. Moore's "Elizabeth Manning Hawthorne" (1994). Also of note is Nina Baym's "Nathaniel Hawthorne and His Mother: A Biographical Speculation" (1982), published in *American Literature*. The manuscript collection of the Bancroft Library contains an unpublished piece, "My Aunt Elizabeth Hawthorne: A Character Sketch," written by Julian Hawthorne, who may have intended to include it in his *Memoirs of Julian Hawthorne* (1938), edited by his widow, Edith Garrigues Hawthorne. This sketch does not appear in the *Memoirs,* although the form and length of the essay match those of the sections in the book.

For material written by or about Elizabeth Hawthorne, the present study moved to the libraries that house her letters: the Peabody-Essex Museum in Salem, Massachusetts; the Hawthorne-Longfellow Library at Bowdoin College; the Berg Collection at New York Public Library; the Bancroft Library at the University of California–Berkeley; the Beinecke Library at Yale; Boston Public Library; and the Huntington Library. These centers contain the evidence to support the premise that Elizabeth Manning Hawthorne deserves study in her own right.

This project has proved difficult; the information reconstructed from letters, fragments, and details that have never appeared together in a single document have made this collection an exercise in patience and perseverance. The selective transcription by Elizabeth's second cousin Richard Manning Jr. further complicates the reconstruction process. But a study of Elizabeth Manning Hawthorne's lifetime of letters will make for better understanding of lives and letters in nineteenth-century New England and in the United States, and of Elizabeth's own writing life, making a work of this kind overdue and completely timely.

ELIZABETH MANNING HAWTHORNE

Introduction

Boston, the center of a new nation's intellectual life, neighbored a bustling town with a long, dark history. Indeed, mention of Salem even in the early nineteenth century conjured up ghosts of Puritan theocracy and horrifying witch hunts, of a new Jerusalem gone amiss in the face of human fallibility and inexpressible hardship. But the women at their needlework in animated sewing circles and the men who talked all manner of politics as horses clopped by rarely spoke of those times. At the busy port and all over the young country, the nineteenth century dawned and the federal United States grew larger and moved faster than anyone could have guessed. The American Renaissance, centered in New England, would soon begin, occasioning the ungainly, innovative, self-conscious, and exuberant literary adolescence of the United States.

Elizabeth Manning Hawthorne was born in 1802 on a day most scholars identify as the seventh of March, little more than seven months after the August 2, 1801, marriage of her parents, Nathaniel Hawthorne and Elizabeth Clarke Manning. Vernon Loggins remarks that in a seventeenth-century Puritan colony, a birth so soon after a marriage would have sent the parents for interrogation before a local magistrate such as William Hawthorne himself (201). Baby Elizabeth, of course, came from the same long line of infamous Hawthornes who would find their way into her brother Nathaniel's consciousness: William, the stern founding member of the Massachusetts Bay Colony, and his son John, a judge at the Salem witch trials. The family would keep the older spelling of their name, "Hathorne," until Nathaniel changed it to "Hawthorne," a move that his mother and sisters would adopt as well. The Mannings, Elizabeth's maternal family, also had a long, sometimes notorious heritage in New England and in Salem, perhaps most notably the conviction of Margaret and Anstice Manning on charges of incest with their brother Nicholas in 1691 (Loggins 89; Young 125). Little Elizabeth's paternal grandfather, Daniel Hawthorne, had been a seaman, like most eighteenth-century men in his family, and her grandmother, Rachel Phelps, was now widowed. Her maternal grandmother, Miriam Lord, and grandfather, Richard Manning, a carriage-line owner and former blacksmith, lived on Herbert Street, behind the Hawthornes' house on Union Street in Salem.

As a young wife and mother, Elizabeth Clarke Manning Hawthorne lived with her mother-in-law and sisters-in-law, an arrangement not only common in the period, but also convenient because Captain Nathaniel Hawthorne earned a hard living and worked at sea. The two young people spent little time together in their six and a half years of marriage: Nina Baym sets the couple's time as a family at less than seven months (9), but Loggins's chronology suggests a total of nearly three years between their marriage in 1801 and the captain's death in 1808 (200–04). A ship's run could last a few months or a year and a half, and periods spent at home, from a few weeks up to a year, followed Hawthorne's sailings. The elder Nathaniel first saw his daughter, later nicknamed "Ebe," when she was a year old, for he had set sail four months after their August wedding and stayed away until 1803. Little Nathaniel, called "Natty," born in 1804, also arrived while his father was away, and the last child, Maria Louisa, often simply called "Louisa," was born in 1808, shortly before word of Captain Hawthorne's death arrived.

Many sailors of the period died at sea, and the Hawthorne family lost many men. The elder Captain Daniel Hawthorne, fortunate to have survived, had retired to his home after a long career in shipping. After his own peaceful death, both of his sons, Daniel and Nathaniel, would perish within four years of each other. Captain Nathaniel Hawthorne died of malaria in Surinam during the winter of 1808, and Mrs. Hawthorne, Loggins notes, may not have known of her widowhood until his ship, the *Nabby,* sailed home to Salem in April (206). Elizabeth recollected in a letter to her niece Una years later: "[O]ne morning my mother called my brother into her room . . . and told him that his father was dead" (November 12, 1865). This singular event would change the course of the family's life: as was also common in the period, Mrs. Hawthorne would move back to her girlhood home with the children, who would now grow up supervised by their mother's siblings in the Manning home on Salem's Herbert Street. Baym suggests in "Nathaniel Hawthorne and His Mother" that a coldness existed between Mrs. Hawthorne and her husband's family because of Elizabeth's untimely birth and argues that this sentiment had something to do with the move back to the Manning home (8–10), but Loggins describes the move rather as "the sensible course" for a family now forced to live dependently. The late captain's sister Mary Forrester already supported the widow and unmarried daughters of the elder Captain Daniel Hawthorne, and life in the affluent Manning family must have seemed an attractive alternative to the home that, touched by many deaths and shriveled prospects, "could not have been gay" (199, 210).

"After the loss of our father we lived with our Grandfather and Grandmother Manning, where there were four uncles and four aunts, all for many years unmarried, so that we were welcome in the family," Elizabeth recalled in a letter to James T. Fields, her brother's publisher and friend. In response to the suggestion that the children were "very strictly brought up," she writes, "I do not remember much constraint, except that we were required to pay some regard to Sunday, which was a day of amusement to most of the people" (December 1870). Other letters written by Elizabeth suggest a more complex, and more genuine, familial relationship when they portray the Mannings alternately as critical of and attentive to her, as capable of "open rebuke" and of "a great deal of solicitude" (May 1822). Hawthorne biographers seem to agree that the extended-family living arrangement, no doubt like all such households, both strained and relieved those involved, particularly the three Hawthorne children. Loggins believes that most relatives in the Manning household—Grandfather Richard and Richard Jr., Maria, Priscilla, Robert, William, and Samuel—were good to the children, but he describes the grandmother, Miriam Lord, and the eldest aunt, Mary, as embittered by disappointment and harsh to their young charges (217–18). Thomas Woodson agrees, describing Mary Manning as "a devout Calvinist, strict with children, and parsimonious like her mother," but also credits her with encouraging her nephew's reading and with paying for part of his education (12). Margaret B. Moore disagrees with these scholars, noting evidence suggesting that the thrifty Mrs. Manning simply dealt responsibly with money and that Mary Manning was purposeful but cheerful (*Salem* 57). Biographers gathered the extant material on the Manning family from various sources and intended to study Nathaniel Hawthorne's childhood and his fiction, but like any records, these often fail to capture the depth of human life and personality. No single source of information on the Manning family, including Elizabeth Hawthorne, is likely baseless, but any such information merits scrutiny.

The Mannings, a prosperous, upwardly mobile middle-class family with a carriage-line business and a work ethic that the market rewarded, could enjoy relative wealth, but as former artisans, belonged to a lower social class than the poorer branches of the old, venerable Hawthorne line that the children represented. Ironically, the move made for a drop in social class but a rise in economic means, and the new household, crowded and bustling with activity, must have posed a striking contrast to the home that the children had left only a few yards away.

Biographical accounts of Mrs. Hawthorne's life in her family home vary.

Julian Hawthorne wrote descriptions of her provided by his aunt Elizabeth Peabody into the biography of his father, *Nathaniel Hawthorne and His Wife* (1884) and, Baym argues, established the traditional view of Mrs. Hawthorne as a recluse (6). Julian Hawthorne wrote, "[F]rom an exaggerated, almost Hindoo-like construction of the law of seclusion which the public taste of the day imposed upon widows, she withdrew entirely from society, and permitted the habit of solitude to grow upon her to such a degree that she actually remained a strict hermit to the end of her long life, or for more than forty years after Captain Hawthorne's death" (4–5). In Julian Hawthorne's opinion, then, his grandmother distorted, misunderstood, or abused the conventions of widowhood and overreacted by sequestering herself away from all people, even from her own children, who had "no opportunity to know what social intercourse meant; [whose] peculiarities and eccentricities were at least negatively encouraged; [and who] grew to regard themselves as something apart from the general world" (5). He thought it miraculous that the children emerged reasonably sane and healthy from such a home.

Elizabeth Peabody, a contemporary and neighbor of the Hawthorne children, wrote years later about her recollections of the same local opinion of Elizabeth Clarke Manning Hawthorne. As noted above, Peabody seems to be the source of Julian Hawthorne's description, one he could not write by himself, having been a small child when his grandmother died in 1849. Peabody's account seems to suggest a popular perception of the widow, but it was written in 1885, many years after her own childhood and long after Mrs. Hawthorne's death. "I . . . remember how warmly used to be discussed the peculiarity of the widow Hawthorne who had shut herself up after her husband's death and made it the habit of her life never to sit down at a table[,] but always eat her meals above in the chamber she never left. For this, she was constantly criticized and condemned by the neighbors, including connections of the family, whom she would not see" (418). But when Mrs. Elizabeth Palmer Peabody came on invitation to visit, she reportedly found Mrs. Hawthorne "a most intelligent, well read, and lively woman" (419). Indeed, Mrs. Hawthorne may have secluded herself selectively, possibly to avoid social situations that did not suit her. Furthermore, she was once again a newcomer in a family she had left and who had continued without her, a situation perhaps making her a peripheral figure when she returned. What does seem clear is that although the Hawthorne children had no father, neither did they live in a home headed by their mother. The sudden change from the Hawthorne house, the shock of their father's death, and the variety of relations and temperaments with which they were now obliged to integrate themselves surely made for a close immediate family and a long adjustment period, and, in Edwin Miller's opinion, forged a bond "perhaps too close for the emotional well-being of all concerned" (33). With Ebe, Natty, and Louisa the only youngsters in a large family of adults, the traditional ratios of older to younger were reversed: more than three adults could monitor each of the three children. These numerous adult-child relationships made the Hawthorne children perhaps the most attended, but perhaps also the most supervised, of any youth in Salem.

"[T]he public schools were not good," Elizabeth wrote years later to her niece Una, and so the Hawthorne children went to some of Salem's many private schools (November 23, 1865). Arlin Turner believes that the family sent Elizabeth, age six, and Nathaniel, age three, to school only a few days after learning of their father's death, because their grief-stricken mother could not cope with them (*Biography* 19). Sister and brother studied first together with Elizabeth Carlton, a schoolmistress in Salem (Moore, "Elizabeth" 1), after which time Nathaniel studied at a private academy under Joseph Emerson Worcester, a famous lexicographer, and then at boarding school in Stroudwater, near Portland, Maine (Loggins 221, 232). He later went on to study at Samuel Archer's school in Salem, and finally with Benjamin Oliver, an attorney who prepared him for the entrance examinations at Bowdoin College in Brunswick, Maine (*CE* XV 113, 117).

Elizabeth studied under various schoolmistresses in Salem. Loggins writes that Elizabeth must not have attended the refined girls' classes run by Mrs. Elizabeth Palmer Peabody in the two-room school housed in the Peabody home, because "an education without such frills as drawing, music, and French was considered adequate [to the elder Mannings]" (221). Moore, however, writes that Elizabeth's teachers, besides Mrs. Peabody, included William P. Cranch and Amelia Palmer Curtis, who was Mrs. Peabody's sister ("Elizabeth" 1). Indeed, Elizabeth Peabody the younger explains in a letter that around 1810 her mother "had given up keeping school to her sister Amelia" and that Ebe came to study there (418). Evaluating Elizabeth's performance, Mrs. Curtis wrote that her pupil showed "exactness in learning" and "amiable manners" (qtd. in Moore, "Elizabeth" 1). Herself a classmate, the young Elizabeth Peabody recalled being impressed with eight-year-old Ebe's reading ability and intellect. "[T]old that the smart little Elizabeth was a bookworm, [my mother] took the occasion to write to Mrs. Hawthorne a note to ask her if she would allow Elizabeth to come to our house to be taught . . . Mrs. Hawthorne was so much touched by the note that she . . . complied with her request . . . (But my

youthful admiration for the astonishing learning of Elizabeth reacted to dis-
courage me who had no power of utterancy at all—at that time)" (418–19).

Furthermore, Elizabeth Hawthorne's youthful letters show that she liked to
read, enjoyed school, and wrote skillfully. Her family saw her as an apt pupil:
knowing that she took an interest in astronomy, her uncle Robert Manning
teased in a letter, "[M]y dear when will the next Eclipse take place, can you tell,
how many stars is there, what is the moon made of, all these things you must
learn before you will be a female Newton" (qtd. in Stewart 4). Well-suited to
learning and exceptionally well-educated, especially for a girl of the period,
Elizabeth read, wrote, and studied on her own after about age thirteen, when
her formal education ended. Her independent scholarship formed one of her
principal occupations in youth and, as the letters show, in adulthood.

Loggins writes that Elizabeth and Nathaniel, whom he describes as "a queer
pair," must have been difficult adolescents for their family to understand and
manage. Eerily recalling the adult Hawthorne's annoyance with the "damned
mob of scribbling women," Loggins himself uses the word "scribbling" to
describe Elizabeth's writing, but notes that Elizabeth and her brother often se-
cretly "exchang[ed] the poems and essays they had created" (230). Both children, Loggins writes, spent long hours alone, day and night, reading, fantasiz-
ing, and writing. "Nat turned the pages of his father's log books, and penciled
comments in the margins, but never gave a thought of going to sea himself.
Though the stables were full of horses, he had no interest in driving or riding.
He preferred to get into an abandoned stagecoach, which he called 'dead,' and
fancy himself journeying with the 'ghosts' of the travelers whom it had long
since served. He memorized pieces from books and went through the skylight
up to the roof and declaimed them to space" (229).

Although Loggins suggests that Elizabeth encountered more opposition to
her solitary habits than did Nathaniel, it seems that the girl's behavior was not
much different from his: "Ebe was also in the habit of sequestering herself in
some corner. When anyone came near, she assumed the look of a bereaved
spouse and went on with her reading or scribbling. If cleaning the house depended on her, the place stayed dirty. When it was suggested that she do a bit
of mending or darning, she would say, in her superior manner, 'It's Louisa who
wishes to learn to sew'" (229–30).

If the Mannings indeed accepted Nathaniel's reclusiveness more than
Elizabeth's, it may have been because he was a boy and two years younger than
Elizabeth, who approached an age when many young women thought of so-

cializing and preparing for adult life. What plans Elizabeth had, one can only conjecture. Loggins describes her as an unpleasant girl who was often lost in thought: "Many a young man who saw her out walking, or sitting at meeting at the First Church must have looked upon her longingly. But those with whom she talked found her cold, hard, and painfully proud . . . Only in her ambition was she emotional. Men of her social level in Salem saw that in her great dreams none of them were included, and the aristocrats who were struck by her attractiveness remembered that she belonged to Herbert Street" (230).

But though her letters show a sharp-tongued young woman, they also show one who was clever, witty, and social, frequently visiting or writing friends and relatives in other cities of the region. Furthermore, some incidents alluded to in the Hawthorne family letters and fragmentary gossip of the period suggest that Elizabeth may indeed have had romantic attachments, but nothing in Elizabeth's own letters implies any potential romance, any heartbreak, or any regret. Indeed, anything reconstructed about her habits suggests that she was not of a mind to marry. If she had an interest in a man, she did not write of him in the letters that survive. No evidence exists, furthermore, of any romantic attachment to a woman.

In 1818 Mrs. Hawthorne took Ebe and Louisa to live in Raymond, Massachusetts—which later became part of Maine—where the family owned large tracts of land and a country home. Nathaniel was sent to boarding school in December, but complained of homesickness to his uncle Robert, who allowed him to stay out of school after winter break until summer, when he then went to Salem (Loggins 231–32). Elizabeth's formal schooling had ended, and, now sixteen years old, she could socialize when she felt so inclined and spend time outdoors in nature, a habit she kept all of her long life. Her letters show her to be less impressed with Raymond's society than with Salem's but "very well content in the midst of the woods" (November 4, 1818). She traveled to Salem or Newburyport (Massachusetts) when she felt sociable, for the Mannings' carriage line made transportation convenient, but she seemed happy to return to the relative peace of Raymond afterward.

Letters situate Elizabeth in New England society of her milieu and show her to be a fastidious young woman of stylish and elegant taste. Mrs. Hawthorne explained that her daughter liked her gowns "fixt fashionable": silken, lined, and trimmed (*CE* XV 109). Elizabeth wore a fine, brimmed straw hat for which her uncle William had paid fifteen dollars and which her brother described as "so large that the most piercing eye cannot discover her beneath it" (150). Perhaps disappointed in the shops of Raymond, the sixteen-year-old Elizabeth wrote to her aunt in Salem, "I should like to have you buy me a pair of white worsted stockings, and a parchment memorandum book with morocco covers" (November 1818). She made extended visits to her Hawthorne relations, the Archers and the Forresters, and other friends in Newburyport, Ipswich, Salem, and Raymond, even complaining, "my engagements are so numerous that I have no leisure to write" (June 28, 1821). Her brother, no doubt referring to her socializing, made a similar observation in writing to their mother: "Elizabeth is too deeply immersed in the vortex of Dissipation to visit Raymond very soon" (153).

Nathaniel was a different matter. His elders had plans for his education, which had been suspended for much of 1819 while he and his sisters enjoyed the freedom that they lacked in Salem under the eyes of their grandmother, aunt Mary, and uncle Robert. But Loggins implies that Mrs. Hawthorne lacked the will or authority to raise a son and characterizes her as "always weak," and so "adept in shielding her son from the stern discipline Robert believed in" that "the wise uncle had to be tactful in doing for his nephew what he thought was right" (224, 232). Robert Manning brought Nathaniel to Salem, away from his mother and sisters, selected a tutor for him, and supervised his studies for two years until he was admitted to Bowdoin College.

A letter from Nathaniel to his sister Louisa in 1819 mentions Elizabeth's writing: "Tell Ebe she's not the only one of the family whose works have appeared in the papers" (*CE* XV 115). While the nature, number, dates, and venues of these publications remain unknown, the fact that some of her work may have seen publication suggests that she spent much of her time writing and that she felt confident enough in her work to submit it for anonymous publication. Her brother's reference to her work suggests that the two competed in this regard, even if it remained unspoken until his letter.

While her brother studied in Salem, Elizabeth and Nathaniel shared their writing with each other by mail, although how regularly remains a mystery. He wrote in 1820, "I am very angry with you for not sending me some of your Poetry, which I consider as a great piece of Ingratitude. You will not see one line more of mine, untill You return the confidence which I have placed in you" (*CE* XV 131). By this time, both published young poets clearly took their writing at least somewhat seriously. Louisa left Raymond in 1820 to visit Salem and keep her brother company, and the separated family members wrote letters, or, as the collected Hawthorne correspondence frequently also indicates, failed to write them: "What has become of Elizabeth? Does she ever intend to notice me again? I shall begin to think she has eloped with some of those 'Gay Deceivers' who abound in Raymond, if she does not give me some proof to the contrary," Nathaniel teased in 1821 (138). Elizabeth remained in Raymond until her mother moved back to Salem in 1822. Loggins explains that Mrs. Hawthorne hoped to marry her daughters into Salem society, marriageable men being sparse in Raymond, but that Elizabeth, "more studious than ever, soon let her mother and grandmother know that a husband was the last thing in the world she was seeking" (237).

Nathaniel saw neither his mother nor Elizabeth for two years until he was at last, in Loggins's words, more mature and no longer "marred by effeminacy" at the hands of his immediate family (236). If Loggins and others are to be believed, Uncle Robert saved his nephew's writing career by insisting that Nathaniel study and prepare for college and by spiriting him away from his mother, who would ostensibly have allowed the boy's lazy impulses to guide his progress. It seems to follow that these same biographers could then conceivably make a case for Robert Manning's having ignored Elizabeth's writing career, something in which her uncle apparently took less interest. Although she was very well read, better educated than most people, and certainly better than most women of her time, one can only conjecture what direction her writing might have taken with the learning and guidance that men in her circumstances routinely received. But no higher education would even exist for women in the United States until the establishment of Georgia's Wesleyan College in 1836 and Mount Holyoke in Massachusetts in 1837, long past Ebe's teenage years.

Once Nathaniel began studies at Bowdoin, his correspondence with Elizabeth continued, sometimes with the familiar theme of their irregular letters: "Most assuredly you are the last person from whom I should have expected a rebuke on account of the shortness and infrequency of my letters. If you will please to recollect you will find that my letters exceed yours considerably in number this term, and as for length (though neither of us have anything to boast of) mine are at least equal to yours" (*CE* XV 174). Many surviving Manning-Hawthorne family letters contain similar complaints, a preference for receiving letters over writing them being a virtually universal human trait. One can propose an argument for Elizabeth's jealousy of Nathaniel's education keeping her from staying in touch with her beloved brother, but her letters to him no longer exist, and his letters to her, his presumably beloved sister, seem likewise occasional at best. Nathaniel explains further in the letter cited above, "My only reason for not writing has been that I have had nothing to write." Indeed, much of what makes his letters, and Elizabeth's, engaging is what ordinarily makes good cor-

respondence: the transmission of news. Their thirteen-year-old sister, Maria
Louisa, whom Woodson characterizes as "lack[ing their] dedication to literature" (19), viewed her task differently, writing, "Ebe has gone down to Aunt
Forresters this evening and has commissioned me to finish her letter we were
very glad to see Ebe but did not expect her we all want to see you very much
I should think you would be very lonesome without any body with you there
is no news here" (*CE* XV 148). Louisa's composition differs radically from
those Elizabeth wrote at thirteen. This letter highlights the similarity between
Nathaniel and Elizabeth's writing styles and emphasizes the sophistication of
both young writers.

All accounts of Elizabeth's physical appearance agree that she and Nathaniel
resembled their mother, a beautiful woman with gray eyes; dark, curly hair;
arching eyebrows; and fine facial features. Many of Nathaniel's biographers describe the brother and sister as strikingly similar: solitary, well read, witty, and
Elizabeth more so than her brother in all of these aspects. Unsaid, but perhaps
implied, though, is that she was therefore stranger for being a solitary, well-
read, witty *girl*, particularly in such a large family. Julian Hawthorne, who
knew his aunt well, would later remark that Elizabeth had "an understanding in many respects as commanding and penetrating as that of her famous
brother" (5). Rose Hawthorne Lathrop would later make a similar observation
of her aunt: "I . . . was astonished at her magical resemblance to my father in
many ways" (473).

Perhaps also implicit in such observations of her behavior and temperament
is that she was all the more peculiar for having purportedly written nothing,
while her brother, of similar inclinations and temperament, became one of the
best-known novelists in American literature. To measure Elizabeth's potential
against his is to expect an oeuvre of the quality and renown of Nathaniel's; to
compare her accomplishments with his is to be disappointed, puzzled. When
young, she showed all of the promise her brother showed, apparently spent
more time writing than he, and seemed much more inclined to make a life of
writing than was he, whose letters show him to be wistful, longing to trade his
books for a gun, to exchange his studying for boyhood romps in the wilds of
Maine. One explanation may be Nathaniel's future obligation to make a living
to support his mother and sisters and, eventually, his wife and children; such
pressure prompted his uncle to insist that he learn a trade or that he further his
education, one that, given such opportunities for women, would prove much
longer and more rigorous than Elizabeth's. This same pressure to earn must have
become Nathaniel's motivation to write. Elizabeth, on the other hand, as a spin-

ster in a middle-class family, had fewer obligations or opportunities than did her brother. She too was a writer, but one who could allow her writing to remain an avocation, who may have had fewer publication opportunities, and one who could not have been offered the education given to her brother.

When Nathaniel graduated in 1825 and returned to live in the house on Herbert Street with his mother and sisters, most of the other occupants had either moved away or died. Both Richard and Robert Manning had married and set up housekeeping elsewhere, and Priscilla had married John Dike, a widower with two children. Grandfather Richard and Aunt Maria had died long before Nathaniel left. With his uncle Robert gone, Nathaniel set up a study in his old room and began the famous years of secret writing that would prepare him for his career as a novelist. Loggins writes that Ebe was "enthusiastic over the course he had adopted. She too was enthralled by the will to become an author. Now she saw herself and Nat struggling on side by side to success and fame" (238). Loggins has observed what many biographers have also commented on the parallel paths that Elizabeth and Nathaniel seemed to be following that would eventually diverge, leading him to prosperity and renown, her to dependence and anonymity.

Nathaniel's return to Salem from Bowdoin College in 1825 marked a new phase in his development as a writer, a phase that included his sister. For twelve years, from his graduation until the publication of *Twice-Told Tales* in 1837, Nathaniel wrote steadily in his childhood bedroom converted into a study, producing fiction with varying degrees of success. Nathaniel's first known work—a novel with an academic setting, titled *Fanshawe* and published anonymously and privately in 1828—met with some success, but later proved such a disappointment to its author that he attempted to destroy all remaining copies of it, Elizabeth said. Within a few years he began to see his short stories published in the *Token* and *New-England Magazine*. Through his publications, Nathaniel made the acquaintance of Samuel Griswold Goodrich, who had established the *Token* and who offered him the editorship of the *American Magazine of Useful and Entertaining Knowledge* in 1836. Thus began the collaboration with Elizabeth in an odd situation that brought neither brother nor sister money or fame, but that constitutes a very interesting chapter in Elizabeth Hawthorne's life.

The *American Magazine of Useful and Entertaining Knowledge,* published by the Bewick Company of Boston, ran from 1834 until 1837. Turner explains that many of the company's members, engravers by trade, used the magazine chiefly as a means to publish their illustrations (1). The serial purported to entertain and enlighten its readers, but Nathaniel apparently became disillusioned with his editorship when the writing proved dull but pressured and the employer failed to pay. Thus, Nathaniel's eventual attitude toward the entire undertaking grew perhaps not unjustifiably negative. His job included creating commentary for the engravings—which he crossly termed "wood-scratching"—and preparing articles of general interest based on his own research. This second point had much to do with Elizabeth's involvement in the project, for she had access to books that her brother lacked. Nathaniel wrote to Louisa in January of 1836: "If Ebe has concocted anything, let her send it. I wish her to make extracts of whatever she thinks suitable; for I have merely the liberty of reading at the Atheneum, and am not allowed to take out books—so that I have but a narrow range of works to extract from" (*CE* XV 228). He wrote directly to Elizabeth four days later, "[Send] your concoctions, prose and poetical. I make nothing of writing a history or biography before dinner. Do you the same" (230).

And concoct she did, contributing, among other pieces, most of a biographical article on Alexander Hamilton. Turner explains that Elizabeth's contribution closely follows her source, John Church Hamilton's *The Life of Alexander Hamilton,* and that her integration of quoted material appears unpolished (29n, 30n). Elizabeth had borrowed the biography of Hamilton on January 4 and had used seventy pages of the text to prepare the article that she sent to Boston (32n). Nathaniel's letters indicate, though, that the piece long remained unfinished. "Tell Ebe to finish her life of Hamilton," he wrote to Louisa in February, and to Elizabeth in March, "Send up your life of Hamilton forthwith . . . If not finished, send what you have written" (*CE* XV 238, 242). The incomplete biography arrived, and Nathaniel wrote the next day:

You need proceed no further with Hamilton. As the press was in want of him, I have been compelled to finish his life myself, this forenoon. I did not receive the packet till last night (Tuesday.) I should have given you earlier notice; but did not know myself that the engraving was coming into this number. I seldom have more than a day or two's notice. I approve of your life; but have been obliged to correct some of your naughty notions about arbitrary government. You should not make quotations; but put other people's thoughts into your own words, and amalgamate the whole into a mass. You may go on concocting and extracting and send me some more of both varieties, as soon as convenient. (243)

The May issue of the *American Magazine of Useful and Entertaining Knowledge* appeared, complete with woodcut and biography of Alexander Hamilton.

Brother and sister, with some exceptions, apparently wrote alike. Both made use of fairly pedestrian summary and of lofty rhetoric; both harnessed hindsight and presented it as fate; both seemed to wink at the pseudo-sagacity of the task. The young Elizabeth, unenthusiastic though she may seem at close range, took specifics from a dry book and crafted them into a life that resonated much more than did John C. Hamilton's own study of his father. And while she also copied passages rather lazily from the source, the piece ultimately published in the magazine sparkles, revealing her hand and her competence.

Despite the difficulties that Nathaniel and Elizabeth encountered while writing *The American Magazine of Useful and Entertaining Knowledge,* they soon embarked upon another task that Goodrich offered: authorship of a children's textbook, *Peter Parley's Universal History on the Basis of Geography.* Nathaniel accepted the job in Boston and on May 5, 1836, wrote: "[Goodrich] wants me to undertake a Universal History, to contain about as much matter as 50 or 60 pages of the Magazine. If you are willing to write any part of it (which I think you might, now that it is warm weather) I shall agree to do it. If necessary, I will come home by- and bye, and concoct the plan of it with you. It need not be superiour, in profundity and polish, to the middling Magazine articles" (*CE* XV 245). A week later he followed up with more news: "Our pay, as Historians of the Universe, will be 100 dollars the whole of which you may have" (247). Accounts conflict as to the extent of Elizabeth's participation in the project. In her letters written in old age, she herself never claims authorship of the book or indeed of any articles from the *American Magazine.* But Nathaniel's surviving correspondence makes plain her collaboration with him on the articles and the book, regardless of whether she chooses to acknowledge it herself. Catalogs in various libraries, including the New York Public Library, list Elizabeth, not Nathaniel, as the author of the textbook, and James Walsh asserts in "A Note as to the Authorship of *Peter Parley's Universal History*" (1918) that the work has traditionally been attributed entirely to Elizabeth (519). The book, Jane Stanbrough explains, "went through countless editions, was used in schoolrooms throughout the [nineteenth century], and made its publishers a fortune" (268).

Designed to teach young children the rudiments of history and geography, the textbook begins with a discussion of these two disciplines and continues with a description of landmasses and their inhabitants. The vocabulary and sentence structure suit young learners, but, in a twentieth-century view, also eerily reduce the whole of human history to pat exposition, impoverishing the complexity, mystery, and pathos of humanity by narrowing the scope drastically, even for a children's book. *Peter Parley's Universal History* reflects the attitudes of the period, a sense of superiority over other peoples and modes of life, different systems of economics, and unfamiliar forms of worship. The book explains, for example, that American Indian tribes lived in savagery and most Asians in barbarism, while people of Europe and the United States flourished in civilized societies, markedly different from the other foreign cultures, some of which the author describes as "very cruel." Young readers of this text no doubt noticed, if unconsciously, the subtext: people of the United States and Europe, who in marked contrast were enlightened and urbane, could gather, organize, and disseminate information about people less civilized than them-selves. The textbook allows any schoolchild to feel king of the primitive world he surveys, a planet much improved by his country's influence and industry, with many more backward lands ripe for further American capitalization and cultural export.

The author anticipates the first of these objections, offering the following disclaimer above the copyright notice:

The idea of embracing in the compass of this little volume any thing like a tolerable outline of Universal History, would doubtless excite a smile on the lip of a college professor, should he ever [condescend] to peep into our humble title-page. But let our object be clearly understood, and we hope the attempt we have here made may not be deemed either ridiculous or presuming. A work which gives in detail the history of mankind, must necessarily be voluminous. It is, therefore, beyond the utmost stretch of the youthful intellect to compass it . . . And yet it is very desirable that every person should, at an early period of life, have imprinted on his mind, in bright and unfading colors, a clear outline of the story of mankind, from its beginning in the plain of Shinar, down to the present hour. (5)

This "Advertisement," furthermore, bears a resemblance to *The American Maga-zine of Useful and Entertaining Knowledge*—specifically, in its tone. The writers of the magazine use the embedded clauses and modest tone familiar to readers of the periodical and absent in the text of the book, where the sentences rarely exceed a few words. The pseudonymous authorship and rhetorical task of this children's primer reveal a variety of discourses. Peter Parley—a pseudonym for Samuel Griswold, itself a pseudonym for Nathaniel Hawthorne, a front for Elizabeth Hawthorne—assumes an attitude appropriate when teaching young readers, one that he, or she, drops briefly to introduce a book that learned people may find simplistic. The multitude of voices and rhetorical tasks belies the most apparent, and the most apparently simple, one.

The Goodrich book had a short development period. Even if the writing began in May, the preparation took no more than four months, and probably less, as the project saw completion by September. Elizabeth and Nathaniel's writing collaboration ended soon thereafter. The young Hawthornes, Elizabeth, Nathaniel, and Louisa, continued to live with their mother in Salem, and all began socializing with the Peabody sisters, Elizabeth, Mary, and Sophia. The courtship of Nathaniel and Sophia would soon begin, as would Nathaniel's sojourn at Brook Farm, and the small wedding, unwitnessed by any Hawthorne family members, would take place in the eight years after completion of *Peter Parley*, Elizabeth's last known successful publication effort.

In 1850 Elizabeth's life shifted into the mode she kept for the remainder of her life. Until then she had lived with her mother and her sister, Louisa, on Herbert Street, or, briefly, with them and the young married Nathaniel and Sophia Hawthorne in a house on Mall Street. With their mother's death, Louisa and Elizabeth moved away from the home they had shared with Nathaniel and Sophia, Louisa moving, Loggins explains, to her aunt Rebecca Manning's and Elizabeth to Montserrat, a district of Beverly, north of Salem (282). The bulk of Elizabeth's surviving letters date from this thirty-two-year period when their author had assumed a new role, that of boarder, in addition to her habitual ones of maiden aunt, occasional visitor, and reluctant correspondent. Nathaniel's biographers portray Elizabeth as given to seclusion, with long rambles in nature, especially the woods. And indeed, a woman of very modest means, she rarely traveled, and never far; a keeper of her own idiosyncratic hours, she rarely visited, and never long. But her letters reveal activity that many such scholars apparently overlook: her long talks with local figures, her visits to family in Salem and Concord, and her shopping trips to bookstores in Boston.

After first staying a few months near Manchester, several miles north of Salem, Elizabeth boarded with an elderly couple, Harriet and Samuel Cole, in a house in Montserrat. As she later wrote to her Manning cousins, the first few weeks there did not bode well:

When I first came here I was sick, and Mrs. Cole used to come up, bringing an armful of wood, and sit down upon it and stare at me and tell me that I was in a consumption. I disliked everything, especially herself, so much that I felt quite indifferent to whether I were or not. I longed to tell her, but refrained, that when I was buried, I desired to have the coffin put out of the window, to get me out of the house as soon as possible. Since that I have taken a great deal of comfort here, and I learned to like Mrs. Cole, who was as good and kind as possible; and the whole family were thoroughly reliable.

But it required a constant effort, for a long time, to understand and accommodate my-self to them. She always called me "Miss What's your name." Whenever she disliked any of my proceedings, she scolded, and very often I replied appropriately, so that we soon learned to appreciate each other, which can never be done by the practice of con-stant civility. (April 9, 1877)

In time, Elizabeth grew very comfortable with her hosts, writing to Nathaniel three months after her arrival at the Cole house:

I am now perfectly recovered, rather in spite of the excessive care which Mrs. Cole, with whom I board, took care of me, than owing to it. I am with an excellent family, who do everything to make me comfortable, and very well accommodated: as well as at Manchester and at a much lower price. We supposed it would be much easier to com-municate with Salem, as this place is only 2 ½ miles from the Beverly Depot, and within sight of the Rail Road. . . . There are many advantages in my present position; I can lose myself in the woods by only crossing the road, and the air is very pure and exhilarating and the sea but a mile distant. (May 3, 1851)

Indeed, Elizabeth's relatively few needs had changed little since her adoles-cence. In her new living situation she had a room in which to read her books and magazines and to write her letters, emerging if and when she chose; she had her meals provided for her, for she apparently never learned to cook, or saw any need to; and she had immediate access to expanses of nature—the woods, the ocean. Although she mentions articles of clothing, some of them very fine, she generally troubled herself little with her attire, wearing, according to her niece Rose, "a quaintly round dress of lightish-brown mohair, which would not fall into graceful folds" (Lathrop 475). Having little money and preferring to spend it on books, she sometimes went without necessities:

As to my coming to Salem, that does not seem a practical proceeding, because I have no shoes to wear. And, what makes the case worse, there are no shoes to be obtained in Beverly, though so many are made here, and though almost every man seems to be a shoemaker. Everybody goes to Salem to buy shoes, and some people even to get them mended. So I must wait patiently till Providence sends me a pair. I have been to the library once, and mean to go again tomorrow. I can walk along on level ground, with-out exposing my shoes, but they would be seen in getting into the Horse Cars. I have a list of eighteen things, of which I am in the last extremity of need, which I mean to purchase in Salem whenever I can get there. (May 25, 1865)

Elizabeth managed to satisfy her worldly needs or go without them cheerfully, perhaps not seeing them as urgent. The letters show that she often went without something that truly mattered to her: letters and visits from people close to her in family relation or in taste.

Elizabeth liked company, but on her own terms, enjoying unannounced social calls from her Manning cousins, but occasionally feeling imposed upon by sightseers: "There are beautiful things, bright green ferns, and the loveliest mosses, and crimson berries to be found in moist places in mild winters, that one quite overlooks until the taller plants are dead. Just before Christmas I was much annoyed by persons who came for me to show them such spots. When I was reading comfortably with a good fire, was it not provoking to be dragged out into the cold?" (February 17, 1869).

She complained about the level of conversation normally available from the Coles, who believed in ghosts and, she wrote, sometimes failed to appreciate the novels she read to them or referred to the author of *Our Mutual Friend* as "Old Dickenson." Although Elizabeth had grown fond of Mrs. Cole and her daughter Jane, she sometimes longed for talks with readers and thinkers on her own level. "If we lived within walking distance of each other, I should intrude upon you whenever I felt the want of conversation, which is the great want of my life," she complained to Robert Manning (December 31, 1861). A few weeks later, playfully scheming to add variety to her life, she confided to Rebecca Manning:

I have a plan for next Summer, which, if I find it practicable will give me a change of air and scene. It is to commit treason, or manage to be suspected of it, and sent to Fort Warren. Then I shall have the sea breeze and society, if any, that will at least be novel to me. I shall besides, live without expense and can buy books with the money I must elsewhere pay for board. Do you think they would allow me a comfortable room, by myself and what do you think I should do to entitle myself to occupy it? Perhaps you would like to go with me. (January 1862)

These passages, while they seem to confirm that Elizabeth spent much time alone, sometimes without the kind of society that she liked, also show a sense of humor that contradicts the usual portrayal of her as a hermitic figure, reminiscent of Hepzibah Pynchon in *The House of the Seven Gables* or Hester Prynne in *The Scarlet Letter*.

Indeed, the corpus of letters suggests not that Elizabeth shunned human interaction, but that friends and relatives could not visit with the frequency that she, who had much leisure with neither family nor employment obligations, would have liked. She had gained a reputation as a lover of nature and, significantly, as a person with whom to experience it. On her short trips to and from Salem, she often encountered her acquaintances in the horse-drawn streetcars and reported very pleasant commuting visits with such locals as "Our schoolmistress, Miss Robins" (December 1864) and feminist writer Lucy Larcom (October 11, 1869). In characterizing Elizabeth as an unpleasant recluse, biographers not only ignore evidence to the contrary but also portray her in an unnecessarily negative light. Of course, letter-writers normally tell correspondents of their society and activity more than of their solitude and repose, and to argue that the middle-aged Elizabeth participated in all the social activities of her milieu would be to err in another direction. But just as some biographers have perhaps overstated the solitary life of her mother, they may have thus exaggerated Elizabeth's own, perhaps in an attempt to show continuity with the Puritan Hawthornes in a dark family that shaped the gloomy romancer.

Elizabeth's letters frequently note the seasonal changes—autumn leaves, which she sometimes encloses in the envelope, or blooming laurel, which she urges her Manning cousins to come and enjoy. Much in tune with her surroundings, she misses her walks once the harsh New England winter weather makes them impossible, and rejoices when a temporary "January thaw" or springtime allows her to spend time outdoors. She writes to her cousin Rebecca Manning:

With great labour I have succeeded in digging up the fern-roots for which you asked me. I am afraid the largest one will not live, for I was obliged to tear away the fibres of the roots, which seemed to extend for half a yard round. One of the others came up easily enough, as it grew upon a rock that formed the roof of the abode of some wild animal, whom I expected to see come out of his hole to ask what I was about. The one with broad leaves is the Royal Flowering Fern. Wordsworth calls it the Queen Osmunda. It has tall brown blossoms, and in the Spring the young leaves are very pretty. To accomplish this work, which was harder than you can imagine, I took the large iron spoon with which Mrs. Cole mixes bread and cake,—without asking her, for she had company,—and it bent itself almost double, which, however was better than breaking, and muddied itself. I took it upstairs, and stood upon the handle to straighten it out, and washed it as well as I could in cold water, but if the next batch of bread had had a flavour of the soil I should have known the reason why. Thus I corrected its perversity, then restored it to its original shape, and replaced it in the closet whence I took it. You must set the roots in a moist place, and put in all the dead leaves and stalks, to make the earth as much as possible like that from which it was taken. There is a little three-cornered fern among the rest and some golden thread which has pretty green leaves. (October 11, 1869)

This passage illuminates several of Elizabeth's characteristics: her writing ability, her wit, her knowledge of plants, her delight in things wild, her affection for her cousin, her eye for detail, in short, the richness of her personality and of her connection with nature. This reverence for the outdoors, even the wilderness, became a trait very frequently commented upon. Annie Fields, one of Nathaniel Hawthorne's biographers, writes of a spontaneous visit she and her husband, James, paid to Elizabeth: "[I]n spite of the fine weather and her woodland life habitually, she was at home, and came down immediately as if she were sincerely glad to see us . . . She is a woman of no common mould, however. Lucy Larcom calls her a hamadryad, and says she belongs in the woods and should be seen there" (qtd. in Howe, 69). Nature, then, more than any single human being, was the entity with which Elizabeth formed a lifelong, intimate bond. She knew and loved her environs well, noting the smallest flower peeking from under the dry leaves, and gazing through her window at the tree branches in bloom on a background of summer twilight.

The letters also situate her in the literary context of her locale. Elizabeth's correspondence shows commentary on such important figures as Ralph Waldo Emerson and Henry David Thoreau, and acquaintance with Annie and James T. Fields and such minor figures as Gail Hamilton, Jean Ingelow, and Lucy Larcom, to say nothing of such family relations as Una Hawthorne, Julian Hawthorne, Rose Hawthorne Lathrop, Elinor Barstow Condit, George Parsons Lathrop, Elizabeth Palmer Peabody, and of course, Nathaniel Hawthorne himself, most of whom published work known to any reader of the period. Indeed, Boston and its outlying towns, which included Salem and Concord, made up the intellectual and literary center of the federal United States and remained an important area after the locus shifted to New York. Geography made Elizabeth well placed to grow up with and live among literary figures, and family and social class made these acquaintances valuable to her personally and, of course, to her brother's profession.

The principal recipients of the letters that remain were Elizabeth's niece Una Hawthorne and her Manning cousins, especially Rebecca. Evidence exists of correspondence in middle age with her aunt Priscilla Manning Dike, but no letters remain except the ones written in childhood. Elizabeth's writing covers a variety of subjects, some of general interest—current literature, political events—and some specific to her home and family. Readers see her describing the scenery of Montserrat, or taking sides in the family controversy over George Lathrop's book on Nathaniel Hawthorne.

The letters to Una contain, among other things normally discussed by a favorite aunt and her favorite niece, just the sort of unflattering observations that Richard Manning Jr. chose to excise. The harsh remarks that Elizabeth made sometimes pertained to her cousin Richard's wife, Elizabeth Yeaton Gould, mother of young Richard Manning, known respectively as Lizzie and Little Dickie in the corpus. Elizabeth Hawthorne would surely not have said anything impolite about Lizzie in letters addressed to Lizzie's husband, but she made candid statements to Maria, Robert, or Rebecca, and their letters appear along with those written to Richard, all selectively typed for posterity by the middle-aged Little Dickie, who destroyed the originals. Furthermore, Elizabeth's letters to Una show a passion and a candor that is absent in letters to any other correspondent, and whether the original, uncensored Manning letters showed this difference, readers cannot know. In all fairness, Elizabeth's legendary dislike of Nathaniel's wife, Sophia Peabody Hawthorne, figures in none of the letters to Una, Julian, or Rose, but does appear in correspondence to the Mannings.

As with any dialog between any people of any time, the intended recipient shapes the discourse. The surviving letters as they exist today show a woman who was more complex than the character normally portrayed in material about her brother. Eccentric and imperious, Elizabeth was also loving, social, thoughtful, engaging, witty, and amusing, a writer of letters that fascinate any reader who had overlooked her as little more than Nathaniel's solitary, peculiar sister.

Elizabeth kept hours that she herself describes as unusual, sleeping late into the day and reading or writing long into the night, as she had done since her adolescence, and this idiosyncratic schedule serves as an important example of the life she led: one shaped partly by financial necessity, but mainly by her own personal needs. Although poverty sometimes pinched her, Elizabeth apparently lived mostly as she chose, seeing friends and acquaintances when it suited her, walking in nature and collecting plants as the seasons tempted her, writing letters when she resolved to, rather than according to the conventions of the day.

Elizabeth boarded in the same house from the time she moved to Montserrat until she died in 1883. Her letters chronicle the dramas of the Cole family, and later, of the Appleton family, who purchased the late Coles' house, including the pets and pests that dwelt there. She lived to age eighty, and despite her advancing years and stooped posture, enjoyed good health until her death from the measles, a disease she had feared for years.

Biographers sometimes fail to attribute properly what they know about Nathaniel Hawthorne's young life. Much of this comes from Elizabeth, specifically, from her letters, which scholars began using even while she lived and have continued to use in the decades since she died. James T. Fields, who wrote retrospective pieces after his dear friend Nathaniel's death, asked Elizabeth for her memories to help flesh out his articles, and Julian Hawthorne, writing years after his aunt's death, quoted her letters extensively. Robert Cantwell, Moncure Conway, Annie Fields, Vernon Loggins, Edwin Haviland Miller, Randall Stewart, Arlin Turner, Mark Van Doren, George Woodberry, Brenda Wineapple— every major biographer of Nathaniel Hawthorne has used material that came from her. Some, such as Miller, do so with specific references to Elizabeth's contribution, and some do so without, such as Woodberry, who writes, "The pleasant, handsome, bright-haired boy was four years old when his mother called him into her room and told him that his father was dead" (4). The event, recounted in Elizabeth's letter to Una dated November 12, 1865, which reads, "one morning my mother called my brother into her room . . . and told him that his father was dead," appears in Woodberry's biography without footnote or other mention of its source. Twenty-six pages later, Woodberry cites Elizabeth more carefully as the source of a quote on Nathaniel's writing, but with no reference to her letters (30).

Philip Young, writing in the 1980s, follows Woodberry's rather careless example of citing only sporadically, and rarely completely. For example, Young refers to, but does not cite, an opinion of Elizabeth's that he found in a letter. In it, Elizabeth mentions the Hawthorne family's residence in Rome, "where [Sophia] kept her family that she might gratify her own love of art; permanently injuring also her husband's health by the same means" (February 18, 1877). Young's summary—"[S]he blamed her sister-in-law for keeping him too long in Rome" (31)—captures Elizabeth's sentiment, but in failing to document the source properly, as bibliographic norms would have required in the 1980s, he practically erases the corpus of her letters. While such informal modes of documentation, standard in research of earlier periods, usually gave way to the more thorough methods used today, they obscured Elizabeth's role as her brother's first biographer.

Elizabeth herself, however, chose to remain unknown, partly out of respect for Nathaniel, who had often expressed a now well-known wish that no biography be written and, as did his wife, destroyed or altered letters and other documents lest they be used for this purpose. "[I]t was my brother's especial injunction that no biography of him should be written," Elizabeth reminded Richard Manning more than six years after Nathaniel's death, but she was able to reconcile herself to something more modest: "Perhaps there would be nothing objectionable in publishing a record of his places of residence" (December 31, 1870). She decided that she could trust James Fields, who had proposed not a biography but a smaller piece in the *Atlantic Monthly*. "Say that you had your information from a friend of his, older than himself, who had known him all his life," Elizabeth suggested after recounting many different incidents from her brother's youth (December 26, 1870). Rose Hawthorne Lathrop agrees that the aging Nathaniel had strong feelings on the subject of a biography: "My father began to express . . . his dislike of biographies, and that he forbade any such matter in connection with himself in any distance of the future" (477). But Rose, like Elizabeth, developed a loyalty to Nathaniel's legacy that finally trumped her devotion to his privacy, and both women helped create a record of his childhood and adult life. While their personal interest in the matter necessarily casts some doubt on their accounts of Hawthorne family life, they too offer perspectives to compare with the ones shared by other family, friends, and colleagues in shaping images—always plural—of the romancer.

Elizabeth also assumed a different role in the Hawthorne hagiography: evaluator of information or informants, some of whom she considered reliable, others not. Writing to James Fields, she disputes the notion that her elders raised her and her siblings harshly, asserting, "I do not remember much constraint," and in response to a memory of Rattlesnake Mountain related by a purported friend from Nathaniel's childhood, she writes, "I believe that to be true, because I remember the place, which was one of his favorites" (December 1870). The articles that Rose's husband, George Parsons Lathrop, published in *Scribner's* made Elizabeth furious and prompted angry rebuttals from her in letters to Una and the Mannings, especially regarding Elizabeth Peabody. At first Elizabeth practically dismissed Peabody's complicity in the biography, writing to her cousins, "I think she is benevolent, and a well wisher of every human being, but I suspect no one who knows her relies upon her word" (April 1876). But her temper and her tone soon changed radically, possibly because she feared that the reading public would believe Elizabeth Peabody. Elizabeth Hawthorne wrote to Rebecca Manning:

I want you to write to Miss Elizabeth Peabody about George Lathrop's misdemeanors, if you choose to call them by so mild a name. Tell her how every one who speaks of his publication in Scribner thinks it nothing less than atrocious; I should like to have you say that you have heard it suggested that it was she who gave him an erroneous impression of Hawthorne's life in his own family previous to his marriage; perhaps not of its details, but of its general aspect; but that you cannot believe her capable of such misrepresentation, and wish to give her an opportunity to deny it. She will not be in the least surprised by a letter from you, or indeed from any human being—or from any divine or demoniac being . . . But if you write you must compliment her as much as you please, and ask her to use her influence to prevent any further folly being perpetrated in print . . . At any rate it would help to make a fuss, and I have much faith in a fuss. (May 19, 1876)

Although the letters Elizabeth Hawthorne wrote to Elizabeth Peabody in the 1830s suggest a cordial, intellectual acquaintance, those she wrote to various recipients after learning of Nathaniel and Sophia's engagement show a growing dislike of the Peabody sisters that lasted the rest of her life. "[Elizabeth Peabody] says insanity is in the Hawthorne family, and was beginning to show itself in Hawthorne himself before he died," she wrote derisively to the Mannings (January 1877), and asserted in two separate letters to them that her brother distrusted Peabody, who "put herself in a false position towards him" (February 18, 1877) and who "was not on good terms" with him (December 1880). Ironically, Edwin Haviland Miller, a contemporary and judicious biographer, hypothesizes that Nathaniel experienced a lifelong struggle with depression that culminated in a declining mental and physical state shortly before his death (512), and Brenda Wineapple writes of the bodily and psychological debility he suffered before dying (366–75). Miller cites a letter from Sophia pleading with James Fields not to speak to her sisters about her husband's mental condition (519) and ties Una's final psychological collapse to her father's thirteen years before (526). Readers thus see Elizabeth's account—whatever she may have observed—differing from Sophia's, and from Elizabeth Peabody's. And although Peabody waited until Sophia died to make this observation, she made it while Elizabeth lived. "In defending her brother from detractors," Miller explains, "Elizabeth Hawthorne hit upon a truth which she probably did not fully appreciate. Biography, like autobiography, is of necessity a fiction, that is, a construct arranged by an interpreter" (xvii). Not only did Elizabeth feel personally invested, but she also knew the multiplicity of interpretations that a life-writing project could yield—and indeed, has yielded—of Nathaniel's life, and, eventually, of hers.

Apart from letters written in the midst of scandal, in the uncertainty of illness, in the wake of death, or through memory, Elizabeth rarely makes mention of Nathaniel, living or dead. Their closeness in childhood, adolescence, and young adulthood apparently gave way to an emotional, and usually geographic, distance after his marriage. Three letters to Nathaniel survive, along with references to his rare visits to her or hers to him in Concord, but Sophia's presence in Nathaniel's life repelled Elizabeth, who blamed her for diminishing the quality of his writing. She wrote to James Fields that marriage earlier in life "would have spoiled the flavor of his genius," and she revealed in her next sentence that she had not truly meant to use the subjunctive mood: "This is your remark, Mr. Fields, nobody's else, certainly not mine; it is something that the keenness of your insight shows you, and you will never discern a more absolute truth" (December 26, 1870). To her Manning cousins, she expressed the same idea without speaking directly of Sophia: "I never thought my Brother was as well in Concord as in Salem. Certainly he never wrote as well in Concord" (May 1879).

Many biographers have commented on the barely concealed hostility between Elizabeth and Sophia, which lasted until Sophia's death and which Elizabeth kept alive thereafter. Describing Nathaniel as "almost their only tie to the world outside," Miller attributes the Hawthorne women's initial coldness toward Sophia to a reluctance to lose Nathaniel, who would leave them to the dark solitude of the house on Herbert Street (201). And indeed, although no one can know the true character of the Hawthorne household in the period after 1825, when Nathaniel had returned from Bowdoin, most biographers would agree that it differed markedly from the Peabody home a few blocks away. If Mrs. Hawthorne, Elizabeth, and Nathaniel were given to the bedroom-bound lifestyle of their repute, the house would have been very silent. Nathaniel's own account of these years differs with those of some others, but his social and family-business life outside of the house apparently fit the normal scheme and sometimes included Louisa, who, like her brother, loved dances and card games. As a reader, Elizabeth felt bonded to her brother, whose propensities had always resembled, but not rivaled, her own, and as a writer, Nathaniel felt literary kinship to his sister, to whom he showed his short stories in progress. Elizabeth could not have welcomed any interloper, and Sophia could not have felt flattered by the cooling of their once-cordial acquaintance.

Julian Hawthorne believed, and Philip Young agrees, that Elizabeth took steps to prevent her brother and Sophia from forming an attachment to each other. Describing his aunt as a "Machiavelli," Julian writes that Elizabeth warned Nathaniel that their mother's mental and physical frailty would make her unable to countenance the notion of her son's marriage. The lovers thus kept the engagement secret from the Hawthorne women for three years (1:196–97). Young cites an 1838 incident involving flowers delivered to the Hawthorne home, apparently for Nathaniel, from the Peabodys (29). Elizabeth Hawthorne writes to Sophia: "The flowers which Elizabeth sent, so sweet, and so tastefully arranged, I thought would be immediately bestowed upon my brother, who professes to regard the love of flowers as a feminine taste; so I permitted him to look at them, but consider them as a gift to myself; and beg you to thank her, in my name, when you write" (spring 1838). Young dismisses the polite tone of the letter and alleges another motive: "She intercepted and appropriated a bouquet the Peabody girls sent him, explaining that he disliked flowers" (29). Young thus colors the incident, rightly or wrongly. Julian Hawthorne defends his aunt as "quite sincere, moreover, in her belief that Sophia would never be strong enough properly to fulfill the duties of married life" (1:198) and then presents a comedic ending that contradicts all known information about the marriage: "As for the wicked sisters, Elizabeth and Louisa, they seem altogether to have failed to maintain the consistency of their rôle. They shamelessly rejoiced in their brother's happiness, and loved his wife quite as much as if they had never cherished any dark designs against the alliance" (1:201–02). So, no doubt, Julian liked to think, or at least, to write.

Regarding Elizabeth and Sophia, or more precisely Elizabeth and Nathaniel, Philip Young takes the speculation one step further, positing an incestuous relationship between brother and sister. He cites the Manning family history, which includes two sisters' conviction of "whorish carriage" with their brother, who had fled to avoid arrest. Margaret, Anstice, and Nicholas Manning serve as the real-life precedents to Hester Prynne, Young argues, the two real women forced to wear paper signs describing their crime just as the fictional woman wears a cloth letter. With *The Scarlet Letter*, Young continues, Nathaniel has transmuted incest in his family into adultery in his novel, making manifest his forbidden relationship with Elizabeth. Other elements of Nathaniel's fiction—in such tales as "Alice Doane's Appeal" and "The Haunted Mind" and novels such as *The Blithedale Romance*—suggest real-life incest, the degree of which remains a secret, but the existence of which Young argues in majuscules: "Something Happened" (135). Although readers and scholars alike have always speculated about dark, scandalous events in the Manning-Hawthorne family,

Young's small, daring volume raised eyebrows in academic circles. Like his readers, Young must accept that the exact nature and degree of the "Something"
remains unknown, but his treatment of the tangential personalities and events
shows a remarkable, frank, and refreshing thoroughness.

Incest hypothesis aside, Elizabeth and Sophia could have felt at odds because
they differed from each other in nearly every way except for their claim to
Nathaniel. Sophia's weariness with Elizabeth becomes apparent in a letter to her
mother, where she writes that her sister-in-law will not help with housework:
"Elizabeth is not available for every-day purposes of pot-hooks and trammels,
spits and flat-irons" (qtd. in J. Hawthorne, *Hawthorne and His Wife* 1:353). And
Elizabeth, who lacked Sophia's reputation for enthusiasm and congeniality,
made her feelings known too, by not leaving her room in the house she shared
for two years with the young married couple. Eight years after Sophia's death,
Elizabeth wrote, "she is the only human being whom I really dislike: though
she is dead, that makes no difference; I could have lived with her in apparent
peace, but I could not have lived long; the constraint would have killed me,"
Elizabeth wrote to the Mannings (December 1879). Her dislike of Sophia included the Peabodys, but no Hawthornes. She loved the three children the
couple had together, and placed any blame for inferior parenting with Sophia,
who wanted to shelter Una, Julian, and Rose from the burden of literacy and
the evils of candy. Intellectuals make poor parents, Elizabeth complained to the
Mannings, and "usually teach children to go the way that they should not, as
Sophia did, you know; yet it was not intellect that misled her, only the aping
of it" (December 1879). Whatever Sophia's crimes—or indeed, Elizabeth's—
Nathaniel's wife served as a convenient focus for Elizabeth's bitterness over her
brother's choosing marriage and family over their Herbert Street home.

Whatever the relationship between sister and brother may have been in
childhood, adolescence, and adulthood, a close family relation to the young
nation's premier novelist constitutes the central fact of Elizabeth's life in American literature. For no other reason have scholars taken an interest in her letters,
and until recently, for no other reason would she have become the subject of
closer study in her own right.

The letters, collectively, merit further discussion, as does the nature of this
project, a mass of epistolary material never intended to survive or to see print,
here prepared for exposition. Indeed, ironies abound in collections of letters:
their endurance as speaking documents after the correspondents' deaths; their
perusal by those not intended to read them, and even by strangers; their organi-

zation by someone else and according to recipient, topic, or date; the complete or partial erasure of the writer's penmanship by typesetting; their appropriation, scrutiny, and synthesis by an editor; their commodification through marketing, sale, and readership; their critical reception and reputed value as scholarly works; and their generic transformation from private missives to public apostrophe. Although easily and frequently destroyed, letters endure in ways that human beings cannot, and while the letters exist, they provide records of language. Through the imperfect media of language and writing, then, thoughts and feelings expressed and made permanent once, by someone for someone else, take on an existence that differs importantly from the writer's and reader's and that lasts, still imperfectly, until another reader introduces yet another existence for the letters. Letters are filled with references to other people, quite often, as in Elizabeth's case, with information to impart to the proper recipient but to guard from other parties. "Do not tell Mrs. Dike" appears frequently in the letters, as do unflattering reflections on nearly everyone of her family or acquaintance. No evidence exists that the criticized people ever read her caustic remarks, but these same observations became young Richard Manning's impetus to censor the letters he owned and to destroy the originals. Against Elizabeth's wishes, many letters did survive for strangers to consult, and now, to collect and edit. With any foreknowledge of this, Elizabeth would no doubt have responded as she did in a letter to her aunt Mary Manning: "Are my letters shown to Mr. Dike? If they are I shall not write any more" (August 1816).

This collection of selected letters, beginning with the earliest and ending with the last known letter, attempts to trace the progress of their writer. In aspiring to a sort of chronologic verisimilitude, the reconstructed corpus of letters ironically calls attention to its artificial, imposed structure as a series. A collection of these letters into a single work, presented all at once to a readership removed from the writer and recipients, disrupts the epistolary task at every level. Indeed, this disruption, which has required much time and effort, has as its paradoxical purpose a new organization that defies the author while attempting ultimately to serve her and those who follow. The appearance of the letters as printed characters also simultaneously detracts from and adds to the collection. Readers in the twenty-first century encounter much less handwritten correspondence than did those in periods before the keyboard assumed such a preeminent role, and contemporary readers thus appreciate a writer's own penmanship as a rarity, whereas earlier readers, much more accustomed to it, could not. The opposite also holds; as William Merrill Decker writes in

Epistolary Practices: Letter Writing in America before Telecommunications, correspondents would frequently associate a letter very closely with its corporeal
human sender: "the figural identification of the absent correspondent with the
mailed object takes as its occasion the theatrical presence of the object; for
correspondents, that object constitutes the actual bodily extension of the sender
or recipient" (40). Thus, to Elizabeth's intended correspondents, her idiosyncratic hand on a folded page or envelope made receipt of a letter different from
a similar event today, because except for the telegraph, no other method of
communication over large distances existed for them. Modern readers would
instead see such a letter as the most personal and most enduring mode of con-
tact, as well as the one requiring the most effort to send, and might also attribute a degree of quaintness to the letter or its sender. Early-nineteenth-century
recipients could not do so.

Those who compile and edit correspondence written between other people
appropriate it, and sometimes misappropriate it. After much reading, rereading,
analyzing, and reconstructing, an editor commonly develops a sense of ownership of the letters as if she had written them herself, another irony that recalls
the generic shift from familiar letter to edited letter, private to public. The commodification of the published volume parallels the original letters' journey
across time and space, always with the danger of loss or misdirection, to the
place the writer had intended, depended, and hoped. And the letters' new generic existence determines, as it did in the original one, the response. For the
first readers of the new collection determine whether others will read it, and
also determine as much as the author whether the correspondence will continue.

Elizabeth's repeated pleas for her correspondents to burn her letters went at
least partially unheeded, and that fact alone has made a study of this kind
possible. The intervention of McLean's "third person" (that is, someone who
was not a letter writer or recipient), or rather, a series of them, has given these
letters a contemporary life that most nineteenth-century correspondence, being
lost, cannot know. But the existence of the letters, certainly in collected, edited
form, also implicates the recipients—the intentional as well as the incidental
ones. As Decker writes, "The fact that [a] study enlists us as readers of other
people's mail, which we not only read but interrogate in pursuit of knowledge
answerable to interests foreign to the concerns of the correspondents, compels
us to ponder the pretexts by which scholarship, no less than the popular media,
erases the line between public and private domains" (5).

Letters, especially when the writer asks that the recipient destroy them, sometimes reveal attitudes normally kept for private conversation and written down only when the writer has no access to the different safety of conversation. Elizabeth sometimes warns recipients of her letters not to repeat her observations or reminiscences, and other times seems to trust them to keep her confidence: "This is a profound secret," she seems to whisper to Una about the once-youthful Nathaniel's love interests (February 14, 1862). And after angrily relating several of Sophia's inadequacies to Robert Manning, she reflects, "As we are neither of us married, we might safely deposit even secrets, if we had any, with one another. To Richard, who has a wife, I do not speak with the same freedom" (March 6, 1870). Interestingly—and perhaps typically—enough, Elizabeth apparently kept cordial relationships with the people she criticized, not allowing her anger to sever any family or friendly ties for long.

Some opinions expressed in letters seem unremarkable in their time but offensive later. Twenty-first-century readers may prickle at Elizabeth's negative attitude about the Irish and about Southerners, and may gape at her categorical dismissal of people now known as Native Americans. Decker gently argues for a degree of indulgence: "Subjected to interrogation, the writings of the most enlightened writers predictably manifest ventings of small mindedness and residues of bigotry. Even when we come upon the intensely virulent expression, it may be productive to suppose that there is a place for musings that are not willfully published" (6).

Elizabeth herself decided to preserve and publish facts of her brother's life despite his wishes, and in doing so provided information derivable from no other sources, such as his authorship of *Fanshawe* and "Alice Doane's Appeal." Apparently, her "injunction to burn my letters" (January 1869) met with a similar response from the family to Nathaniel's prohibition against his biography. She could not have expected or wanted scholars to conduct biographical research on her. Elizabeth felt competing obligations to her brother, or rather, to his legacy and to his privacy, and she sought to champion the former without compromising the latter. Although she made no mention of feeling she had betrayed Nathaniel, seeing personal letters used in George Parsons Lathrop's work stung Elizabeth, and her unwitting implication in proscribed biographical work surely lent vitriol to her criticism of Lathrop. The ethical dilemma of publishing Elizabeth's letters, then, recalls the drama that erupted in the extended Hawthorne family. And while at present Elizabeth Manning Hawthorne hardly constitutes a major figure in American letters, scholarly attention has turned to her on several occasions and may continue to turn up material so that, like her brother's, her reputation grows.

What prompted these family interlopers to save Elizabeth's letters was the fame of Nathaniel Hawthorne. But Elizabeth's corpus of interpersonal writing has a focus of its own, and her brother's complete absence from a large majority of the letters shows it to be much more than fraternal hagiography. This absence, ironically, gives the letters a value all their own, independent of what could be—and was—gleaned about Nathaniel. Their very scarcity of information on the novelist, outside of the few letters designed to transmit information about him, makes room for discussion of myriad other topics that show Elizabeth to be much more than a famous person's sister. Initially, her sisterhood recommends her and her letters to students of American literature, but the quality and richness of her writing also free her from the bonds of the much-researched, possibly dysfunctional family that could not in itself make her an important writer.

As an activity—and sometimes a chore—letter writing, frequently a daily affair, took up much leisure time in a middle-class family of the eighteenth- and nineteenth-century United States. Many prominent people's letters survive from these periods and contribute not only to what is known about their accomplishments—artistic, political, reformative, military—but also about themselves and those around them. The correspondence of Margaret Fuller, Elizabeth Palmer Peabody, Emily Dickinson, Alice James, and many other such figures has provided valuable insight not only into American history and literature but also to collections similar to this one and ultimately constitute important literary works in themselves.

Like many other such works, the collected letters of Elizabeth Hawthorne act as a window into nineteenth-century American life. Such historical events as the War of 1812, the Civil War, and the presidencies of Abraham Lincoln, Andrew Johnson, and Ulysses S. Grant appear in the letters as seen and read about in a home of the period rather than writ large, reminding us that history focuses on the actions of the most powerful, less so on the quotidian. Retrospect often privileges memories held in societal common, whereas national politics sometimes ironically constitute the least important aspect of a human life. What Elizabeth writes, and what she leaves unwritten—about abolition, women's suffrage, latest publications, and fashion—shows twenty-first-century readers the mores, literary tastes, history in the making, and political climate of the period now seen as the dawn of the modern United States. That Elizabeth wrote of current events as they took place and as she read of them in the print media endows these letters with an authority and authenticity that documents written in retrospect necessarily lack.

All writers express a multiplicity of voices and selves, and the number of Elizabeth's addressees, the length of her life as a correspondent, and the variety of topics she broaches give voice to much of her complexity. The letters show readers glimpses of a person's inner life: a middle-class woman, unusually educated, less-unusually unmarried, and perhaps most important, at leisure to pursue a life much as she would have liked. Elizabeth evolves as a writer and a thinker, and the letters, which begin in her adolescence and end shortly before her death, document the change, recording penmanship, introspection, and commentary from less to more sophisticated. Further, the sheer size and span of this set of documents constitute a principal value of this artifact.

The literary quality differentiates this compilation from a purely historical piece, and incidentally also lends more merit to this corpus as a historical document, because it shows Elizabeth's opinion and discernment about people and events that she knew personally or through the press. This same perspicacity marks her commentary on the literature of the period: novels by the Brontës, short stories by William Dean Howells, poems by Henry Wadsworth Longfellow, and essays of all kinds. Elizabeth muses on the private lives of George Eliot and Lord Byron, anticipates the latest book from Anthony Trollope, and expresses disappointment with Wilkie Collins, to say nothing of the less-well-known authors she mentions. This constitutes unknown but fairly sophisticated criticism of the literatures and societies of the period at a local, regional, national, and even international level. This corpus of letters, appropriately called an oeuvre, invites readers of the twenty-first century to welcome a long-overlooked but very valuable literary figure.

About the Text

G. Thomas Tanselle, in *A Rationale for Textual Criticism,* distinguishes between editing works written for private purposes and those written for public. Whereas private documents, including letters, are normally "best served" by an "attempt to present the texts exactly as they appear in the surviving documents," such documents occasionally merit an approach usually reserved for public documents, such as novels: "some letters, for example, may be in effect polished essays, which readers should have the chance to experience in texts purged of the idiosyncrasies of the documents" (63–64). A variation of such an approach has guided the editing of Elizabeth Hawthorne's letters. Naturally, this edition improves the legibility of the letters so that readers may read them more quickly and easily without navigating the pinched hand, small sheets of paper, and apparent disdain for margins. However, I have intentionally preserved some of the peculiarities of the various manuscripts, notably, the variant spelling. The result is an edition of selected letters that is less characteristic than the holographs in that its emphasis is on content rather than on visual interest. This approach has lent itself well to reproducing the letters, however, because Elizabeth Hawthorne intended mainly to correspond with family and thus revised much less than would the writer of a work that was meant to endure or reach a large audience. Consequently, I have not had the responsibility to reproduce many strikeouts and interlinings. By far the most useful guidance in editing these letters came from the editors of Nathaniel Hawthorne's letters for the *Centenary Edition of the Works of Nathaniel Hawthorne,* Thomas Woodson, L. Neal Smith, and Norman Holmes Pearson, with the assistance of Bill Ellis. Smith and Ellis prepared the Textual Commentary for that edition's *Volume XV, The Letters 1813–1843* and set an example that served as my model. I believe that I present a faithful edition of Elizabeth Hawthorne's selected letters.

The letters included here trace Elizabeth's growth as a writer and correspondent from age eleven to eighty. All of them, either in the form of holographs, longhand copies, typed copies, or retyped copies, reside in various archives, all of which have kindly lent copies of every extant, known letter or fragment written by Elizabeth Manning Hawthorne.

REPOSITORIES

The Bancroft Library at the University of California–Berkeley

The Hawthorne Family Papers were purchased by the library in 1953 and 1954 from John Howell Books, acting for Albert R. Vallière, an heir of Julian's widow, Edith Garrigues Hawthorne, who died in 1949. Elizabeth Hawthorne's papers in the collection are longhand transcriptions of fifty-eight letters, plus one letter in holograph, that Elizabeth wrote to her niece Una. The penmanship of all the copied letters is the same, but the transcriber is unknown. The collection contains two letters to Sophia Peabody: one transcribed along with those written to Una, and one in Elizabeth's own hand, the letter written on May 23, 1842. Seven fragments also exist, transcribed probably by Julian.

The Beinecke Library at Yale University

Yale owns six of Elizabeth's full letters, plus seven fragments, to Una, all in holograph and microfilmed. Their provenance is unknown. The letters show dates of 1870 to 1876.

New York Public Library

The Henry W. and Albert A. Berg Collection of English and American Literature houses the only three surviving letters written by Elizabeth to Nathaniel Hawthorne, along with two letters to Una; eight to Sophia, including a holographic version of the May 23, 1842, letter; one to Rose; two to Elizabeth Palmer Peabody; one to Miriam Manning; one to Julian; and one to Rose and Una together. The collection also contains seven fragments.

Boston Public Library

The Sophia Peabody Hawthorne papers contain six holographic letters that Elizabeth Hawthorne wrote in old age, all of them addressed to James T. Fields. Their provenance is unknown except for the date of their acquisition, June 26, 1937. Elizabeth wrote these letters in December of 1870 and January of 1871 after a request by Fields for memories of Nathaniel from Elizabeth's childhood.

The Huntington Library

The Hawthorne Family Papers contain thirty-nine holographs, written from 1870 to 1876. The library purchased these letters from Edith Garrigues Hawthorne, Julian's widow, in March of 1936.

The Peabody-Essex Museum

The Hawthorne-Manning Collection contains eleven holographic letters, ten written in old age to Richard C. Manning and one in middle age to Maria Louisa Hawthorne. The collection also includes a typescript made by Richard C. Manning Jr. of 149 letters and fragments, from holographs written from 1864 to 1883, that he later destroyed. Richard Manning Jr. gave carbon copies to Manning Hawthorne and donated the set of typed letters to the Peabody-Essex Museum, whose staff retyped them. Manning Hawthorne donated his set to the library at Bowdoin College.

The Hawthorne-Longfellow Library at Bowdoin College

The Hawthorne-Manning Collection houses nineteen holographic letters from Elizabeth Hawthorne's youth, dated 1814 to 1827, all included in this edition. Manning Hawthorne, who received them from Richard C. Manning Jr. made a gift of them to the library in April of 1975.

STATE AND LEGIBILITY OF THE MANUSCRIPTS

The holographs that I have seen at Boston Public Library, Bowdoin College Library, and the Peabody-Essex Museum remain in excellent condition. The paper has aged well, although the ink has faded, and wax seals have degenerated and possibly damaged the paper by saturating it. Broken seals have also left holes and tears in the paper, but the documents are quite legible. Almost anyone's handwriting requires patience to learn, but Elizabeth's is not egregiously idiosyncratic and indeed sometimes provides clues in dating, namely when a wrist injury in 1870 temporarily changed her penmanship.

THE CORPUS

The broad variety of manuscript materials used in this collection distinguishes it from much other textual editing work. Except for a few letters cited illustratively, Elizabeth Manning Hawthorne's correspondence has never seen publication, certainly not as a corpus. What became clear in the course of preparing this collection was the difficulty in gathering all of the known letters, transcribing them, organizing them chronologically when many of them bore no dates, and deciding upon a level of editing.

CRITERIA FOR INCLUSION

Some 288 finished or nearly finished letters written by Elizabeth Hawthorne exist, as do many fragments, and I know of no other extant letters or repositories. In this edition I have included 118 letters, fewer than half of those known to have survived. I have chosen the letters that show Elizabeth in her context: the family, the community, the region, the nation, and the international scene. The correspondence here illustrates the author's developing self, harmony and tension in the Manning-Hawthorne clan, local and regional happenings, popular and classic literature of the period, and news that became history. All of the letters have personal, historical, or literary merit, but in the name of practicality, for this edition I have chosen those that showcase Elizabeth's literary talents and wit, that furnish historical information typically overlooked, and that refer to people and events familiar to those who will read the correspondence.

In writing a book that focuses on Elizabeth rather than her brother, I have had to choose which letters pertaining to Nathaniel should be included. Indeed Elizabeth's material referring to Nathaniel has seen publication for many decades and appears elsewhere. Elizabeth's sibling relationship to a famous novelist prompted the Manning and Hawthorne families to keep and indeed to preserve the letters as sources of information on Nathaniel. To showcase Elizabeth's writing ability, biography, and relationship to Nathaniel, I have included one of the three extant letters that Elizabeth wrote to her brother. To highlight the degree and importance of Elizabeth's contribution to the biographical corpus on her brother, I have included all six extant letters written to James T. Fields about Nathaniel's childhood and youth. Readers will recognize the now-famous biographical details not always attributed to his sister.

CHARACTER OF THE HOLOGRAPHS

In the fashion customary in her youth, Elizabeth Hawthorne used no envelopes, but folded her letters, sealed them with wax, and wrote the address on the face, which was intentionally left blank for that purpose, writing what seems most insufficient to a twenty-first-century postal customer, for example, "Miss Sophia Peabody/Boston." She wrote in a variety of inks, possibly colors, although the fading reduces to guesswork any attempt to ascertain the original tint. She used different colors of sealing wax, such as red and black, and pressed the seal with an embosser. Later, along with other correspondents of the period, she began to use postage stamps and envelopes, allowing her to write all over both sides of the leaves. In old age, Elizabeth began to ignore margins, writing from top to bottom and from end to end of a page.

EDITORIAL POLICY
Format

Elizabeth Hawthorne followed a fairly regular format typical of the period. She normally headed her letters at the upper right, although what she wrote varied. She usually began with the town in which she wrote: Salem, Raymond, Beverly, or Montserrat, although she used the last two interchangeably. She did not write the state and rarely wrote the day of the week. Next she normally wrote the month, sometimes abbreviating variously, so that January appears as "January," "Jan," "Jan.," or "Jan ^{y}." Afterward, she wrote the date, also variously, so that "10," "10th," and "10th" all appear. The longhand transcriptions held in the Bancroft Library invariably show the "10th" format. Sometimes she included the year, but often she did not. She followed the heading with a salutation at the left margin, sometimes with a comma, sometimes without. In her youth, she normally wrote "Dear," ("Dear Uncle" to Robert Manning); in old age she wrote "My dear" ("My dear Sir" to James T. Fields). Elizabeth rarely began a new leaf simply to finish a sentence, paragraph, or letter, preferring instead to write in the margins, sometimes overwriting existing text at a right angle. She wrote a closing, such as "your affectionate Aunt," as space allowed, sometimes leaving it out altogether, and sometimes capitalizing the first word, that is, usually "your." She normally capitalized "Aunt." She also signed her letters as space permitted, sometimes writing "E. M. Hawthorne," for example, but preferring "EMH" or "E. M. H." in old age. Sometimes, apparently because she felt rushed or had no more space on the page, she left the letter unsigned.

For this edition I have reserved the upper right of the page for the heading, reproducing what I find on the manuscript and adding the year, bracketed, where it is absent. I have attempted to copy the heading—with capitalization, spelling, and abbreviation—to reflect the various manuscripts. I have copied sentences that appear in margins and at right angles, placing them at the end of the letter, because Elizabeth used these blank areas probably only when she had exhausted the customary writing spaces. The closing and signature I have regularized to the right margin, but kept the capitalization and punctuation as I read it on the manuscript.

Indentation

Elizabeth opened the body of her letters with a deep indentation, but indented very little thereafter. I have identified paragraph breaks by checking for sentences that begin at the left margin after the previous sentence ends short of the right margin, especially if a long dash follows the previous sentence. I have silently omitted these long dashes. In a few cases I have made a paragraph break to improve the legibility of the text.

Punctuation

This issue presents some difficulty, not only because the Bancroft and Peabody-Essex transcribers have punctuated some of the letters in a manner unlike that in which Elizabeth punctuated the holographs, but also because Elizabeth wrote certain marks very much alike. Periods and commas look sometimes like dots, and other times like small arcs. Elizabeth occasionally capitalized after no punctuation mark ending a complete sentence. Nineteenth-century writers made more use of the dash, including with commas, than today's writers do, and Elizabeth made frequent use of it. The Bancroft and Peabody-Essex transcriptions show very few dashes, in contrast to the holographs, and I have copied mid-sentence dashes as I read them in the manuscripts.

When transcribing the holographs, I have followed the example of the *Centenary* editors, who worked with the letters of Nathaniel Hawthorne and silently used the context to decide on punctuation issues. For the Bancroft and Peabody-Essex transcriptions, I have copied what I read rather than try to guess the content of a lost holograph.

Orthography

Elizabeth Hawthorne spelled quite well. Many apparent misspellings are variant orthographies, now archaic ("staid" for "stayed") or now identified as British ("honour"). I have not changed these, nor have I attempted to regularize the text if two or more variants appear in the corpus ("labour" and "labor," for example). I have corrected in brackets apparent misspellings (such as "beleive"), because they distract unnecessarily, while variant spellings add flavor to the text. Such unusual spellings also provide an objective correlative to the nineteenth-century American political and cultural struggles with Britain. I have used brackets to regularize names (such as "Greeley") with the intention of reducing distractions. I attribute most spelling errors to typography rather than to ignorance, and to the typists rather than to Elizabeth Hawthorne.

Capitalization

Elizabeth followed common practice and capitalized in a manner that may be strange to current readers, possibly stranger for being inconsistent. She sometimes capitalized common nouns such as "Newspaper" in mid-sentence, for example, and I reproduce her choices here. When she departed from capitalization norms, for example, by beginning a sentence in lower case, I generally allow her form to stand.

Word Changes or Additions

I use brackets and notes to signal my editorial changes in words (such as "Yes" for "You") or additions of words for clarity ("can not" for "can") or to indicate the addition of presumed words or letters lost by holes, tears, or blots in the manuscript. I use the signal [*illegible*] when necessary. In one case, the text of the letter abruptly ends before the closing. Where that is the case, I have indicated the truncation with [*text ends*]. Parentheses in the body of letters come from the author herself or from the transcriber.

References to People

Elizabeth writes of many different people, some in her family or acquaintance, and others local or national figures. To reduce the need for endnotes, I have made lists of those frequently mentioned and introduced some of them in the section prefaces.

Presentation of the Letters

In the upper-left corner before beginning a new letter, I indicate the repository that owns the manuscript. Next I list a number for reference, indicating the sequence of each letter in the reconstructed chronology. Next appears the recipient's name, almost always stated in the letter or address, and occasionally deduced from the context or from notes appended by others. In the endnotes, I commonly supply information about the people and events mentioned in the letter and note any changes made to the manuscript: spelling, capitalization, or punctuation. These notes also record any peculiarities such as marginalia or markings presumably made by others than Elizabeth.

Familial Referents

MANNING ELDERS, MATERNAL RELATIVES
Miriam Lord Manning (1748–1826): "Grandmother," "Grandmaam"
Mary Manning (1777–1841): "Aunt Mary," "Miss Manning"
William Manning (1778–1864): "Uncle William"
Elizabeth Clarke Manning Hawthorne (1780–1849): "Mother," "Maam"
Richard Manning (1782–1830): "Uncle Richard"
Susan Dingley Manning: "Aunt Susan," "Mrs. Manning," wife of Richard
    Manning
Robert Manning (1784–1842): "Uncle Robert"
Rebecca Dodge Burnham Manning: wife of Robert Manning
Priscilla Manning Dike (1790–1873): "Aunt Priscilla," "Aunt Dike," "Mrs. Dike"
John Dike (d. 1871): "Mr. Dike," husband of Priscilla Manning Dike
Samuel Manning (1791–1833): "Uncle Sam"

MANNING COUSINS, CHILDREN OF ROBERT MANNING AND
REBECCA DODGE BURNHAM
Maria Manning (1826–1917)
Robert Burnham Manning (1827–1902)
Richard Clarke Manning (1830–1904)
Rebecca Burnham Manning (1834–1933): "Beckie," "Becky"

HAWTHORNES
Nathaniel Hawthorne (1804–1864)
Maria Louisa Hawthorne (1808–1852)
Una Hawthorne (1844–1877)
Julian Hawthorne (1846–1934)
Rose Hawthorne (1851–1926)

PEABODYS
Elizabeth Palmer Peabody (1804–1894): sister of Sophia and an intellectual and
    educator

Mary Tyler Peabody Mann (1806–1887): sister of Sophia Peabody Hawthorne and wife of Horace Mann

Sophia Amelia Peabody Hawthorne (1808–1871)

OTHER FAMILY MEMBERS MENTIONED

Judith Hathorne Archer: one of Elizabeth's aunts from her father's side

Mrs. Caroline Archer: a Hawthorne cousin

Nancy Forrester Barstow: one of Elizabeth's cousins from her father's side

Gordon Coit: a cousin

Elinor Barstow Condit: a Hawthorne cousin

Aunt Eunice [Hathorne]: one of Elizabeth's unmarried aunts from her father's side

Rachel Hathorne Forrester: one of Elizabeth's aunts from her father's side

Kezia and Sally: Susan Dingley Manning's relatives

Sally Lord: Miriam Lord Manning's sister

Richard Clarke Manning Jr. (1867–1957): "Little Dickie," son of Richard C. Manning and Sarah Elizabeth Yeaton Gould Manning

Sarah Elizabeth Yeaton Gould Manning (1833–1911): "Lizzie," wife of Richard C. Manning

Ruth Manning Rust: "Aunt Rust," sister of Richard Manning

Ann Savage: a Hawthorne cousin

Mrs. Lucy Lord Sutton: a cousin of Elizabeth Clarke Manning Hawthorne

Nonfamilial Referents

Abbie: the Coles' granddaughter

Alcott, Mr. [Amos Bronson]: philosopher and a friend of Ralph Waldo Emerson

Almon, Miss Mary, "May": unidentified Salemite

Appleton, Mr. and Mrs. Tom: Elizabeth's landlord and landlady after Jane Cole's death

Appleton, Tommie: Mr. and Mrs. Appleton's son

Berry, Mrs.: unidentified

Blaisdale, Mrs.: unidentified teacher

Bradford, Mr. Alden: editor of *American Magazine of Useful Knowledge*

Bradford, George: one of Una's teachers

Bradley, Rev. Mr. Caleb: ran a boarding school where Nathaniel once attended

Bridge, Mr. Horatio: lifelong friend of Nathaniel Hawthorne

Browning, Herbert: unidentified (although Elizabeth refers to him as "a son of the Poet")

Burchstead, Mrs.: unidentified neighbor

Cabot, Mrs.: unidentified

Carlton, Elizabeth, or "Betsey": a schoolmistress in Salem

Carlton, Eunice: unidentified, probably Betsey's sister

Charlie: unidentified

Cheever, Rev. Mr. George: a schoolmate of Nathaniel at Bowdoin

Cole, Jane: daughter of Samuel and Harriet Cole, Elizabeth's landlady after Harriet's death

Cole, Samuel and Harriet: Elizabeth's landlord and landlady from 1850 to 1877

Cole, Hattie: a daughter-in-law of the Coles

Cole, Israel: son of Samuel and Harriet Cole

Cole, Jennie: unidentified

Cole, Mrs. Israel: Israel Cole's wife

Cole, Sammie: son of Samuel and Harriet Cole

Cole, Zachariah: son of Samuel and Harriet Cole

Curtis, Mr. G. W. [George William]: editor of *Harper's Weekly* and a lifelong friend of Nathaniel

Davis, Mrs.: unidentified neighbor

Dingley, Jacob: surely a relative of Susan Dingley Manning
Dora: unidentified
Emerson, Mr. Ralph Waldo: American author, poet, and philosopher
Evans, Mrs.: unidentified
Felt, Mrs. Margaret Heussler: married to Jonathan Porter Felt
Fields, James T.: Nathaniel Hawthorne's publisher and friend
Foster, Mrs.: unidentified
Frances: unidentified
Gay, Mr. March: unidentified
Giddings, Daniel: widower of Miriam Lord Manning's late sister, Sarah Lord
Giddings, Sarah: Daniel Giddings's oldest daughter
Gray, W. S.: cashier of the Essex bank
Hamilton, Gail: American teacher and writer
Higginson, Storrow: Una Hawthorne's first fiancé, nephew of T. W. Higginson
Higginson, Col. T. W.: an abolitionist and a supporter of Emily Dickinson
Hodges, Mrs.: an acquaintance of Elizabeth Hawthorne
Holmes, Dr. [Oliver Wendell]: a physician and poet
Ingles, Mr.: unidentified
Jewett, Ellen: unidentified
Kellogg, Mr.: unidentified
Lancaster, Mrs.: unidentified
Lander, Miss [Louise]: a sculptor with whom the Hawthornes socialized in
    Rome
Larcom, Miss Lucy: local and regional literary figure and feminist
Larson, Mr. Louis: unidentified
Loring, Mr., and Mrs. George Bailey: cousins of Sophia Peabody Hawthorne
Mulock, Miss: Dinah Maria Mulock Craik, English author
Needham, Eliza: unidentified
Page, Susan: unidentified
Payne, Miss: unidentified
Peabody, George: Sophia Peabody's brother
Peckham: attorney involved in suit over publication of Nathaniel's biography
Pickman, Miss [Love] Rawlins: an aunt on the Peabody side
Poole, Jane: an employee in the Manning-Hawthorne household
Robbins, Miss: schoolmistress
Russel, Mr. and Mrs. J.: unidentified neighbors
Sanborn, Mr. Frank: Concord schoolteacher and abolitionist
Shepard, Miss Mary: Salem schoolteacher

Sontag, Madame [Henriette]: famous German operatic and concert soprano

Spiller, Mr.: unidentified

Storey: local, prominent family that included Moorfield Storey, first leader of the NAACP, and Augusta Storey, an acquaintance of the Mannings

Story, Charles: unidentified, possibly same family as Storey above

Sumner, Mr. [Charles]: U.S. Senator and opponent of slavery

Taylor, Mr.: minister at Manchester

Thackeray, William Makepeace: British author

Thoreau, Mr. Henry David: American writer and philosopher

Ticknor, William D.: Nathaniel Hawthorne's publisher and friend

Trollope, Anthony: Victorian writer

Upham, Mr. [Charles Wentworth]: an ordained minister and important political figure

Washburne, Mr.: a minister

Webster, Albert: Una Hawthorne's second fiancé

Weld, Mr.: unidentified

Wesley, Miss: unidentified

Wheatland, Dr.: unidentified

Wheeler, Mr.: a cabman living in Montserrat

Whipple, Mr.: a storeowner in Salem

White, Mr.: a milkman

Williams, Mr. [Isaiah Thornton]: attorney and Swedenborgian

Worcester, Mr. Joseph Emerson: a famous lexicographer and teacher under whom Nathaniel studied

Wyeth, Mrs.: unidentified

The Letters

Of the three sections of letters herein, this one represents the longest span of time, twenty-eight years, and features twenty-seven letters. Elizabeth wrote the first letter at age eleven to her uncle Robert, and the last to her future sister-in-law, Sophia Peabody, a few days before Sophia's marriage to Nathaniel. This section of letters shows the marked changes in Elizabeth's writing style and social habits from childhood to middle age. It also traces the changing living arrangements that the Hawthorne family made between Salem and Raymond, and it shows the acquaintance between Elizabeth and two of the Peabody sisters, Elizabeth and Sophia.

After her husband's death, in 1808, Elizabeth Clarke Manning Hawthorne's brother Robert Manning assumed much financial responsibility for her and her three children, acting as something of a surrogate for the late Captain Hawthorne. The Hawthornes moved from the Manning home in Salem to a new house in Raymond, Massachusetts, in a section of the state that in 1820 became part of Maine. Mrs. Hawthorne's brother Richard owned a house, a store, much land, and livestock there, and the earlier letters of this section show correspondence between family members in Raymond and those in Salem, typically including Grandmother Miriam Lord Manning, Aunt Mary Manning, and Aunt Priscilla Manning Dike. The Hawthornes did not move permanently, returning instead to Salem in various stages. In this twenty-eight-year period, while Nathaniel moved frequently—going to boarding school, to Bowdoin College, to Boston, and to Brook Farm, with periodic residence in Salem—Elizabeth simply moved to Raymond twice, then back to Salem with her mother, whom the children called "Maam" (a term similar to today's "Mom").

Elizabeth writes of current local events such as the War of 1812, of such periodicals as *The Analectic* and *The Polyanthus,* of her travels to her Hawthorne relatives, of contemporary authors such as Ralph Waldo Emerson and Thomas Carlyle, and of her brother's leg injury that is well known to his biographers. Letters written in Elizabeth's late thirties show her on cordial terms with Elizabeth and Sophia Peabody, exchanging reading material and making plans for evening walks.

In childhood and adolescence Elizabeth signs her name "Hathorne," but because she frequently uses initials rather than a signature to close her correspondence, readers cannot see until the end of this group of letters that she begins to write her name "Hawthorne," as Nathaniel does. Readers will note the occasional resentful tone and sharp wit and the emergence of an engaging, graceful writing style, brush strokes in the self-portrait that Elizabeth paints with her correspondence.

Salem [Wednesday] Jany 12th 1814

Dear Uncle.

I wish you a happy new year, & thank you for the sheep. Did you know there was a new library in Salem? It is kept in a trunk at school Miss Pearson gave us a book called The Village Maid New year's day in the forenoon, & in the afternoon the library [commenced]. I don't know as Nathaniel's foot will ever get well if you don't come home. [He won't] walk on it & the doctor says he must; so do come soon. Do you like to sleep in a room with a fire in it as well as you used to? How does Uncle Richard do? Does he like the eastwind as well as he thought he should? I have not had one sleigh ride this winter. Grand-maam has a bad cold & keeps up chamber, but she is better than she was. The rest of the family are tolerably well.

Good-bye, Dear Uncle
E. M. Hathorne[1]

—∿—

Salem, July 27th 1814

Dear Uncle,

We have received the Analectic magazine for July & the Polyanthus for June. They will be sent down to you with my letter.[2] As you do not think it advisable for us to visit Raymond this summer, Mary & [Priscilla] intend going to Che-bacco to stay a week or fortnight.[3] [Don't] forget the letters you [promised to write] us. We have had a great many string beans & cucumbers out of the gardens. [Maam planted a] number of small cucumbers, but as it is sometime since rain has fallen, they do not grow very fast. How does Richard's garden flourish? How do the lambs do? Have the bears taken any more of them? Mary says that the seven dollar prize at Mr Whipple's will be lost for want of the ticket.[4] Do you recollect of lending Temper to any one? If you do, Maam would thank you to send her word. It is time for me to leave off, for I have exhausted all my materials.

Good-bye, dear Uncle.
Elizabeth M. Hathorne[5]

Bowdoin College Library
Number 3: To Robert Manning

Salem September 10th 1814.

Dear Uncle.

You must not expect me to write you a very long letter though it is a good afternoon; for Maam & the three children intend going to Ipswich by daylight Monday morning & I must put up some clothes. We have sent away a trunk of books, including some of yours, & three more trunks, containing the most valuable things. Grandma'am, Priscilla, and Mary will stay to the last, I believe, if they are left alone. Half of the inhabitants of Salem are moving into the country towns.⁶ Nathaniel wants Ma'am to let him stay to see the English, but as he is one of the three children, he must go. I believe we do not receive many more letters from you than you do from us. We want to know where you are. We expect a letter from you every day. [Don't] disappoint our expectation any longer. Good-bye, dear Uncle.

E. M. Hathorne

PS Tell Richard that we shall not accept his offer & drive him from his house into a log hut. Mr Ingles has just arrived & will set out on Monday or Tuesday, he will bring the things which you desired.⁷

Bowdoin College Library
Number 4: To Richard Manning

Salem May 29th 1815

Dear Uncle,

I hope you will continue to be pleased with the dogs; what do you call them? Robert earnestly requests that you will not cut off their ears & tails.

Nathaniel is much stronger than he was, he rides out quite often. Ma'am thinks of visiting Raymond with him when strawberries are ripe. I should like to see Aunt Susan. [Don't] you intend to bring her to Salem? Ma'am, Mary & Priscilla send their love to her. There are two schools kept in this house. [Don't] you think it rather uncommon? Mary keeps an afternoon school, Nathaniel keeps school for Louisa, who is his only scholar. I expect she will soon leave him. Robert bought the "account of Rachel Baker" some time ago, but he waited for a favourable opportunity to send it.[8] I shall send my letter as far as Portland, by private conveyance.

I hope you will write soon to your affectionate niece
Elizabeth M. Hathorne

Dear Brother I intended writing to you by Mr Dike, who conveys this as far as Portland, but have not had time, so Elisabeth permits me to say a few words in her letter we were much gratified, with receiving yours of the 3[d] of this month, but I am obliged to those with requesting you to write concerning your health, and concerning your house, and if it would be agreeable to you to receive a visit from Maam.[9]

—៣—

Bowdoin College Library
Number 5: To Mary Manning

Raymond August 1816

Dear Aunt,

I do not know what can be much more foolish than to write a long letter about nothing, this, however, I am required to do; much against my will, I can assure you. Perhaps you will call it a good exercise for my patience. it may be the same to read it.

We have no rusberries; if we had, mother would make the jelly with can I say with pleasure? I have [received] a letter from Eliza Needham.[10] Are my letters shown to Mr Dike? If they are I shall not write any more. Nathaniel will bring you a most beautiful tansy cheese.

I like riding about very much, but if my time is at my own disposal, I shall not make one visit while in Raymond: I always dislike them, but never so much as at present. People can talk about nothing tolerable but their neighbor's faults: That theme rouses them from the languor which otherwise overwhelms them, & then no tongue is silent. Yet I believe this is not exclusively the case here. The society here almost equals that of Salem, & it is much pleasanter living here. Write us word of how Sally Lord does.[11] Can you reconcile Aunt Rust to spend her life in this cold, unfruitful country?[12] Can you be reconciled yourself? Stay here one summer you will not be reconciled to live in any other place.

I close my letter with an earnest request that you will ask no more letters from me, for I was never so much engaged as at present.

Elizabeth M. Hathorne[13]

Raymond, Oct^br 28th 1816

My dear Grandmother

We have not received any letter since the 4th day of October, & my mother left Portland on the 14th. Maria Louisa attended school constantly while she remained there. I was rejoiced to see Sebago once more, for I was no better pleased with Portland than I expected to be. It was very smoky, disagreeable weather from the time you left us, until I returned to Raymond on the 12th day of October. We are not yet in suspense respecting our situation for this winter. Mr. Spiller will remove this week, much to the satisfaction of all concerned. We shall expect a letter from Nathaniel by the next mail. We wish to know what school he attends, whether he will continue to study Latin, & many other particulars respecting him & our other friends in Salem. Perhaps Samuel has commenced his journey, but if he has not, Priscilla will remember to send the things my mother mentioned in her letter, particularly Spenser's Fairy queen, & the first number of the large edition of Shakespeare, which contains his portrait. If she can conveniently send one dozen blue silk buttons, some blue cord for the sleeves & some narrow ribbon for the collar of my pelisse. Do not forget to send the books with the other furniture. If convenient, & if goods are cheap in Salem, my mother wishes you to send by Samuel an olive bombazet for me, & Scotch plaid for herself & Maria Louisa.[14] Those articles were dear in Portland. Can none of the family spend time to write a few lines? I shall write to Nathaniel soon, perhaps next week. All the family here are well, & desire to be remembered to you. We wish to know whether Sally and Caroline [Archer] are gone to Baltimore. Give our love to them, & request them not to write to me. I am much obliged to them for neglecting to do so. I should be glad to receive a letter from Eliza P Needham, from Jane Poole & from some others. I remain &c.

Elizabeth M. Hathorne[15]

Salem August 18, 1818

Dear Uncle:

I came home Saturday, and should have written to you the next day, but, as I had been absent three weeks I had so much to say & to hear, that I had no time till now. Mr Dike received your letter Saturday evening. We were sorry to hear that the house will not be finished till November; because so long a journey in cold weather will be disagreeable. We are all well now, but Louisa has been sick. You must not complain of our not writing, for two letters have been sent you, and we can tell you nothing but what you know already. Mr Dike desired me to say, that he was afraid he should not have it in his power to visit Raymond this summer, because he expected two vessels very soon, and should then be too much engaged. For several days past, the weather has been cold enough for September! We hope you will not have the head-ache while you are in Raymond; but it is rather strange that you should not; is it because you do not feel the Eastwind there?

I am become quite an early riser since you left us, & very sociable, been to Mrs Forrester and Mrs Barstow, and Mrs Archer, so you can't expect my letters to be quite as long as if I staid at home all the time.[16]

I want to know how Mrs [Richard] Manning was pleased with her gown, and handkerchief. &c &c and to see her, and Uncle Richard, and Kezia and Sally.[17] I shall write to Mrs Manning and Kezia and Sally soon and they must write to me. Having nothing more to say, I remain &c &c &c &c &c &c &c &c

Elizabeth Manning Hathorne

—w—

Salem August 24, 1818.

Dear Uncle,

I hope I need not "look out for breakers" if I write to you every week that would be very hard. I suppose you received my letter of last Monday or Tuesday, I forget which. Who did you carry to meeting with you, you and Mr and Mrs Manning could not all go in one chaise. It is so long since we heard of your going to meeting, that Mrs Manning has been seriously alarmed lest you should have forgotten how to behave. Mr Samuel Manning intends to send the trunk this week, and will let you know in what packet. We have received all of your letters, but we don't know whether or not Mr Dike intends visiting Raymond this summer.

I had a very pleasant visit in Newberryport, I like it much better than Salem. I staid there three weeks: a fortnight longer than I at first proposed. We have had, since you left us, one number of the Analectic Magazine, one of the Port Folio, and one of the Atheneum. I have written to Caroline Archer and I go to see my relatives and acquaintances quite as much as is desirable.[18] Do you think you shall be at home as soon as the first of September? We have had no rain for this last three or four weeks, except a little this morning.

W. S. Gray, the cashier of the Essex bank, has failed, and is gone to Windsor, in Vermont.

I am commissioned with a large stock of loves and tendernesses, and good wishes, &c &c &c &c &c &c &c &c &c &c, but I always omit everything of this kind; it is enough to say that we are all well, and I hope you are the same. I remain, &c &c &c &c &c &c &c

E. M. Hathorne

Mrs Manning, Kezia, and Sally are most respectfully desired to write to me.

Miss Mary Manning absolutely disavows all thoughts upon the subject of you going to meeting; she neither knows nor cares anything about it.

—m—

Bowdoin College Library
Number 9: To Priscilla Manning Dike

Raymond November 4, 1818

Dear Aunt,

We were very much disappointed at not receiving a letter from you the first week after our arrival, and had almost determined not to write till you had set us the example, but did not wish to lose so good an opportunity as now presents itself.[19] Mr Manning has just returned from Portland, where he went to see Mrs Lancaster, who inquired for you, and intends visiting us soon, that is, she says so.

I think we shall be very well content in the midst of the woods, when we are settled in the new house;[20] but it would be much more agreeable to us to have Grandmother remove [here] this winter; therefore we shall be obliged to you if you will raise no new objections to that event, as we are not sufficiently disinterested to gratify [our] wishes at our own expense.

Mr Gay brings you a pot of butter from Mrs [Manning] of her own manufacture; and on his return to Raymond he will take charge of Jane [Poole],[21] for which Uncle Robert has engaged to pay him, and that his horse & himself shall be provided for by the family while he is in Salem.

I think you will have no reason to complain of us, when you see all the letters we have written. I like Salem much better than I did when I was in Raymond before, but I do not wish to return. We have all of us been well since our arrival, we hope you will not neglect writing another week, should be pleased to receive letters from any of our friends, desire to be remembered to them all, and I remain, &c &c &c

E. M. Hathorne

PS   Mother desires you to send us some butter crackers, & if we send a box, to return it, & to give the inclosed to Miss Manning.[22]

—ℳ—

Bowdoin College Library
Number 10: To Mary Manning

Raymond Wednesday Nov. 1818

Dear Aunt,

We received your letter of the 4th of November, and were glad to hear the family was well. I wish you would not say so much about "<u>Brother Robert</u>" and "<u>Sister Susan,</u>" &c &c, we have determined not to write again if you do so any more.

We hope Mrs Dike has another girl, as we should be sorry to take Jane from her, and yet we find it quite impossible to get good help here

Mother is very careful of her health, & you need not be afraid of our going into the house too soon, we have had fires there all this week, & it is now perfectly dry, in every part, & we shall remove next Monday, or, at farthest Wednesday or Thursday.

Do not omit sending the letter paper, let it be as nice as this, which I am writing on, and larger. We could not get any in Portland, but we bought some in Salem at Mr Whipple's.

I should like to have you buy me a pair of white worsted stockings, and a parchment memorandum book with morocco covers.

Mother is very much obliged to you for your attention to the bills, but there was 25 cents due to Mrs Berry for some yarn, which she forgot to mention in her letter, & Jane will know whether it was paid for when she purchased it. Mother desires you will send by Mr Gay [numbers] of the <u>Registers</u> and <u>Gazettes</u> you have received since we left Salem, and save all the papers you have to send by Uncle Robert, because Mr Manning never saves his papers.

The chimneys of the new house draw smoke very well; we are more pleased with it every day.

Mother desires you will give our love to Aunt Eunice, & tell her we were very sorry we could not call & see her. I did not call to see Mrs Archer, before I came away, because I did not know where she lived. Tell Miss Hathorne I hope she has not forgotten her promise of writing to me.[23] We hope you will write this week, & I remain , &c &c

E. M. Hathorne

P.S. We are all well, & I hope you are the same. Mother desires you will burn this before you read it. You must let Jane wear your knot shawl, and as many more clothes as you can spare & you must give her a good pair of gloves & some crackers in her pocket, to eat on the road

Send a small phial of essence of peppermint which is by the closet window, & a piece of soap which Mother left in the closet. Send the trunk as soon as possible & if it is not sent Jane's feather bed with it. & the brass candlesticks in it. & any thing else you can think of. & don't forget the muslin.[24]

—*m*—

Bowdoin College Library
Number 11: To Priscilla Manning Dike

Raymond Dec 15. 1818.

Dear Aunt,

Mother desires me to say she is much obliged to you for your letter to her, and intends answering it very soon. Nathaniel went to Mr Bradley's this morning; and when Uncle Robert is gone, I am afraid we shall be very dull and lonesome.[25] I do not feel at all surprised that people think it strange we should remove from Salem, but I assure you we are extremely well contented here, and that nothing could induce us to return.

I must not say what I think of the inhabitants of Raymond, because I believe they have agreed among themselves that they are the most <u>polished</u> and <u>enlightened</u> people in the world, and therefore to call them ignorant and savage would be quite unpardonable. There are some decent families in the town, but the best of them are <u>merely</u> decent. I suppose your eloquence has succeeded in preventing Grandmother's removal this winter, but we hope you will not exert it to postpone that event any longer; we shall expect a visit from you all next summer, and then perhaps you will not pity us quite as you seem to do now.

Mrs Manning wishes to be remembered to all the family.

We have all been well since we came here; I thought it unnecessary to say anything about our health, as we were not sick. I should write to grandmother next week; I think Miss Manning has received letters enough from me. Jane appears to be much pleased, says she does not wish to return or to write to her father. Uncle Robert will tell you anything else you may wish to know about us, and I hope you already know how much we wish to see you all, therefore I have nothing else to say at present, but remain

Your affectionate niece.
E. M. H.

Was my letter to Uncle Sam received? I should be happy to receive letters from any of my friends, and will engage to answer all of them.

—∞—

Bowdoin College Library
Number 12: To Robert Manning

Raymond Jany 13th 1819

Dear Uncle

We received Mrs Dike's letter last week, and I intend to answer it soon: Miss Manning's letter to Uncle Richard was received at the same time.

We are all well, and safe, and though we wish to see you, we shall continue to remain tolerably contented till your return.

Uncle Richard went to see Nathaniel last Tuesday, and found him well.

The sleighing is not as good as it has been, and the weather has not been very cold since you left us.

Shall you return as soon as the first of February?—and do you intend to bring a boy with you? The one we have now does as well as can be expected from a <u>savage</u>; but he is too small to be of much use. I hope my letter to Uncle

Sam was received, and, if it is not too great an effort, I should like to have him write to me in return. Will not Mrs Dike visit us next summer, when Grandmother leaves Salem? I think she will be pleased with Raymond in summer, though it is certainly much to be lamented that so pleasant a place should be inhabited by people so rude and uncultured.

We hope all our friends in Salem are well, and we shall expect letters from them.

I am &c &c &c

E. M. H.

—⦙⦙⦙—

Bowdoin College Library
Number 13: To Priscilla Manning Dike

Raymond, Feby 24th 1819.

Dear Aunt,

It is now nearly a fortnight since we received a letter from our friends in Salem, so we hope Uncle Robert's return will not be much longer delayed.

We hope you are all as well as we are, & that you intend soon to write to us.

I am,

&c &c &c

E. M. H.[26]

—⦙⦙⦙—

Bowdoin College Library
Number 14: To Miriam Lord Manning

Raymond June 23 1819

Dear Grandmother,

We have received no letter from Salem since Uncle Sam and Nathaniel left us, and we wish much to hear from them.

We are all of us well; Uncle Robert's health has improved considerably since he came here, and Mother's is better than it was in Salem.

Maria Louisa wrote to Aunt Forrester, and intended to send her letter by Nathaniel, but it was mislaid and forgotten. She will write again soon, and I shall expect to receive a letter from Miss Hathorne. Miss Manning desired us to mention them in our letters, so we hope they are all well &c &c. Nathaniel must write next week if he has not written already.

We have had very fine weather for some time past, and we hope you enjoy this delightful season as much as we do. Strawberries are plenty, we often wish to send you some, but it would be still pleasanter if you were here to eat them.

I shall write to Miss Manning and Nathaniel soon and hope to receive letters from all our friends, Mother and the rest of the family desire to be remembered to you all. Jane behaves very well, and I am

Your affectionate Granddaughter,
E. M. H.

—⟋⟍—

Bowdoin College Library
Number 15: To Priscilla Manning Dike

[1819]

Dear Aunt

I have only time to say that I am well, & hope you are so too. I did not know I should have an opportunity, or I would have written before.

EMH.

—⟋⟍—

Bowdoin College Library
Number 16: To Elizabeth Clarke Manning Hawthorne

Salem, May 14th, 1822

Dear Mother,

I received Maria [Louisa]'s letter on Friday, and was very sorry to learn that you intend to come to Salem but I presume your determination is fixed, & I <u>know</u> that in one week after your return you will regret your present peaceful home.[27] Not all the pleasures of society, great as they <u>are represented</u> to be, can afford the slightest compensation for the tumultuous and irregular life which one is compelled to lead in a family like this. I wish I had remained in Raymond. I am obliged to visit every day and all day, because if I am half an hour at home, my ears are assailed by long and severe lectures, which may possibly be just, but are certainly most injudicious & ill-timed. Without doubt I am wrong in many instances, but if all my errors were crimes, the remarks upon my conduct, & the language which <u>my friends</u> employ towards me,[28] could not be more harsh than it is at present. If I attempt to converse with any one of the family, if I ask the slightest question, a reproof is invariably joined with the answer I receive. Bodily Labour comprises their only idea of intellectual and moral excellence, and an angel would fail to obtain their approbation, unless he came attired in a linsey-woolsey gown & checked apron, and assumed an honourable and dignified station at the washing tub.—If I remain at home, the whole family express their astonishment at my "moping in the house when the weather is so fine," & if I go out two days in succession, I am, with equal justice and elegance, accused of "spinning street yarn." If I do, I am blamed for devoting my attention exclusively to one person, who unfortunately never happens to be the right one. I shall never be able to give satisfaction to them, yet I believe all this is done and said in kindness, & that they really feel a great deal of solicitude for my welfare; but they do not understand the art of government. I am perfectly willing to be ruled and managed, but it must be done dexterously, and not by open rebuke, or repulsive frowns. But I will not weary you with anymore complaints, hope if you come, that the journey will be conducive to your health.—Maria [Louisa] will excuse my answering her letter, as I shall so soon be under the disagreeable necessity of seeing her. You know not how much I wish to go once more to Raymond, it is so pleasant in the country at this season, and I am obliged to remain in town. My compliments to Mr and Mrs [Dike]. Have you seen any of Mr Kellogg's family lately?

I am
Your affectionate daughter,
E. M. H.

I have not heard from Nathaniel for a long time.[29]

—⁂—

Bowdoin College Library
Number 17: To Richard Manning

Salem March 30th 1826

Dear Uncle,

I write at Aunt Mary's desire to express the surprise felt by all the family at learning that you had received a letter from Claremont of the kind you mention, and to assure you that nothing has been said by any one here which could induce Mr Daniel Giddings or his children to apply to you for assistance.[30] Sarah Giddings, the oldest daughter, staid in Salem at a Mrs Felts for three months last summer.[31] She called to see Grandmother, and afterwards dined here once, but was not invited to make us a longer visit. I do not think your name was mentioned to her. Grandmother requests me to say to you, that she hoped none of her children will be troubled as she has been, with the company of distant relations, and that if Mr. Giddings' children are in want, let them work as she did at his father's, and if they cannot maintain themselves so, let them go to the poorhouse. We are told that this Frances, whom you are desired to take, is already grown up. She has been in Newbury Port at Charles Story's, till they were obliged to send her home. Her sister Sarah has also staid with her relations in Newbury Port three or four months. We suspect that Sarah Giddings and her mother wrote the letters which you have received. Mrs. Giddings has a sister in Hopkinton, where Sarah spends a great part of her time. Grandmother advises you to avoid all connection with the family, as they are an artful, designing set of people.

We regret that Mrs. Evans has made you so long a visit. Perhaps you know that she was at that time a little deranged. In such a state of mind, she must indeed have been troublesome. She came to Salem a short time before she went to Raymond, lost her trunk upon the road, and Uncle Robert was obliged to go to Dover in search of it. It is strange that her husband should suffer her to go about as she has done, without anyone to take care of her, intruding upon all her acquaintances.

I am very sorry Aunt Susan's health is so poor; please to give my love, and that of the family, to her. Grandmother, and all your friends are very desirous to see both you and her. I hope that she will not forget to answer my letter. It will give me great pleasure to hear from her. Uncle Robert will write to you either this week or next. I must beg you to excuse the length of this letter, and am your affectionate niece

E. M. Hathorne

—⚏—

Bowdoin College Library
Number 18: To Mary Manning

Salem December 17th 1827

Dear Aunt,

It is so long since we have heard from you, that we begin to be afraid that you, or some of our friends in Raymond, are sick. The travelling is so bad that I suppose you will not think of returning at present. We wish to see you, but as all the family are perfectly well, should regret your taking an unpleasant journey. It has rained almost incessantly for a fortnight past, and the roads on this side of Portland are said to be nearly impassible.

Maria, Uncle Robert's little girl, has spent a week with us, and was very well contented, and sorry to go home. She talks a great deal, and is learning to read. Robert is well, and grows fast.

I suppose Uncle Robert told you every thing new in his letter, and nothing worth relating has happened since. Mother has had a present of a pair of spectacles, with tortoise shell bows, and gold clasps and sections. They clasp on the back of the head. You never can guess who gave them to her, but it was not a Dutch Burgomaster.

Maria [Louisa] has had an invitation to pass the winter in New York with Mrs Wyeth, and the next summer in Syracuse, with Mrs. Archer, but chooses to remain at home, at least for the present. Mrs. Dike is very well, and frequently walks out, when the weather will permit, which has not often been the case, of late. Rebecca has had a bad cold, but is recovering. I hope colds have not been so prevalent in Raymond, as with us. Hardly any one has escaped them here.

Have you heard any thing of Mrs. Sutton and her family, since you saw them?[32] Capt. Sutton has written to her to go to Buenos Aires; but I do not know whether she is going this winter.

Give our love to Uncle Richard and Aunt Susan. I hope they are well, and should like to see them. It must have been equally agreeable to you and to them, to be together on Thanksgiving-day. I believe it is the first time you were even absent from home on that occasion. We had a very pleasant time here. Mother has been better, for the last two months, than for several years before.

If we do not hear from you soon, we shall think the report of your marriage to the Dutch Burgomaster is true, and shall order three loaves of Simmons' best wedding cake, in your name, to celebrate the event. I am

Your affectionate niece
EMH[33]

—⁓—

Bancroft Library
Number 19: To Sophia Peabody

[Spring 1838]

My dear Miss Sophia,

For many days I have wished to write and tell you how much I regretted not having thanked you immediately for those beautiful tulips; but, as Mary supposed, I was ashamed to appear before you, either in person, or by note. I have not seen so great a variety for several years, and I kept them as long as possible, and looked at them almost continually till, in defiance of my efforts to preserve them, they faded. The flowers which Elizabeth sent, so sweet, and so tastefully arranged, I thought would be immediately bestowed upon my brother, who professes to regard the love of flowers as a feminine taste; so I permitted him to look at them, but consider them as a gift to myself; and beg you to thank her, in my name, when you write. I hope this warm weather agrees with you, and that next week it will be cool enough for Mary and me to walk. I wished to go this afternoon, but the thermometer stands at 98° in the sun, though it is after 4 o'clock. I did not know till last evening that your brother wished for Miss Payne's letters. I send them now, with the book of fruits, which your Mother said she should like to see, and the Quarterly Review. I do not know whether you can read this scrawl, but I have forgotten how to write.

Believe me yours,
E. M. H.[34]

New York Public Library
Number 20: To Sophia Peabody

[1838–1840]

Dear Sophia

I can hardly venture to expect you in this unpleasant east wind, but I presume there will be music, and your company would give us a great deal of pleasure.

I hope your family are all as comfortable as usual. Mother and Louisa both have the head ache.

As my messenger is waiting, I can say no more now, but I wanted to see you last evening it was so delightful.

yours,
E. M. H.

New York Public Library
Number 21: To Sophia Peabody

[Summer 1838–1840]

Dear Sophia,

I have delayed answering your kind note, in the hope of a change in the weather, that I might be able to propose a walk, but there seems to be no prospect of it. I have looked over these numbers of Shakespeare with much pleasure; some of the designs are very pretty.

Perhaps your Mother would like to look at these [numbers] of the "Magazine of Horticulture." there is an article by her friend Mr. J. Russel. Will you give my love to Elizabeth, and tell her that Nathaniel desired me to return this Portfolio, (which he has kept much too long,) with his thanks. For my own part I do not expect ever to see Elizabeth again, though I should like to have one more walk with her. She not only refuses to come to spend an evening with me herself, but appears to think the east winds will prevent you from coming, but we must hope for better times. I am very glad you mean to walk this summer.

I am writing in the dark. what very pretty notes you always write!

Do you know whether Mr. Taylor is to preach in town tomorrow, & if so, where?

yours affectionately
E. M. H.[35]

—⟁—

New York Public Library
Number 22: To Sophia Peabody

[April 1839]

Dear Sophia,

This is the first opportunity I have had to thank you for those beautiful flowers, or for the volume of Carlyle, which I am reading with delight. I cannot but sympathize with his idolatry of Goethe, and do not doubt that it arises from his comprehending him better than other people; but if we consider Goethe as he is generally represented, Carlyle's reverence for him seems almost as strange as the same feeling toward Voltaire would, in a good Christian.

I send you the last number of the Foreign Quarterly review. It contains some remarks upon Photogenic Drawing, and perhaps other things that you may like to see. I will also send Sir Philip Sidney's Arcadia, though I do not know whether you will want it now, but I think this is the right kind of weather for reading it. And speaking of the weather reminds me that I ought to apologize for not letting you know, as promised, whether I could come and talk with your mother last Friday. I could not obtain a messenger, in the forenoon, but I presume it was of [no] consequence, as it rained. When Mary is at home I hope for many delightful walks with your mother and with her.

If it is good weather tomorrow evening, will you not come and spend it with us?—If we cannot hear the music here, we can walk upon the common if you feel well enough. I do not propose a walk with your mother, while it is so warm. The heat of the summer is too oppressive. What a long scrawl I have written!

yours,

E. M. H.[36]

—⟋⟍—

New York Public Library
Number 23: To Sophia Peabody

[Summer 1839]

Dear Sophia,

I return the fourth volume of Carlyle, with many thanks to Elizabeth. I should have returned it sooner, but wished to keep it for Nathaniel to read, which he did with great pleasure

Here are half a dozen peaches for George, if he will accept so few.[37] We would send him more if we had them. Do you not think this weather delightful? I hope you enjoy it, and that you will soon be in such excellent health as to luxuriate, like me, in a north-east storm.

Louisa desires me to ask you if you are reading Mr Emerson's "Nature," as she has promised to lend it to a friend in Newbury Port, and will have an opportunity to send it tomorrow morning. Poor child! she has the tooth ache again, or she would have called, herself to ask you. I hope we shall see you and Elizabeth soon. I am in haste

yours,

EMH

—⟋⟍—

New York Public Library
Number 24: To Elizabeth Peabody

[Autumn 1839]

Dear Elizabeth,

As you were out on Saturday Evening, I hope you will be able to come and spend this evening with us—will you not?—I should be extremely happy to see Mary, though I despair of it; and though I cannot venture to ask Sophia, perhaps you can for me.—Pray tell me particularly how your Father is. we are all anxious to hear, and whether George is as before when we heard last.

I am, in haste,

E. M. H.[38]

—∿—

New York Public Library
Number 25: To Elizabeth Peabody

[Spring 1840]

Dear Elizabeth,

If you do not want this volume of Balzac, I should like to keep it for Nathaniel to read, next Sunday. You have never told me whether your Mother had completed her translation. Her stories of <u>old maids</u> always amuse me more than any others. But do you believe that such conversations as are related in some of his volumes could ever have been uttered?

I have not half of Nathaniel's tales, nor duplicates of any. I thought we had some in newspapers, and have been looking for them, but without success. If I could have found them, I should have sent you what we have in magazines. I wish I had copied the Seven Vagabonds, and others in that Token. "Dr Heidegger's Experiment["] was published in the Knickerbocker, and that must be the Fountain of Youth to which you allude. Just before I received your note I had been cutting out his articles in order to make a volume. I regret as much as you do that he would not be prevailed upon to collect them himself. Do not tell him you hope the <u>Whigs</u> will do any thing for him. He might think himself bound in honour to make some demonstration of his zeal for democracy: and I know besides that they never will—"to the victors belong the spoils".

My mother desires me to thank [you] for the beautiful flowers you have twice sent her. Will not you and Sophia come some pleasant evening to see us. Remember I spent an evening with you in December, and you have not been here since a long time before that.

I have staid at home all the pleasant weather till to day, when I have been to Marblehead. The reason I have not called for you is that I felt as if nothing less than a very long walk would do me any good. If you are not engaged every afternoon in the week why cannot we go to the beach some day at one or two o'clock. Those were the pleasantest walks I have ever taken, with you to the beach. Or would not your Mother and Sophia like to go.

I send you the last number of the Quarterly Review. You will find "Journalism in France" entertaining.

I am yours
E M Hawthorne[39]

—⚋—

Number 26: To Sophia Peabody

Salem. May 23rd 1842

My dear Sophia,

Your approaching union with my brother makes it proper for me to offer you my assurances of a sincere desire for your mutual happiness. I hope nothing will ever occur to render our future intercourse other than agreeable, particularly as it need not be so frequent or so close as to require more than reciprocal good will, if we do not happen to suit each other in our new relationship. I speak thus plainly, because my brother desired me to say only what was true: though I do not recognise his right to speak of truth, after concealing this affair from us so long. But I believe him when he says that this was not in accordance with your wishes, for such concealment must naturally be unpleasant, and besides, from what I know of your amiable disposition, I am sure you would not give us unnecessary pain. It was especially due to my mother that she should long ago have been made acquainted with the engagement of her only son: it is much more difficult to inform her of it at this late period, with only a few weeks to prepare her feelings for his marriage.

I anticipate with pleasure the renewal of our acquaintance, with the opportunity of becoming better known to each other. In the mean time, accept my best wishes, with those of my sister, for the continuance of your health and the accomplishment of your hopes of happiness, and believe me to be yours,

with regard,
E. M. Hawthorne[40]

—⚋—

New York Public Library
Number 27: To Sophia Peabody

Salem, June 15th 1842.

My Dear Sophia,

I am sorry to be so soon obliged to begin a note to you with an apology; but so it must be,—for not immediately replying to your very kind letter. Indeed a <u>note</u> in itself requires an apology; it ought to be an epistle of proper form and length; but I have an aversion to letter-writing which I trust you will take into consideration upon this and all future occasions.

We are all very desirous of seeing you, dear Sophia, but my brother gives us no hopes of enjoying that pleasure at present. My mother desires me to beg that you will both visit us this summer, even if you cannot come before your marriage. I dare say we shall, and must seem very cold and even apathetic to you; but after you have known us a little while it may be that you will discover more warmth and sympathy than is at first apparent. My mother, in deed, in disposition resembles her son; and you need not doubt that she is prepared to receive and love you as a daughter. Neither are my sister and myself wanting in that sisterly affection to which you feel that you are entitled, and which it will be a source of great happiness to us to find returned. I deeply regret that I said any thing in my note to give you pain; if we can all forget the past, and look forward to the future it will be better. The future seems to promise much happiness to you, for certainly I think your disposition and my brother's well suited to each other; but have you no dread of the cares and vexations inevitable in married life, and in <u>all</u> life, I allow, only in some situations we have in a great degree the power to withdraw from and forget them? I confess I should not have courage to incur any responsibility not forced upon me by circumstances beyond my control. I should not like to feel as if much depended upon me. In this, however, I am aware how much I differ from almost every one else, and how strange it must appear to you, especially just now. And this reminds [me] of the innumerable engagements that must press upon you and so occupy your time that you can have no more to share for me; so I will no longer detain you. My mother and sister send their love to you, and I am

yours affectionately
E. M. Hawthorne.[41]

The Letters

This group of letters, by far the largest at sixty-nine items, covers twenty years. Elizabeth wrote all of these letters in the period between the Hawthorne marriage in 1842 and Sophia's death in 1871. Readers who remember the warm acquaintance between Elizabeth and Sophia, evidenced by the letters in the last group, will note the scarcity in this group of any correspondence between the two women until Nathaniel's death. If Elizabeth wrote to Sophia between August of 1842 and autumn of 1864, no letters survive. This series of letters begins in 1851, after a nine-year gap in the extant correspondence of Elizabeth Manning Hawthorne.

In the period 1824 to 1834, Elizabeth's uncle Robert Manning married Rebecca Dodge Burnham and had four children—Maria, Robert, Richard, and Rebecca—with whom Elizabeth, old enough to feel like their aunt, later corresponded. These letters to the Salem cousins make up a sizable portion of Elizabeth's surviving correspondence, including those in this section and the next one.

During part of the Hawthorne marriage, Elizabeth, Louisa, and Mrs. Hawthorne lived with Nathaniel and Sophia, making correspondence unnecessary but also prompting Elizabeth to live upstairs and not show herself, even when the young, growing family needed help. Nathaniel and Sophia's marriage lasted nearly twenty-two years and produced three children, Una, Julian, and Rose, all of whom Elizabeth adored and eventually corresponded with, especially Una, who received a large proportion of the letters that Elizabeth wrote and that appear in this edition.

This section of letters begins almost two years after Mrs. Elizabeth Clarke Manning Hawthorne died in 1849. Nathaniel, Sophia, and the children moved to Lenox, Massachusetts, then Newton, before buying their first home, known as The Wayside, in Concord. Louisa went to live with Priscilla and John Dike, her aunt and uncle, and Elizabeth moved to Manchester, and then to Beverly, where she would live for the rest of her life as a boarder in a farmhouse. Nathaniel had published *The Scarlet Letter* and *The House of the Seven Gables,* and he and Sophia expected their third child, Rose, who arrived in May of 1851. Elizabeth refers to her translation of Cervantes's tales, which she never published. The surviving correspondence does not record the death of Louisa Hawthorne in a steamboat wreck in 1852 (see Miller, 384).

In 1853 President Franklin Pierce named his college classmate and old friend Nathaniel Hawthorne as U.S. Consul in Liverpool, so the family chugged away by steamer to spend seven years abroad in England and on the Continent. Elizabeth's letters to Una reflect her warm relationship with her niece and make reference to events in the United States and abroad. Many in the family fell sick in Rome—Una with malaria, and Nathaniel weakened, Elizabeth said, for life. The Hawthornes returned in 1860 to their Concord home at The Wayside, with Nathaniel gloomy and eventually ailing. He wasted away and died in May of 1864, and Sophia took the children, all by then in young adulthood, to live in Germany in 1868. Sophia died in London in 1871.

A few years after Nathaniel's death, Elizabeth wrote six letters to her brother's publisher and friend, James T. Fields, who had asked her for early biographical material. Elizabeth complied, furnishing many anecdotes that are well known to Hawthorne scholars. Fields and the later generations of biographers apparently took seriously Elizabeth's request for anonymity, because her name rarely appears in the myriad retellings of these childhood incidents. The letters to Fields much enriched biographies of Nathaniel, books that were written despite what Elizabeth describes as "my brother's especial injunction" against them.

New York Public Library
Number 28: To Nathaniel Hawthorne

Montserrat, May 3 [1851]

Dear Brother,

Your letter gave me an unexpected pleasure, for I really had but little hope of ever hearing from you again. I wish I could see the children, especially Una; I cannot bear the idea of their ceasing to be children before I see them. Why cannot you bring Una with you? I thank you for your invitation, but I do not like to go further from home than I can walk.

I have read "The House of Seven Gables," as everybody else has, with great delight. People who abjure, upon principle, all other works of fiction make an exception of yours. I cannot tell whether I prefer it to "The Scarlet Letter," and there is no need of drawing a comparison. The chapter entitled "Governor Pyncheon" seems to me unequalled, in its way, by anything I can remember; and little Pearl, too, is unique,—perfectly natural, but unlike any other child, unless it be Una. Louisa says that Judge Pyncheon is supposed to be Mr. Upham, but I imagined him to be a such more insignificant person,—less weighty in every sense.[42] There may be some points of resemblance, such as the warm smiles, and the incident of the daguerreotype bringing out the evil traits of his character and his boasts of the great influence he had exerted for Clifford's release. The greatest charm of both books, for me, is the perfect ease and freedom with which they seem to be written; it is evident that you stand in no awe of the public, but rather bid it defiance, which it is well for all authors, and all other men, to do. I would like to see the preface to the new edition of the Twice Told Tales, and shall be very glad of the engraving of your Portrait. Why cannot you have a daguerreotype taken of yourself and the children for Louisa and me. Nothing would give us more pleasure.

I stayed in Manchester from July to November, at a place called Kettle Cove, where the woods grow to the very edge of the water, and within a moderate walk of four fine beaches, one of which I had entirely to myself. I have walked there for hours without seeing anybody. There was a little fishing village near one end, but out of sight. Kettle Cove is a spot of peculiar characteristics—few people are born there, and few die; and they enjoy uninterrupted health. The very old go off from a sense of propriety, to make room for those who have a right to their places. They are more susceptible of enjoyment than any people I have ever met with; they wander about in the woods, and pick berries, and fish, and congregate together to eat chowders in the open air, on the grass,—old men and women 70 and 80 years of age, and those of all intermediate ages down to two or three. The weather is also cooler in summer and warmer in winter than is usual in these latitudes, being sheltered from the north by an amphitheater of hills, and only open to the sea. I never knew before how much beauty and variety a mist, brightened by sunshine, can impart to a landscape. The hills and the houses at a distance look as if they were based on air. There is a house in the Cove which I think would have suited you, and which you might have had. you certainly must have been happier near the sea; I would never go out of the sound of its roar if I could help it. There would have been no want of society, at least in the Summer. Mr Ticknor lives about a mile off and there is another Boston Family in the neighborhood. But you could have been alone, when you chose, more than I suppose you can now. Perhaps you never heard that our earliest peculiar ancestors, whose remembrances you have made permanent in the Introduction to the Scarlet Letter, preached, besides all his other great doings. Mr Taylor, the minister at Manchester, a man addicted to antiquarian pursuits, called to ask me if I knew anything about [them]. He said "he thought it possible I might have paid attention to my ancestry', and told me that this old Major, with about a dozen others, whose names he mentioned, used to go by turns to Manchester to preach. He had the information from Mr. Felt.

I came to Montserrat, which is a part of Beverly, the 3rd of January, in very severe weather, and partly from a cold, but more because the air of Salem where I was obliged to stay more than a month, and the confinement, did not agree with me, after almost living out of doors, as I did at Manchester, I was sick for nearly two months, more so than I have ever been in my life; I could eat nothing but gruel, and lost all my strength. But I am now perfectly recovered, rather in spite of the excessive care which Mrs. Cole, with whom I board, took care of me, than owing to it. I am with an excellent family, who do everything to make me comfortable, and very well accommodated: as well as at Manchester and at a much lower price. We supposed it would be much easier to communicate with Salem, as this place is only 2 ½ miles from the Beverly Depot, and within sight of the Rail Road. But Louisa has not been here since March, and I have not seen her since the first week in April, when I went to Salem. I have written three times to her and to you once before this, and have each time been unable to send the letters till they were too old. I dare say I shall have no opportunity to send this to the post office for a fortnight. But there are many advantages in my present position; I can lose myself in the woods by only crossing the road, and the air is very pure and exhilarating and the sea but a mile distant. Direct your letters to the care of Mr Samuel Cole, Beverly. I shall get them some time or other. I have been very busy about Cervantes's Tales.[43] I want to consult you about what I think a few necessary alterations, when you come.

yours,

E. M. H.[44]

—⁂—

[Autumn 1851]

Dear Sister,

I return the Wonder Book, which I admire; I read it to Hannah [the Coles' granddaughter], for as she is always here, it is more convenient to read anything to her, and her criticism is, after hearing the whole, that the book is not worth printing. After I had read the Seven Gables, she said, "[Yes]; I think it's worth reading;" as if it were rather doubtful, and it was hazarding something to say too much in its favour. Mrs. Cole does not like the Scarlet Letter, because the minister gets into so much trouble and she does not like "that young one," meaning poor little Pearl. Such are the opinions of the best judges here in Montserrat. I hope this Wonder Book will reach you without delay you do not say when you received my note, which Alfred carried on Monday evening. Alfred is going to school at Hampton Falls, tomorrow. I was glad of the Mouslin [muslin], and of the Newspaper. I am sorry you cannot all come and spend the evening yet, but I dare say we shall have sleighing, so some time this winter, and then Richard must come and bring you all. I hope you will be able to get here next week, for I want to see you and I want the things very much. Mrs. Cole has talked of coming and I doubt not would like to, but Mr. Cole is not easily moved: so it is very uncertain whether we come this winter. I suppose Una will not come to Salem as they are settled. I think it a very poor plan for them to go to Newton when it will be absolutely necessary to remove again in the spring. I think they might have decided to leave Lenox time enough to find a permanent residence this autumn. I suppose it is Sophia's plan; it is so much like the Peabodys never to be settled. If Nathaniel buys a place, she will have some excuse for leaving it in a year or two. Some of the Newspapers say that he is going to Lynn; Jane saw a paragraph to that affect in the Bee: do you think it is true? I should think not. I believe I told you how sick Miss Wesley was: she is decidedly better; Jane went to see her the other day; she was able then to sit up while her bed was making. When you come over, cannot you bring me an Orange to send her? I should like to let her see that I have not forgotten her. Jane wanted to carry her one, but there were none in Beverly.

Among the numerous things that I want are a larger Inkstand and more pens and ink. we had two or three glass inkstands; do you know where they are? The one I use now is very small. that was excellent ink that you sent me last and the pens were the best I ever had; the only steel pens and ink which did not seem to have a natural aversion to each other.

I am sorry Miss Betsey Carlton has been so sick: it seems as if I should never have an opportunity to go to see her. I intended the two last times I went to Salem, not to go home without visiting her, but you know I could not.

The book you want is too big to send by Israel, and Mr. Appleton does not go now as he did in Summer, so it must wait until you come. If we were fifty miles apart, it would not be much more difficult to communicate with each other. Mrs. Cole says I have been here nearly a year and Mrs. Dike has not been over since; I do not wish her to come this winter for she would assuredly take cold. I am very glad to hear that she is better. I have not been out for nearly a month; when I did go I was almost frozen; though I wrapped up as well as I could. I felt as if I had nothing on. I cannot believe that it was ever warm, or ever will be again. My chamber, however, is what I consider comfortable; though perhaps you would not think so, for it is a long time since the ther- mometer has been as high as fifty degrees; but I feel better than if it were warmer. I have agreeable society, too; two kittens and I know not how many mice, for I hear them running about after I am in bed. It is impossible to get rid of them; as soon as the kittens are gone they come out of their holes; and if I stop up one hole, they come out of another.[45]

—⚭—

Bancroft Library
Number 30: To Una Hawthorne

Montserrat, Nov. 10th [1853].

My dear Una,

I am so anxious to hear from you again, that I do now what I ought long ago to have done, that is, answer your letter. You are all very happy, I hope, and I should like to know just what you are doing, especially yourself and Julian. I believe I am less acquainted with your proceedings than anyone else is. I have heard that you are settled in the country,[46] but you must tell me in what sort of a place, and whether you think it as pleasant as Concord or Lenox, and whether Julian finds as pleasant walks there as he did at home. The autumn scenery, I suppose, is sombre compared to ours. I have gathered some bright leaves, which I send you that you may remember how beautiful it is to stand in the woods and look up to the clear blue sky through such gorgeous foliage lighted up by the sunshine. We have had more sunny days than usual this season. All October has been pleasant. On the twentieth of that month I gathered violets, and even yet I sometimes find flowers. I frequently think of our walks at Concord. I am afraid you are forgetting a little what the progress of the seasons is here, for in your note dated the 18th of August, you say that "you suppose the leaves are falling at home." Since that there have been many weeks of summer, for September was not like autumn. We have had a profusion of berries, particularly blueberries, half as large as grapes. I never saw such, nor so many, before. I have eaten uncounted quarts of them. I wished for you and Julian to enjoy them with me: There have been several pic-nics in the woods, where the company (acquaintance of Maria and Rebecca's) sat under the trees and feasted upon berries and cream, and afterwards sang. You would have liked to be there, but I hope you have been as much pleased elsewhere, and you must tell me how. Write to me often, and do not wait for me to answer your letters, nor suppose that they make me the less happy because I do not tell you of it by every mail.

I should think your papa might write to me, for I went to Salem about the 1st of July and stayed a week, expecting him to come, as he half promised that he would. Tell him that he would be amused at Mrs. Cole's manner of introducing me to people; to those, I mean, for whom she entertains a peculiar respect, for it is an honour she does not accord to others. "This is Miss Hawthorne; you have heard of her brother who is gone to England,—this is his sister." But she is a very good woman, and extremely kind to me. I went to Salem again in September, and stayed two days, and as Miss Rawlins Pickman had been so kind as to express a wish to have me call and bring your letter, I did so.[47] She seemed much interested about you all, and said that you had promised to write to her. Perhaps by this time you have written.

I went one afternoon to Marblehead, and walked upon the beach, as I have many times done when I lived in Salem. I also visited a house which is, in this country, what some of the grand old mansions that you probably sometimes go to see, are in England.[48] It is about eighty years old. There is nothing here that more resembles them, yet I do not say there is only one comparison in point of splendour. But still it was so expensively built and decorated, that it cost the owner most of his fortune, and the gentleman who showed us over it said that two of his descendants, from the west, came there and wept long and bitterly, at the thought that such a place had passed from their family. I like the plan of it much better than that of modern houses. The rooms are large, and the entries and staircases broad, with balustrades of solid mahogany, beautifully carved. The window frames and sashes are of cedar, we saw a piece of the wood broken off of one of them; the doors of the best rooms are of mahogany, and there are two hundred little knobs in one room, each of which cost a dollar, besides other carving. It was all done in England, and not by machinery, as I suppose such things are now, but with a knife. In one room we found the prettiest little dutch tiles round the fire place that I ever saw. The staircase is papered with views of Italian scenery, in good preservation, though the house is open till ten o'clock in the evening. In some of the rooms there were pictures, one of which was sold for a thousand dollars. But what is really worth seeing is the view from a little cupola, with seats round it, on the top of the house. I should like to sit there all day.

Thus I have given you a long description of what will hardly be interesting to you. I was not aware, till I looked at the paper, how much I was writing. But you must remember that I see very few things and places. I have not much to tell you of, for nothing happens here. Occasionally I take a little longer walk than usual, and if anybody will go with me, I manage to lose my way, as I did the other day with a young lady who knew me so little as to trust herself to my guidance. I took her to an unfragmented common, just such a place as the Great Pasture near Salem, and we wandered about till near Sunset, when we were lucky enough to find a road; after dark we could not possibly have found our way out, for we could hardly stir without getting into a swamp. We had at least three miles to walk after we came to the road, and we must have walked eleven miles. I was not in the least fatigued, but enjoyed it. It is not worth while to begin upon a new sheet of paper. I am

Your most affectionate Aunt

E. M. H.[49]

Bancroft Library
Number 31: To Una Hawthorne

1858

My dear Una

I received your letter from Rome the other day, but I have had none from Paris; this is the first since you left England. I am sorry there is one lost; because

I find them all very interesting. I am sorry, too, that the violet is lost which you were going to send me from Rome. You must gather me another wild flower. I should like to possess one that grew in Rome. I wish you and Julian could be here for one day, for a ramble in the woods, which you would enjoy, I doubt not, as much as you ever did. There is one kind of violet in this region that is indeed "glowing"; it is the loveliest wild flower I ever saw; there is meaning in its face, but it has no perfume. You would enjoy a walk in the woods with me; I should lead you across rivulets upon bridges of single logs. Sometime or other I hope such a pleasure will be attainable. Tell your father that Miss B.C., his and my old schoolmistress, is dead, at nearly 85 years old.[50] Her last illness was occasioned by a fall, otherwise she seemed likely to live many years longer. He will remember her, as she did him, of course.

E. M. H.

—〰—

Bancroft Library
Number 32: To Una Hawthorne

Salem, Oct. 12th. 1859

My dear Una,

I have just learned that any letters that are to be sent by Miss Lander must be written within an hour, so that I shall not have time to say much to you.[51] I must not forget to tell you that I have been exceedingly gratified by the perusal of your journal. You will have pleasant remembrances enough to last you all your life, even if you never travel again, and a great deal to tell me next summer, if you return home in the spring, as I trust that you will. In the meanwhile, however, what is the reason that you never write to me? If it were not for Miss Pickman, I should know nothing at all about your movements, nor your intentions. She said that you were all very agreeably established near Florence. Mr. Thoreau told a friend of mine the other day, that a letter had been received, (I do not know <u>by</u> whom, nor <u>from</u> whom,) in which it was said that your Mamma's health required a longer residence in Italy. But I hope that it was a letter written a long time ago, as the intelligence conveyed in it differs from what I have heard from other sources. I was amused, and not provoked, that you should complain of me to Richard when you have not yet answered my last letter, written in May. I recommended Laidre to you—have you read it? It is a very charming book. I have seen Miss Lander, and she showed me a photograph of her bust of your father. It looked grand, but very old; but she says that the bust will not look old. Will you not send me your likeness? I send you mine, which I should not think it worth while to do if it would much enlarge the package; neither would I have given more for it than it cost, which was only ten cents. It has a most defiant air, for my head was fastened back, and the lower part of the face is not good, and too much of the figure is visible; but perhaps you will like to see it. I am glad that you like Miss Shepard so well. I suppose that she is not a great many years older than yourself. Can you not tell me something about the new book? everybody is asking about it, and I heard of it long before you told me.[52] Do you know whether it is to be fiction?

Yours affectionately,
E. M. H.

—⋘—

Bancroft Library
Number 33: To Una Hawthorne

Beverly, March 11th. 1860.

My dear Una

As the time draws near when, as I hope, you will all return, I feel as if I ought to have written to you a little more frequently, although you have not always acknowledged the few letters I have written. One, of last July, perhaps you never received, for at that time we did not know whither to direct, nor did Mr. Ticknor. And before that, there were letters which you did not answer. One of yours, too, from Paris, I believe never reached me, which I regretted, for I should have liked to know how you felt in France. But it is of no consequence now, for you can tell me everything next summer, if you do but come home. I want to see you and talk with you. I have many questions to ask. Letters are a very unsatisfactory mode of communication; unsatisfactory even to receive, though much better than no intelligence at all; and I am always gratified when you forget my remissness, and write to me as if I were not, as your father once called me, "an impossible correspondent." But I have an absurd feeling when I write; it is as if I were talking with the consciousness that somebody in the next room was recording every idle word. Thus no words will come to be recorded. But when I heard of your illness, I felt as if I had been unkind, and as if you might have fancied I did not love you so well as I do. We heard of your danger through the newspapers, only about a week before your probable recovery was announced; but I should be sorry to pass another six days in such anxiety; yet I tried to hope there was exaggeration in the account.[53] I thought more of your father than of you; it seemed to me that the affliction would be heavier to him than even to your mother. That I should never see you again was nothing, as I felt even then. But I am recalling a very sad period. At all events, I hope you will not go to Rome again. I am expecting everyday to receive the <u>Book</u>.[54] I am anxious to read it before I see any critique upon it. I do not like to hear anything about a book I am going to read. You must write and tell me whether you like it better than the others; though indeed you have never said a word about any of them.

I do not wonder that your mother needed repose, and I am glad you did not return late last autumn, there is then so much more danger in the passage. If you come in summer, I shall not be half as anxious about you. It seems impossible that you can be sixteen years old, and Julian nearly fourteen. I am ashamed to ask to have Julian write to me, but it would give me great pleasure if he would.

Goodbye.

E. M. H.

—∿—

Phillips Library
Number 34: To Robert Manning

Beverly, December 31ˢᵗ [1861]

My dear Cousin,

If we lived within walking distance of each other, I should intrude upon you whenever I felt the want of conversation, which is the great want of my life. I fear you would grow very weary of me. Now, especially, I should come to see you, every day, to talk with you about the war. What do you think, and how do you feel about it? I have exhausted the capabilities of every other person to whom I have access; I have made them say all that they can say, which has usually proved to be a good deal more than is worth saying. That would not be the case with you. I doubt not that you would suggest something worthy of consideration, and you cannot do less than write to me upon this subject, as we cannot meet to talk about it. It will hardly be a greater effort for you to answer this note than for me to write it. I only do so because I am so desirous to hear from you. I dislike letter writing quite as decidedly as you do. I made a long visit in Concord in the autumn. The air of the place is not so good as that of Montserrat;—neither is the scenery, though the elm-trees are larger and finer than any in Beverly; but the woods are not half so pleasant. There is a beautiful pond, Walden pond, on the margin of which Thoreau once had his abode. I brought home some leaves from a tree which has grown up on the site of his hut. If I can find them I will send you one. Poor Thoreau is deep in consumption: it is supposed that he cannot live long. There is a Mr. Williams in Concord who has produced a new system of philosophy, but I believe he has not succeeded in making it comprehensible to a single person yet.[55] He thinks Mr. Emerson and Mr. Alcott the wisest of mortals except himself, and is trying to dispel the remaining darkness of their minds by the light of his own. Nothing of the kind ever interests me so I did not inquire into the features of this philosophy. Una rowed her father and me across Walden Pond and when we were in the middle of it told me that it was a most dangerous place. But I think I could swim, or float, upon calm water. You are near the beautiful Connecticut [River], and near Mount Holyoke.[56] Rivers and mountains are the things in which I should most delight, and I am far from them both. There is not even a brook, nothing better than a ditch here. But you know all about this place. I wish you would read Parton's "Life of Jackson"; it represents the old Hero exactly as he probably was. If he were but alive now! Nathaniel says that wherever he is, he would undoubtedly rather be on earth at this crisis. I think so too. His early life was far more object[ion]able than I supposed, but somehow or other it fitted him for what he had to do.

I send you this photograph of Webster and wish you a happy new year.[57]

—⁓—

Phillips Library
Number 35: To Rebecca Manning

[January 1862]

My dear Beckie,

I shall be very glad to have Harper's Weekly, and will be careful to return it. There is no Story by Miss Mulock in Harper's Magazine, at least not in any of the numbers that I have: if it is published in future numbers, I will send them to you.[58] It was Elsie Venner, in the Atlantic Monthly, that I asked you for— Also, I want Trumps, which Mrs. Russell lent me, and I left at your house, and Olmstead's Journey Through the Slave States, if you will lend it to me, Eunice will send any thing. I was glad to receive a note from you, and to learn that you had a "Merry Christmas". I have a plan for next Summer, which, if I find it practicable will give me a change of air and scene. It is to commit treason, or manage to be suspected of it, and sent to Fort Warren. Then I shall have the sea breeze and society, if any, that will at least be novel to me. I shall besides, live without expense and can buy books with the money I must elsewhere pay for board. Do you think they would allow me a comfortable room, by myself and what do you think I should do to entitle myself to occupy it? Perhaps you would like to go with me. I fear Robert will not answer my note. One of these days I shall write to him again.

I return John Halifax, as I intended to do last summer.[59] It may be that there is some truth in the theory of Spheres, for I cannot endure Miss Mulock. Her sphere and mine cannot coalesce, not even so much as to enable me to read John Halifax, though everybody says it is a readable book. I once read a short Story of hers, "A Low Marriage", With some pleasure; but she is not natural; it is like going into a close room, to read one of her novels. How different from the author of Adam Bede. I can breathe freely with her. I like her books better than Charlotte Bronte's. I have not read Silas Marner nor any other new book since I came home from Concord, except the numbers of Thackeray's and Trollope's novels, both of which are admirable. Do not you want them?

Yours, EMH.[60]

—⚭—

[January 1862]

Dear Becky,

I return your books. When you send Elsie Venner, will you also send me St. Ronan's Well, or Guy Mannering?[61] If you give them to Eunice she will remember to send them. Come and see me.

EMH[62]

—⚭—

[Winter 1862]

My dear Beckie

I return your Harpers and when you have read them, I should like some more. This number of the Quarterly Review is for Mary Shepard, who asked me for it long ago, and I am ashamed to say I forgot it till I happened to see the book the other day. She too asked me as you do, if I knew who St. Sebastian was. I think it was St. Sebastian she wished to know about. I know nothing, and have no books by means of which I could learn. There is information upon almost every subject in the Encyclopedia Americana, and perhaps you will find him there. It is in the Atheneum, if not in the Institute Library, so that you can consult it. I dare say those Catholic Ladies who teach school in Salem would tell you with pleasure, and if I were you I would open an acquaintance with them. They must be unlike anybody else that you know.

Robert has not written to me, have you heard from him? I mean to write him again soon.

You inquire about Una. She and Julian seem to be amusing themselves with all their might. They go to a dance every week and Una dances every dance, to her great delight. There are one or two other parties of some sort regularly every week; and in the day time they skate and coast down steep hills. She has been to Church every Sunday this Winter, whatever the weather has been. If she were required to go, she would not like it any better than I do. Then she studies a good deal, George Bradford being her Instructor. At Mr. Sanborn's school they perform Pantomimes, exhibit in Tableaux, &c, though not in school hours, but one evening in a week. It is very late, and I must stop.

EMH[63]

—m—

Bancroft Library
Number 38: To Una Hawthorne

Montserrat, Feb. 14th 1862.

My dear Una,

I have been anxiously awaiting the arrival of your composition. Why does it not come? I believe I am writing punctually this time, and it is possible that you have done the same, for the roads are so bad that we have no regular communication with the town, so that letters are not always brought as soon as they should be. You ask my <u>idea</u> of Mark Antony. The word <u>idea</u> is well chosen, for opinion would assuredly condemn him. Therefore, perhaps, Shakespeare, who seems to have put his whole soul into Antony and Cleopatra, has lifted them both out of the region of opinion. But certainly, whether right or wrong, he is "noble courageous, high, unmatchable ," and not strictly so,—he can weep and can enjoy; he is not the unreal kind of man, with human nature left out, that we are often called upon to admire. But I have no talent for criticism. Tell me what Mr. Weld thinks, and what you think, and for your sake, I will so far depart from my usual custom, which is to read nobody's saying upon Shakespeare, that I will take you into consideration. I used to think, when about fourteen, that the most charming way of living would be out of doors, in the woods, as they lived in the forest of Arden; but I fear I told you that, sometime ago. Your father preferred Perdita, in the Winter's Tale; but my favorite was Rosalind in As you like it. [In it] how utterly the customary world is excluded from that forest life. Shakespeare always shows us just as much, and no more, of humanity that we ought to see. He makes us perceive that a glorified state of existence is possible: in "Love's Labour Lost" there is the same shutting out of the world, but there is less poetry; less than in As You Like It, but more than in the most poetical creation of any other author. And is not the Midsummer Night's Dream all poetry? All sorts of rural gatherings, such as the sheep shearing feast in the Winter's tale, are delicate and sweet when he describes them; even pedlars,—how amusing is Autolycus. But I have left myself no time to say what I have wanted to ask you in several letters; but have always crowded it out. How does Rose go down to the depôt so very early, almost before daylight in the morning? Not surely alone. I should be almost afraid to trust her in Boston unattended. That reminds me of the danger to which young ladies' <u>heads</u> are exposed. Perhaps you heard of the poor girl whose hair was cut off and stolen. Be upon your guard when you go into any assemblage. Your hair would be worth stealing. It comes into my mind now about your father, that after a sojourn of two or three weeks at Swampscot, he came home captivated in his fanciful way, with a "Mermaid" as he called her. He would not tell us her name, but said she was of the aristocracy of the village, the Keeper of a little shop. She gave him a sugar heart, a pink one, which he kept a great while, and then (how boyish, but how like him) he ate it. You will find her, I suspect, in the Village Uncle. She is Susan. It was about the year 1833. He said she had a great deal of what the French call espieglerie [mischievousness]. At that time he had <u>fiancées</u> like that whenever he went from home. This is a profound secret, mind

E. M. H.[64]

—⁓—

Phillips Library
Number 39: To Rebecca Manning

Montserrat, April 3rd [1862]

Dear Beckie,

   I return Harper's Weekly with the exception of the number for March [15] which I have sent to the Army, to a Boy, who lived a good while with Mrs.

Cole. He is with Burnside, and I thought he would like to see the achievements in which he had a share recorded. I send you the change to replace the number. I should have bought it if I could have sent down in town, but I suppose you can get it without difficulty. There are times when communication with the inhabited world seems impractical. I have not yet been able to get Harper's Monthly for April, but I suppose I shall have it on Saturday, and will send it to you next week, with the Vol. of the Atlantic Monthly. Will you be so good as to leave the next Vol. at Mrs. Dike's to be sent me when Mrs. Burchstead calls? If you would like "Mademoiselle Mori",[65] which is a readable novel, I dare say you can have it of Mrs. Russell, to whom I lent it. I must carry it to Concord when I go, which I suppose I shall be expected to do early in the summer. I borrowed it there. I have not seen a new Book since I came home. You thought it strange that I should buy books, but you do not know how much I want them in winter when I cannot go to the Library, and frequently cannot send. You ask if paper is scarce here; but how can it be when I use it so economically, always on little scraps, the uncovered portions of Mrs. Dike's notes? Envelopes are an extravagance I am seldom guilty of. I shall be very glad to see you all here, at any time. Come and spend the day.

EMH[66]

—𝕸—

Phillips Library
Number 40: To Rebecca Manning

Friday Evening May 23 [1862]

Dear Beckie

I do not get these Magazines till a week or two after they are published, else I should send them sooner. If it were not that they are cheaper in Beverly,— sixteen cents, while in Salem they are twenty. I should ask you to buy them for me and read them before you send them to me. Communication is very difficult with the town. Una has never once failed to write Sunday Morning, and to put her letter in the office on Monday but I seldom receive it until Saturday. I have not yet got this week's letter. When the library is open I go down myself, but now it has been closed three months, for the Books to be arranged. You will perceive that I am in a forlorn condition. I hope Richard will soon find time to bring you and Maria over. All the flowers are in bloom and everything is looking beautifull. You asked me once if I had your copy of Jane Eyre—I am sorry to say that I have not. I intended to borrow it, but forgot to do so. I think the "Mistress and Maid" grows more stupid, Miss Mulock has no sunshine in her mind: her novels are more dreary than real life, and more uniformly somber.[67] I do not know what her own experience can have been, but certainly she must have had shocking sisters, such as Selina and Penelope, in another of her books. She proceeds upon a false theory, always, as she says in her "Women's Thoughts", to do her very best, whereas nobody can write a good novel without inspiration, which never comes when it is called for. Charlotte Bronte is right about that: she waited till characters and scenes appeared to her; then she could depict them. I see a new novel by the author of Paul Ferroll advertised. "Why Paul Ferroll killed his wife". If it really is by that Author, I mean to have it do you know anything about it?

EMH[68]

—⟋⟍—

Phillips Library
Number 41: To Rebecca Manning

[Summer 1862]

My Dear Beckie

I shall be very glad to learn something more about that poor misguided Magdalen, who seems to be rushing rapidly upon ruin—and if you will lend me, when you have all read it, the last number of the Atlantic Monthly, containing "Leamington Spa" you will gratify me much. Will you not all come to see me again soon, as you did the other day? We shall soon have moonlight Evenings—then I should think you might come.

This "Romola", in Harper, I fear is going to be a failure: there is no life in it, and the "Mistress and Maid" grows more sorrowful every number. Miss Mulock is evidently a very unhappy woman, and deservedly so, for her presumption in assuming to be always wise. If you ever write a book, take care that it be with no intention to be useful.

EMH[69]

—⟋⟍—

Phillips Library
Number 42: To Rebecca Manning

[May 1863]

My dear Beckie

You said you should come to see me all of you—when the flowers were in bloom, therefore I look for you to-morrow, and I have, indeed, for several

Saturdays—and of course you will not come. When you have done with the Atlantic Monthly for May will you lend it to me? If you want Browning's Poems you can have them now, but I cannot send them in this Package, because I have no piece of paper large and strong enough to hold them.

I want the third and fourth Volumes of Ruskin if nobody is reading them, there is something in one of them I wish to see. I am reading Ruskin's Diary— it is rather amusing.

Jane is gone to Rutland, in Vermont, to visit her brother.

I do not think the beginning of the new Story by Charles Reade, in Harper's Weekly, very promising:[70] none of his books please me,—they are so bustling— it is wearisome to be in such a crowd of uninteresting people and none of his personages have any more souls than those paper dolls that Rose offered to cut out for me, and which I have not yet written to accept. I am just reading "Great Expectations" and am interested in it. Why should the title of a Book be marked as a quotation? A Book is a real thing, and has not its being in any body's words—

EMH[71]

—⁄⁄⁄—

Bancroft Library
Number 43: To Una Hawthorne

Montserrat, Sept. 4th 1863

My dear Una,

Do you not think that you are a naughty girl to write to Mrs. Dike instead of to me, and what is worse, to complain of me to one who takes such an awfully serious view of all things as she does? She has sent me a note exhorting me to answer your letters without delay, and for this once I will do so; though you know very well that I never have anything to say. If you were here, I should like to talk with you, and to show you some charming places which you did not visit when you were here. I commend your patience in picking huckleberries. They have been very abundant here; also high-bush blueberries; which are nice, and which perhaps you never tasted, as they do not probably grow in England. We have high-bush blackberries, too, which are cultivable in gardens, where they grow much larger than when wild. Do not forget what I told you about tomatoes; that when the frost comes the vines, with the fruit upon them, are to be hung up in a garret or a cellar to ripen.

There is a Secessionist lady here, who has two daughters married to South

Carolina planters. She knows Mr. Yancey, and other leading men, and admires Yancey excessively.[72] I am quite in luck, for I have longed to see a Secessionist.

I am glad that Julian is to be at home every Sunday; it will be so much better for him, as well as pleasanter for all of you. Hazing seems to me to be barbarous enough to be suppressed by the authorities of the college. How long does it last?

I have hardly enjoyed a summer so much as this since I was of your age. The uniformly warm weather, and the clear and warm nights are delightful to me. When the thermometer stands at eighty life seems charming. I sit on the hill in the woods where you used to sit, and where there is always a good breeze, almost every fine day.

E. M. H.

—ᴍᴍ—

Bancroft Library
Number 44: To Una Hawthorne

Beverly. Nov. 19th 1863.

My dear Una,

I was very glad to hear from you last week—there seems to be very little intercourse between Montserrat and the outer world. I forgot when I wrote last that I had not thanked Julian for his photograph. I shall not compliment him upon his looks, but I am very much pleased to have it. Everyone who sees it supposes him to be a year or two older than he is, and he is certainly very fine-looking and manly.

I received your Mamma's and Rose's very kind letters just after I wrote. I agree with your Mamma as to who upholds the Atlantic; which was certainly dull before your Papa contributed to it; and I wish he would publish something more from his English Journal. Is he aware that he has "earned the undying enmity of all Englishmen by his remarks upon English women"? I never doubted that the English were as sensitive as other people if you could only hit them in the right place. But it may be some compensation to know that the Emperor of Brazil is the warm admirer of both his writings and his photograph, having been made acquainted with both by some Baptist minister; and singling out your Papa's likeness, of his own accord, from a bookfull of portraits of eminent men.

I must not forget to say that we are all much obliged for the book. You would be amused to hear Mr. Dike read and remark. He does not suspect, nor does

Mrs. Manning, that I asked to have it sent to them. They would never forgive me if they did.—I have had a delightful walk today. There are beautiful things still in the woods, bright leaves, and pretty mosses, and fern as green as in summer. They are sheltered from the frost in the deep woods.

I wish your Papa would read, or at least look over, Napier's History of the Peninsular War; I have read it with much satisfaction, finding that other nations blunder, when they are in difficulties, as badly as we do, and that the British Government, according to Napier, did nothing but blunder.[73]

Your affectionate Aunt,
E. M. H.

—〰—

Bancroft Library
Number 45: To Una Hawthorne

Beverly, Jan. 19th 1864

My dear Una,

I was very glad to see your handwriting once more. I was beginning to be a little anxious, because you said that your Papa was not particularly well; and now in your last letter you say that General [Franklin] Pierce had heard of it, and came to see for himself. I want to know as much as Gen. Pierce does, and you must tell me if he is seriously indisposed. But you seem to be enjoying yourself as usual, so I infer that it is no more than a cold, and perhaps the influence of the weather, which has been unusually gloomy this winter. And then there is no society in Concord that suits him. It must be pleasant for you all to have Julian at home for the long vacation. And it will really help you through the winter to think that he is going to stay till the first day of Spring, far off as spring actually is at the beginning of March. But I suppose you will skate, and slide down hill, and amuse yourself in other ways of which I never, even at your age, could imagine the pleasure. I enjoy winter now more than when young, because all I want is to sit quietly and read. If I am disposed to talk, it must be to myself, to whom I do sometimes talk,—indeed it has become so much a habit with me, that when I go to meeting in Salem, I am afraid to forget for an instant where I am, lest I should speak out loud. Think how terrible it would be if I did. So you see I am deprived of the benefit of my own meditations, and even of my own being, in such a situation. Fortunately it does not often happen that I am obliged to stultify myself. My last visit to Salem was not very long. I came home Christmas Day, bringing

with me a cold imbibed in the close atmosphere of the place, which has unfitted me for writing until now. I have been reading Bayard Taylor's "Hannah
Thurston," and could not help saying, "Friend, how comest thou in hither, not
having on a wedding garment?" The characters are people gathered from the
highways and hedges of the outer world, but in no way fit for fiction, indeed there is no atmosphere of fiction in the book, which is as dreary as actual
life.[74]

E. M. H.

Bancroft Library
Number 46: To Una Hawthorne

Beverly, March 20th. 1864

My dear Una,

I feel very badly about your father being unwell, especially because his
health has been so uniformly good. I am afraid I am hard hearted towards
confirmed invalids, but for a well person to become ill is a pity. I wish he could
be prevailed upon to wear more clothes, an abundance of which are necessary
to comfort in this climate. We hardly feel the changes if we dress warmly, but
cold benumbs all the vital powers, and the stomach especially suffers. But perhaps he has not eaten animal food enough—he ate none when I was in Concord. You know the stomach needs to be exercised, else it will lose its vigour. I
think people should habitually eat a good deal, and that a variety of food is
good. He never had a great appetite, and perhaps now it needs to be tempted
with delicacies. He ought to eat fruit, which is always wholesome. I am glad he
is going away for a little while. When he went with Mr. Ticknor to Washington
two years ago, I believe he enjoyed his journey, and was benefitted by it—and
not he only, but the public, for then he wrote the best article that had ever
appeared in the Atlantic Monthly—"Chiefly about War Matters." It is amusing
to see how little time seems to mollify the wrath of the English, who continue
to quote his description of the Fat Dowagers, and would make a <u>war matter</u> of
that, I think, if they dared. I have read the Marble Faun again lately, with ever
more interest than at first. I should like to know whether the gray Champion
seems such a wonderful thing to you as it does to me. It should be read at War
Meetings. Men would enlist after hearing it. It would be well to have it printed

in the form of a tract, and distributed to the soldiers. I know of nothing written in America so effective.

If you have not much to put in your letters, still I like them. But your late letters have been full of incident.

Yours
E. M. H.

—⁓—

Bancroft Library
Number 47: To Una Hawthorne

Beverly, May 20th. 1864

My dear Una,

Rebecca is going to write to you to tell you that I cannot come.[75] I do not think you will be surprised. The shock was so terrible that I am too ill to make the necessary preparations. I should have been obliged to go to Salem and have a dress made, and to see people. Happy are those who die, and can be at rest. When I look forward I can anticipate nothing but sorrow, few people are so completely left alone as I am—all have gone before me. It is sad to hear, as we sometimes do, of whole families being swept away at once by disease, but it is far sadder to be the only survivor. I cannot tell you how much I feel for you all. I suppose you were no better prepared for what has happened than I am. Do write as soon as you can and tell me more. I have been anxious all the week to hear about Dr. [Holmes's] opinion, but I hoped everything [to improve] from travelling. Perhaps it would have been an effective remedy, if poor Mr. Ticknor's unfortunate death had not occurred. But now he will never know old age and infirmity. I shall always think of him as I saw him in Concord, when he seemed to be in the prime of manhood. It is not desirable to live to be old. Poor Julian, just entering the world, how much he will miss his father's care. You and Rose will be with your mother, and safe from evil, but a young man's life is full of peril. I hope General Pierce will counsel and have a care of him, for his father's sake. Dear Una, do let me know, as soon as you feel as if you could write, whatever there is to tell.

Your Aunt,
E. M. Hawthorne[76]

—⁓—

Phillips Library
Number 48: To Rebecca Manning

Montserrat, August 17 [1864]

Dear Beckie,

I have just received your note, and will send the book the first time Mrs. Burchstead calls, which I hope will be tomorrow. I wish Robert and Richard would come over here. The evenings are beautiful now I suppose it will be a good while before Robert comes home again.

Yesterday the Russells came, with the two Miss Brownes, Miss Lucy Larcom and Miss Page, from Danvers, who has been here before. We had a delightful day in the woods near Beaver Pond. If you had been here you would have enjoyed it. They are coming again, if possible, and I wish it could be so arranged that you could come with them. Miss Larcom brought Tennyson's new Poems, and one of them, Enoch Arden was read aloud. It was good, but did not suit me so well as the Idylls of the King. I like to be taken out of common life, in poetry.

If you have not bought the book for Jane, I hardly think you will find a more suitable one than Jean Ingelow's Poems. She need not read it and will not, probably, whatever it be. Adelaide Proctor I do not quite fancy, but it is late and I must stop.[77]

EMH

—⁜—

New York Public Library
Number 49: To Sophia Peabody Hawthorne

Beverly, Nov. 24 [1864]

My dear Sophia,

I am very much obliged by your kind punctuality in sending me the money, which arrived, as it always does when I was much in need of it.[78] I received your letter today: the reason letters are always late in coming to me is that I have requested the postmaster never to send them except by a person whom he knows to be trustworthy. When the weather and walking are good, I frequently go after them myself, but this week it has rained every day.

I am more gratified than I can tell you, that the children think of me and love me; Some time or other, I hope I shall see them. If Rose could have come to Salem, even for one day, it would have delighted me, and I confidently expected that she would. I only went to Salem for the sake of seeing Una and Rose. Next summer, when Una comes, I hope Rose will come, even if she stays but a few hours. And I want to see Julian, perhaps he will come at the same time.

I am glad to learn, from the Newspapers that General Pierce is out of danger. Has he any sister, or niece, or any female relative, living with him? I think, very often, that I am not so much alone and forsaken as I appear. My friends, though dead, may be near me. I dream of them. It is a great pleasure to me, now, that my Brother came here, and walked about, and left the memory of his presence in many spots, which will be always associated with him, and him alone, in my mind. And to you and to his children, it must be a consolation that you had all lived together so long in Concord. If he had died abroad, the desolation of the home where he had not recently been, would have been dreadful.

I am

yours affectionately

E. M. Hawthorne[79]

—⁊⁊—

Phillips Library
Number 50: To Rebecca Manning

[December 1864]

Dear Beckie

If there is not enough of this moss and of the other plants to fill you[r] pudding dish, let me know, and I will get you some more. This is the first opportunity I have had to send it. Mrs. Burchstead stopped once in the road, and sent her boy in, but he did not wait, though the bundle was ready.

I got home very well that evening, though I went [without] over shoes, and half slipped down once in the mud, and had to tug my feet out with a great effort once or twice. Our schoolmistress, Miss Robbins, who boards in the next house, was in the cars, and made room for me. I was very glad that I happened to be acquainted with her. We had a rather pleasant walk, though it was dark, for it took us till six o'clock. We stopped in Beverly and I got a newspaper, which I dropped on the way and went back alone after it, about a quarter of a mile, not discovering the loss till I got home.[80]

—⁊⁊—

Beverly, Dec. 15th. 1864.

My dear Una,

I am sorry to hear that Julian is so unpleasantly situated, but perhaps he will study more diligently for it. <u>Contented people seldom accomplish much.</u> I have knit one pair of socks for him, and one stocking of the second pair. I could not begin them till after Thanksgiving, for want of suitable yarn. I wished to buy some finer than I could get here.

I hope you do not neglect the study of Greek. I almost wish you might be completely isolated this winter, quite [removed] from all human intercourse, and compelled to find your only recreation in reading. For you ought to read Shakespeare, and so much besides. Only reflect how much poetry there is with which it is desirable to become familiar. I do not think you can read too much poetry, and if I were you, I would learn a good deal by heart. You will find it useful in future, to divert your mind from the realities of life, which may not be uniformly agreeable. You ask me to give you a list of poems, but I am apt to forget titles. But Daniel's poems are good: read his History of the Civil Wars,[81] which seemed to me to have more thought in it than any other history I ever read. Then there is Drayton's Battle of Agincourt[,] a long poem in which are set forth the preparations made in England for the invasion of France.[82] I read it with great interest about the time we were preparing for this war. There are some Eulogies of Drayton for every month in the year, like those of Spenser's which you read. Browne's Britannica's Pastorals contain a great deal of good poetry, though I could not read them connectedly, and his other poems are some of them beautiful.[83] If you have not read Bacon's Essays, of course you ought to as soon as possible.

As you suppose, I did groan over the prospect of going to Salem till the idea of it became intolerable; and then, as I had told Rebecca that I preferred walking down to the cars, I took advantage of the rain that was falling on Monday, and wrote word to Mrs. Dike that the bad travelling made it impossible for me to come, and gave the letter to the baker to put in the post-office. So I felt safe, though Jane said she knew they would send for me, which they did, at about half past eleven on Thanksgiving Day, making me very angry indeed, for I wished to be quiet. However, I rather enjoyed the visit, and Saturday afternoon I insisted upon walking home. I had some purchases to make, so it was half past four when I got into the cars, which were full, and I must have stood all the way, if Miss Robbins, our schoolmistress, who was in them, had not made room for me by her. I was glad that I happened to be acquainted with her. She displaced a little boy, who was in the seat next to her, in the easiest and pleasantest manner imaginable, by looking down at him and saying, "I don't know who this boy is." We walked home in the darkness, which came on early that evening, for it was cloudy. I stopped and got the newspaper in Beverly, and dropped it about a quarter of a mile from home, and went back after it alone. The mud was almost as deep, we thought, as it is represented to be in Virginia. I was obliged to tug my feet out with great effort, but after all it was good fun, and did me good, as a hard tramp always does. I could not see the road, so I was not tempted to go out of it, as you say I always do when walking. That reminds me to ask you why you are so soon fatigued when you are walking with me, though you can go many miles upon other occasions? The air in Montserrat is so invigorating that it must be my stupidity as a companion that paralyzes you. But next summer I am resolved to drag you to several places where you have never been; and to reward you, we will invite Gail Hamilton to spend the day with us at Mrs. Cole's, who has proposed it, for she wants to see her. A little while ago, Gail Hamilton brought some friends home with her from Boston, but on her arrival found her mother absent, and though she had the key of the front door in her pocket, it was bolted on the inside, so she invited them into the barn, where they remained till her mother returned, toward evening.

I am ashamed to have written such a girlish letter—at my age I ought to be imparting the lessons of experience, and making myself tedious, instead of absurd.

EMH[84]

—⟋⟍⟍—

Phillips Library
Number 52: To Rebecca Manning

Montserrat, January 26th [1865]

Dear Beckie,

I hope this note and you[r] Books will be conveyed to you tomorrow, but it is doubtful. I suppose you received my note the other day. I want the books I asked you to lend me very much. And I want to see you, but I suppose the cold weather and the snow will continue to deprive me of that pleasure. If it ever becomes mild again, I hope you will come. Every family in the neighborhood is afflicted with the Mumps, except this.

I like Wilkie Collins' Story, Armadale better than the Dead Secret or No Name.[85] In general, I think the adventures of young men are pleasanter to read than those of young women, who should be staid and well conducted, and not, like poor Magdalen, suffer themselves to be made the sport of fortune. Dickens' story fails to interest me, though it seems to improve a little, Lizzie Hexham is an impossible character: with her refinement and innate elegance, what does she need to be taught? Have you read Gail Hamilton's last book, A New Atmosphere?[86] I wish very much to see it, for one of the religious newspapers says it contains some good things but that in what she says of marriage she defies all laws, human and divine, and that she is moreover impertinent, and lectures the public as she should not, with many other charges.

Una says Julian makes such progress that he will be able to join his class in March. He can be diligent enough in seclusion or with people he dislikes, as he does the family in which he is placed.

EMH[87]

—⁕—

Bancroft Library
Number 53: To Una Hawthorne, fragment

Montserrat, Feb. 26th. 1865

My dear Una,

I hope you will certainly come in October, and spend the whole month with me, as you promise. You think it would be pleasanter to go to Richard's than to Mrs. Dike's, but to me it certainly would not; besides, it would be treating Mrs. Dike very ill to go anywhere else in Salem; she would be exceedingly hurt and grieved; she has a sort of gloomy satisfaction in seeing me. Mr. Dike has somehow found out my opinion of him, and will never forgive me, and for that reason Mrs. Dike is always uneasy when I am there.

There is very little to tell about your father. He did not stay long in Raymond, when I was there. By some fatality, we all seemed to be brought back to Salem, in spite of our intentions, and even resolutions. He came to go to school. The first time we went to Raymond was merely for a visit in the summer of 1816, when he was twelve and I was fourteen; then he did not stay long. In 1818, we went there to live, and almost immediately he was sent to school to a clergyman in a neighboring town; but after a few months he again went to Salem, and only made us short visits.—So far I had written in great haste, hoping to send my letter by Jane, who was going down; and with Abbie talking to me all the time, and insisting upon being answered, for she is almost as imperious as you are,—there must be something in me which emboldens everyone to assume a tone of authority.[88] I have forgotten what I was going to say about your father, but I enclose some original poetry of his composition at the age of sixteen, which I found among some old papers. I do not recollect anything in prose of his, except letters, till a much later period. These verses have not much merit; I do not think them so good as that little poem of Julian's "On a Stocking." They were written merely for amusement, and perhaps for the pleasure of seeing them in print, for some of them he sent to a Boston newspaper. It was while in college that he seems from one or two letters, to have formed the [*text ends*]

—m—

Bancroft Library
Number 54: To Una Hawthorne

Beverly, Wednesday, March 1st. 1865

My dear Una,

I have looked over Dickens' story "Our Mutual Friend" in Harper, and I don't know that it would not be better to die and leave it unfinished, than to continue it in the miserable manner in which it has so far proceeded. But probably Dickens would not think so—the spirit seems to be all burnt out of him, and he would not be so willing to give up this life as in his youth, when he wrote the "Old Curiosity Shop." You will understand that this is my inference, and that I can know nothing about his feelings. Wilkie Collins' new story, "Armadale," I think interesting. Do you read any of these things? You enquire if I have read the Sparrowgrass Papers I read some of them when they were first published, I think, in some magazine; they were rather amusing.[89] They are in our library, but I do not believe they would repay the trouble of transportation hither. You ask me if I have read St. Augustine, and a book by Miss Cobbe,[90] which I have not met with. I have read portions of the Confessions of St. Augustine with interest; but for religious reading I prefer Jeremy Taylor, who is too admirable to be praised. Nehemia, Ezra, &c were the delight of my Sundays when I was about fourteen years old, and had not yet emancipated myself from the restraints imposed upon my childhood; for we were forbidden to read any other than religious books on Sunday. And the only argument for the inspiration of the Bible that has any weight with me is, that it is readable, which other books are not. I have read that lecture of Mr. Clarke's, and quite agree with him in what he says of Mr. Emerson. All that Emerson, Thoreau, and others say about the Vedas, Confucious, &c is evidently mere humbug. I have a better opinion of their taste than to suppose that they really do think as they profess to.

Thus far my letter seems very ill-natured, even to me, as I look it over. Your Papa used to call me the severest critic he knew, and sometimes he told me I was not amiable in my tastes; but I believe that was because I excessively admired Milton's Satan, and had other predilections of a similar kind, as I have still.

An old acquaintance of mine, Mrs. Hodges of Salem, whom I have hardly ever seen since I was of your age, has been here. She lost a son at that terrible explosion at Petersburg, [*illegible*] had served since an early period of the war. She has another son in the army. She drove over with her son's war horse, which was with his master at Petersburg, and had been with him at Port Hudson. He was a splendid animal, splendidly caparisoned. It was something to see a living creature that had been in a battle, and I went out to look at him.

E. M. H.[91]

—ɯ—

Phillips Library
Number 55: To Rebecca Manning

Montserrat, March 3rd [1865]

Dear Beckie,

I have sent Una's two last letters to Mrs. Dike. You can get them from her and return them to me. One of them concerns Richard. I was very glad to hear from Maria and you and when the roads become passable, I hope to see you both.

You ask me if I am not rejoiced that the Peace Conferences result in nothing—I supposed they would; but I suspect I am the only person who has any confidence in the President; else why is there such a general feeling of relief and of pleasure merely because he has acted with common sense? I think it was very shrewd in him, not to let the commissioners come to Washington.

I pity the Charleston people more than any other rebels because they seem to have no misgivings, either as to the right of their cause or the probability of its success. But I wish I had a Book from some Secessionist's Library. It would be pleasant to go into some of the deserted houses in Charleston and search for relics. Though I should have preferred to go before the people ran away, if that had been possible. I have always desired to see and talk with rebels, especially after any signal victory or disaster.

I return a Volume of the Living Age (this pen is so bad I can hardly make a stroke with it.)[92] Will you lend me the 72nd Vol. containing the rest of the Chronicles of Carlingford? If you will leave it at Mrs. Dikes she will perhaps send it. "Salem Witchcraft" is such a nice looking Book that I have not shown it to Mrs. Cole. Lest it should be defaced.

EMH[93]

—⁓—

Bancroft Library
Number 56: To Una Hawthorne

Montserrat, March 8th. 1865

My dear Una,

I assure you that I am not in the habit of sending your letters to Mrs. Dike, she would be shocked at a good many of them. This is the first she has seen since you were in Salem. But it seemed the best way of ascertaining whether she had a pair of bellows to dispose of, and I knew she would be pleased that you had been studying Nehemiah &c, I would not on any account show her your last letter, in which you avow such heretical opinions about the Bible. I don't know but she would object to my corresponding with you, for she always treats me like a child of fifteen. The moral and intellectual world stands still to her, or rather, once in a while she catches a glimpse of it whirling round in a bewildering way, while she herself is immovable.

I have not been out yet. I half regret the advent of Spring, it is so pleasant to sit by the fire and read, and not feel that I am losing out of door enjoyments.

Little Abbie, Mrs. Cole's grandchild, is here now, and I read her to sleep every night. Her chamber opens into mine. She likes to hear poetry, and I always endeavor to find something that she can understand, to avoid exciting her brain. I began with Tennyson, reading the Lady of Shalott, and The Sisters, which she liked, but comprehended [not] too much of. So now I am reading Chapman's translation of the Iliad, which is as [confusing] to her as the original Greek would be, particularly the Catalogue of the Ships. She comes to me in the afternoon sometimes, and asks me to read Jean [Ingelow's] High Tide. She repeats Hood's Bridge of Sighs with a good deal of feeling, and is quite forward enough for a little girl of six years.

Goodbye,
EMH[94]

—⁓—

New York Public Library
Number 57: To Sophia Peabody Hawthorne

Montserrat, March 16th [1865]

My dear Sophia

I do not know how to thank you for this inestimable portrait. Richard brought it me and took it out of its wrappings, and when I first saw it I said that you had only sent it for me to see; I could not believe myself so happy as to be the possessor of it. I thought you extremely kind even to lend it to me: but when I read your letter, and discovered that it was actually my own, Richard said he wished I could see myself. I seemed struck dumb with joy and astonishment. He brought it last evening—he, his wife, Rebecca, and a young lady visitor. I do not know whether they suspected what it was, but they were all impatient to see it, and I thought they were going to worship it. it is more like the original, in his best moments, than I ever thought any likeness could be,—than I ever expected to see any thing in this world.

I think the children had better come here next summer—it will be pleasanter than in Salem, and there will be no one to whom we must talk and be civil. I will make arrangements with Mrs Cole, who will be pleased, for she is very desirous to see Rose, and who admires Julian and Una. The Mannings would be happy to have us meet there, and Richard would be delighted to receive us, but I should prefer to see them here. If the weather is dry, we will dine in the woods; if not Mrs. Cole will accommodate us.

You will miss your sister, as you have no other relatives in Concord, and perhaps no very intimate friends. I am sorry for your sake and the children's. I must close my note, with renewed thanks. Somebody is waiting to take it to the Post Office.

> yours affectionately
> EMH

My dear Rose,

I am very much obliged to you for this lovely little sparrow. I look at it every five minutes to assure myself that he has not flown away. He arrived here safely last Saturday. It is so charming to be remembered, in one's old age, as I am. The box is very beautiful, and being ornamented by your artistic fingers, very precious to me.

> in haste, your loving Aunt
> EMH.[95]

—⟋⟍⟍—

Bancroft Library
Number 58: To Una Hawthorne

Beverly, Thursday, May 12th. 1865

My dear Una.

It is a good thing that you have at least begun to read Shakespeare in earnest. I used to read him when I was but twelve years old.

Just now we are all in expectation of the capture of Jefferson Davis. I would consent to be a close prisoner (in comfortable quarters) as long as it might be thought worth while to keep me, if that would ensure his being brought to Justice. Wendell Phillips says that "he would as soon grant the habeas corpus to an adder, or the trial by jury to a rattlesnake" as to Jeff Davis. But I wish him to have a fair trial, as public as possible, that we may be Justified to the world.

EMH.

—⁓—

Bancroft Library
Number 59: To Una Hawthorne

Beverly, May 24th. 1865.

My dear Una,

You tell Rebecca that you hunger for a sight of the sea, and I hunger for a sight of you, and mean to be very happy during your visit. I forgot to tell you that Richard was in Richmond. he went about three weeks ago, and promises me a trophy of some kind, if he can pick up anything. Do you not exult at Jeff's Capture?

Your loving Aunt
E. M. Hawthorne

—⁓—

Bancroft Library
Number 60: To Una Hawthorne

Montserrat, Nov. 12th. 1865.

My dear Una,

I cannot write at the word of command. If you are so imperious, you will be served as despots usually are, with a very limited amount of the product of the brain. Your commands have expelled all recollections from mine. I can tell you nothing at all now of what you desire to hear. All I am capable of saying is what relates to the dull present, and to my stupid self.

I suppose Mr. Storey is a nephew of Mrs. Forrester, it is only through her that he can be connected with our family. She was a Storey, and her husband, John Forrester, was a son of Rachel Forrester, my father's sister. Mrs. Forrester likes to talk of the ancestral glories of the Hawthorne family. Several years ago she brought the Misses Savage a copy of our coat of arms, drawn by one of her daughters. She had made researches in heraldry, but she could not tell what some figures upon it were. Nobody could, from that drawing. But our coat is the one attributed in the White Old Maid to some great family: "Azure, a lion's head erased, between the flower de luce."

I did not return home till Saturday evening, and then came with Mr. Wheeler, a cabman who lives in Montserrat. He said he would come at seven, or half past, but he did not till half past eight. Then, though I had never seen him before, he said with the greatest familiarity (for I opened the door, being on the watch)" "Well, were you tired of waiting for me, and did you think I was not coming?" It was as dark as a moonlight night could be, and rained all the way directly in my face, keeping it dripping; but I always enjoy anything that looks like a hardship, but is not one, so I found the drive rather agreeable. I talked with the man, who gave me his opinions upon several subjects of public interest. It appears to me that there is more to be learned from people of his class than from those in a higher position, of the same degree of natural intelligence. They have ways of their own of acquiring knowledge.

I can tell you when your father was born,—on the fourth of July, 1804, in the chamber over that little parlor into which we looked, in that house on Union St. It then belonged to my grandmother Hawthorne, who lived in one part of it. There we lived until 1808, when my father died, at Surinam. I remember very well that one morning my mother called my brother into her room, next to the one where we slept, and told him that his father was dead. He left very little property, and my grandfather Manning took us home. All through our childhood, we were indulged in all convenient ways, and under very little control, except that of circumstances. There were aunts and uncles, and they were all as fond, especially of your father, and as careful of his welfare, as if he had been their own child. He was both beautiful and bright, and perhaps his training was as good as any other could have been. We were the victims of no educational pedantry. We always had plenty of books, and our minds and sensibilities were not unduly stimulated. If he had been educated for a genius, it would have injured him excessively. He developed himself. I think mental superiority in parents is seldom beneficial to children. Shrewdness and good nature are all that is requisite. The Maker of the child will train it better than human wisdom could do. The few incidents of your father's childhood that I can remember are too trivial to relate except to you, who will be interested in anything. For instance, he was very fond of animals, especially kittens, yet he sometimes teased them, as boys will. He once seized a kitten and tossed it over a fence, and when he was told that she would never like him again, he said, "Oh, she'll think it was William." William was a little boy who played with him. He never wanted money, except to spend, and once, in the country where there were no shops, he refused to take some that was offered him, because he could not spend it immediately. Another time, old Mr. Forrester, for we never called him Uncle, though our aunt's husband, offered him a five dollar bill, which he also refused, which was uncivil, as Mr. Forrester always noticed him very kindly when he met him.

EMH.

—⁊⁊⁊—

Bancroft Library
Number 61: To Una Hawthorne

Montserrat, Nov. 23rd 1865

My dear Una,

There is very little to tell about your father's childhood. When he was twelve years old, we all went to Raymond, in Maine, where my grandfather owned a great deal of wild land. Part of the time we were at a farmhouse belonging to the family, as boarders, for there was a tenant on the farm, and at other times at our Uncle's. It was close to the great Sebago Lake, now a well-known place. We enjoyed it exceedingly, especially your father and I. As soon as our Mother became a widow, Uncle Robert assumed the entire charge of my brother's education, and sent him to the best schools, and then to college. It was much more expensive then than it would be to do the same thing now, because the public schools were not good then, and of course he never went to them. Your father was lame for more than a year, I think when he was about ten years old, from a sprain, or some sort of injury, received while playing bat and ball. He may have been lame two years, I cannot remember exactly; but his foot pined away, and was considerably smaller than the other. He had every doctor that could be heard of, among the rest your grandfather Peabody. At last they agreed that nothing could be done, and it must be left to "doctor Time," who did at last cure him. He had another long illness,—I have strangely forgotten dates,—but I remember he used to lie upon the floor and read, and that he went upon two crutches. Everybody thought that, if he lived, he would always be lame. Mr. Joseph E. Worcester, the author of the Dictionary, who at one time taught a school in Salem, to which my brother went, was very kind to him; he came every evening to hear him repeat his lessons. It was during these two long confinements that he acquired the habit of constant reading. Undoubtedly he would have wanted many of the qualities which distinguished him in after life, if his genius had not been thus shielded in childhood. His favorite amusement was playing with a kitten, who would run through houses of books which he built upon the floor. All through his youth he was very fond of Kittens, very unlike you. I think he must have burned all his early letters, as none remain.

Your Loving Aunt,
EMH.

—ⱴⱴ—

Bancroft Library
Number 62: To Una Hawthorne

Montserrat, Dec. 20th. 1865.

My dear Una,

I am anxious to hear whether you are comfortable in your new abode,—whether you have a good warm room, with a sunny aspect, and a person who understands the business, to make your fire in the morning. How pleasant it would be, (to me, at least,) if you were here with Mrs. Cole to take care of us both, and how much you could read, if you had no other amusement! You could also draw, and do various other things. Could you be contented in an inaccessible place like this, in winter? When we lived in Raymond, and your father had gone to school to a clergyman, a Mr. Bradley, near Portland, and Louisa, after a while, went to Salem for her education, I stayed nearly three years—three winters and two summers there. I like to recur to it now, and I think it was good for me, because I acquired the habit of careful reading. I read the Waverly novels as they came out, for there was a good circulating library in Portland, twenty-five miles off, and a stage went thither once a fortnight, by which I went for and returned books. We had a good many of our own for those times; perhaps I had access to books enough; I read Shakespeare assiduously, as I might not have done, if more had been within my reach. Also, I wrote verses, which seemed to me very pretty and were extolled by an intimate friend, with whom I corresponded. I found a bundle of her letters the other day,—and besides, I found two or three of your father's, which I will show you next summer. One or two of them were written during a short tour in Connecticut with one of our Uncles, in 1831, I think, and are very amusing. Your father's lameness was cured by cold water, if by anything. You ask if he had not a pet monkey; he had, and it died, and we buried it in the garden; Louisa, who was very little, said it was planted. We also carried a Cat to the grave with a long procession, and he wrote its epitaph upon a piece of slate. It was this:

"Then, oh Thomas, rest in glory!
Hallowed be thy silent grave,—
Long thy name in Salem's story
Shall live, and honour o'er it wave."

He must then have been about thirteen. You perceive that the lines are melodious, and show a familiarity with the language of poetry. I remember one verse, (there were more, but I have forgotten them), which he wrote long after, at sixteen, perhaps:

"Lady fair, will you not listen
To my ardent vows of love?
Love that in my eyes doth glisten,
And is firm as Heaven above."

                                                              EMH.

—⁊⁊⁊—

Bancroft Library
Number 63: To Una Hawthorne

                                        Montserrat, Wednesday, Feby. 26. 1866
My dear Una,

I hope you will not think me hard-hearted, or wanting in sympathy for you, if I say that I cannot reconcile myself to the plan of going to Concord. The more I think of it, the more I shrink from it. I should miss your father, and altogether there is a gloom about Concord. I feel sure I should not live a year, if I let myself be pulled up by the roots, and transported thither. Let me live peaceably in my native air; it is by imbibing that, that my health has been so remarkably preserved. I should lose ten years of life by removing into another atmosphere, and while I lived, I should never be well, and you would have the trouble of an infirm old woman for an inmate. Another reason why it is inexpedient for me to leave this vicinity, is the state of Mrs. Dike's health. She is extremely unwilling to have me go away, because she knows pretty well that she should never see me again, and she is not likely to live many years. She has something to leave, of which I should be glad to have a share; but if I go where I cannot, in any case, be with her, she will take it as proof that I care nothing about her, and she may give me reason to regret it. I have a plan of my own which I have been revolving in my mind for a good while. It is to take two rooms in Salem, a parlor and a sleeping room, with a lounge in the parlor on which you could sleep; and then you could come to see me, and stay as long as you liked, and there would be no one to "say us nay." Then I think we may be happy together. My plan is to buy dinners, and to prepare my tea for myself. I think I could make it cheaper than boarding. I am going to write immediately to Rebecca to look out for rooms. I think that there is a house in North Salem where I could be accommodated, and that perhaps the Mannings would supply me with dinner. Besides dinner, I only want bread and milk and tea. Do not you admit that my plan is good? Mrs. Cole has just told me that she and Mr. Cole have come to the conclusion that they cannot keep me another winter. Mrs. Cole says (and I cannot but own she is right) that at her age she ought to seek repose, and that it would not surprise her if Mr. Cole was taken away suddenly; she is in constant dread of it, and is herself becoming more infirm everyday. In short, she wishes me to go soon. I mean to try my plan first. Tell me if you do not think you should enjoy visiting me?

EMH.

—⟱—

Bancroft Library
Number 64: To Una Hawthorne

Beverly, May 11th. 1866

My dear Una

I have waited in vain for an inclination to write, so now I write from a sense of duty, and I think my letter will be disagreeable to you. I shall find fault with many things. In the first place, you always spell <u>development</u> wrong, you write the word <u>devellopment.</u> It is a mere trifle, but it gratifies my present ill-natured mood to mention it. Next reformers are by no means the salt of the world, they are only more pugnacious than other people, who observe, and amiably tolerate many shortcomings to which they are supposed to be blind, rather than raise a cloud of strife which will darken the sunshine of social intercourse. At this moment I am a reformer. Nothing pleases me. Of course I am speaking of the common sort of reformers, who are so only in pretence, being in reality the worst nuisances. Of true reformers, I think you are mistaken when you say that they run to extremes. Christ and the apostles never did so. All the rules for the conduct of life to be found in the New Testament, are moderate and practical. There you never find "the reverse of wrong mistaken for right." I do not know much about other reformers. John Howard certainly never went to extremes in his efforts for the reform of prisons; neither, I think, did Martin Luther, and his co-workers. Moderation, indeed, is an essential element in every improvement. You know the rule—it is quoted often enough—hasten slowly. Next, as to "the extra breath of immortal fire" with which you suppose them endowed, "burning with a light more dazzling than that of day." That is mere humbug. When the light of day shines, we do not see such smoky and lurid flames as they kindle, which never would rouse anybody from slumber, but from the alarm that they create of a conflagration. But you know that when you walk in a dark street in the evening, when a few lamps are burning at the opposite end of the street, and you are approaching them, how they dazzle your eyes, and how much worse they make it than utter darkness. It is because they are nearly on a level with the eye. We can only be safely guided by light that comes from above. The light of the sun does not mislead. As to woman's rights, I have always found privileges much better things. There are some laws, though I suppose not many in this country, that are unjust to our sex. If women are paid as much as men for the same work, and have the free disposal of their earnings, I think there is no other right worth contending for. But you know nobody will pay more to men or women than they can avoid, and there always seem to be plenty of women glad to work cheaper than men. The female teachers of schools are many of them well paid now, and probably women of active minds will somehow contrive to obtain all important rights. Indeed, cultivated women have never been much oppressed; the difficulty seems to be in raising whole classes of people, men and women too, to the level of cultivation. But as there is no obstacle to that in this country, I see no reason for any solicitude about rights or privileges. I do not like your saying that you "suppose many women would vote as well as most men." It would not be easy to say a more severe thing about the intellect of our sex. It is placing women whose mental endowments make them the eminent and enviable few, just on a level with the herd of mediocre men. This nearly finishes my fault-finding. I shall only say, further, that I do not think the best way of discovering truth is to be continually seeking for it. If you keep your mind tranquil, as much truth as you need will be photographed upon it.

Does your mother heartily approve of your staying at Lexington this summer? The more I think of it, the odder it seems to me. I have always felt as if young women who were obliged to leave their mothers and their homes before marriage were to be pitied; but as you do it from choice, I hope it is not so hard a case [as] for those who are constrained to do so.

Richard and his wife called yesterday, and we took a little walk together. We found plenty of Columbines, and of those bird-foot violets, I believe they are called, the loveliest of wild flowers. Did not you tell me that they were especial favorites with your father? I never see them now without thinking of him. He did not profess much love for flowers in general; less than he felt, no doubt. Once, when he expected to leave Salem soon, he told us on his return from a walk, that he had switched off the heads of all the columbines he passed, as he never meant and never wished to see their successors again. But as it happened, he did not go away, and visited the same spots for several years after that.—I am longing for a letter from you, a long letter, such as you used to write. I wanted to ask Mrs. Foster if she would take you in October, but did not venture, because she might be fortifying herself against it all summer. It will be better to make a sudden assault, when she is not thinking of it. If she refuses, I know not what will become of me. I should like a general overturn in the neighborhood, with the exception of the Coles. Something favorable to us might turn up.

I have written away my ill-humour. I am quite amiable now, and can tolerate even cant. Send me your next composition. If you really prefer staying at Lexington, you will not mind what I say. I have got a new bottle of ink, which scatters itself upon the paper, and makes yellow blots, as you will see. Write immediately.

EMH.[96]

—ᗰ—

Phillips Library
Number 65: To Rebecca Manning

Montserrat, Friday May 25 [1866]

My dear Rebecca,

If you do not come over soon all the violets will be gone. I hope that consideration will bring you as soon as possible after you receive this. I think they are not quite abundant as they were some years ago, on the hill where we have gathered so many, but there are enough in more remote spots. Almost all the wild flowers are in bloom now. If you do not come tomorrow I trust you will not defer it longer than the first of next week. And besides the flowers you will like to see, I want to see you—all of you. As to my coming to Salem, that does not seem a practical proceeding, because I have no shoes to wear. And, what makes the case worse, there are no shoes to be obtained in Beverly, though so many are made here, and though almost every man seems to be a shoemaker. Everybody goes to Salem to buy shoes, and some people even to get them mended. So I must wait patiently till Providence sends me a pair. I have been to the library once, and mean to go again tomorrow. I can walk along on level ground, without exposing my shoes, but they would be seen in getting into the Horse Cars. I have a list of eighteen things, of which I am in the last extremity of need, which I mean to purchase in Salem whenever I can get there. My gown is made, for we have a dressmaker in Montserrat.

Una says in her last letter that she cannot imagine why I use the word odd in reference to her staying at Lexington. She says it is much more odd for girls not to go to school, as has been her case all her life, than for them to go. She feels that she is benefitted by it in many ways, and if she goes home she must leave her gymnastic course unfinished with no prospect of ever resuming it, and she thinks that on many accounts it was good for her to leave home; though she deeply regrets leaving her Mother, who misses her very much. So I shall not say any more about it. Rose says in a letter she wrote me the other day, that "Aunt Lizzie, Nat Peabody, and Uncle Nat have come here for the summer, They are delightful people and we are ever so glad to have them here". I think she must mean only that they have come to Concord, to live perhaps in Mrs. Mann's house. Rose sent me another photograph of Julian. Do you want it?

I should like to read Clare's Poems, and, if books were not so dear I would buy them. But then there are others that I want more. I like Miss Marjoribank and the Claverings.[97] It is rather a disadvantage to begin to read a story in the middle, but there is a pleasure in guessing at what has gone before. For what is to come, we may easily guess at something of that in the Claverings at least. Trollope's young men are so fickle that we may anticipate a good deal of wrong-doing in Henry Clavering. Do not you think that Fanny Clavering will in the end marry this Mr. Saul? The way in which he makes his offer is amusing, and must have been provoking, too. I should have hated him, but Fanny will learn to like him.

If you have arranged to come to Montserrat tomorrow (Saturday) and if you get this before you set out, do not be prevented by my saying I am going to the Library. I hardly ever go until after tea, and if you come I can walk down with you.

EMH[98]

—⁓—

Bancroft Library
Number 66: To Una Hawthorne

Beverly, February 10th [1867]

My dear Una,

I take it for granted that there is no truth in this newspaper paragraph, but I should like to have authority for denying it when it is mentioned to me.[99]

You know you promised to return that little Photograph you carried away,— the group I mean of yourself, Julian and Rose. It is the only likeness of you all in your early years, and I value it very highly. You cannot be so unkind as not to send it. Then I want to beg a lock of your beautiful hair, a full length lock, though I will be satisfied with a thin one, even one of only half a dozen hairs. It will be a pleasure to me to look at it. Also, if you have any of those tintype's of me, will you send one to Dora, who asked me for something of the kind. She asked as if she really wished for one. I promised to send her one, though I hate to have anybody see them, but I find I have none.

I will return the Programme of those dramatic performances when I write. I am afraid it would make this letter too heavy. I wish Julian would write to me.

I hope your Mamma is quite well now. Colds are extremely annoying. I do not think they are indigenous in Montserrat: none of us here had them this winter. Little Abbie is here, and I read her to sleep every night with Fairfax's Tasso. It will not be my fault if she has not a good taste in Poetry.

I see that Miss Rebecca Harding is arrived.[100]

—⁓—

Phillips Library
Number 67: To Robert Manning

Montserrat [May 1867]

My dear Cousin,

Rebecca desired me to telegraph the first appearance of the violets, but it will be easier to write. I have just found unusually beautiful ones in a place where

I never found them before. They seem to be spreading all over this region; it is said that they grow where the woods have been burned. In the same vicinity there were pink and white Anemones "the pied wind flower" perhaps. The trientalis is leaved out but not bloomed.[101] You must all come over as soon as possible, if the sun ever shines again. As for me, it is not well for me to go to Salem, for I never can get home comfortably. Monday evening it rained, and I went to Mrs. Davis's and left my bonnet there and borrowed a <u>cloud</u> to wear home.[102] It was not much better than a cloud of the sky, and the sensation of the raindrops on the crown of my head was very unpleasant. And when I sent for my bonnet a day or two after, Mrs. Davis and all the family were absent and the house shut up. I shall have to borrow one of Jane's bonnets.

I do not know what a <u>characteristic</u> letter is, and if it is possible to find a "Complete Letter Writer", I must provide myself with one, to learn what it befits me to say. This delicate paper ought not to be scrawled over in my careless way, besides, You must not let Mrs. Dike know that I write you, because she will think herself entitled to equal attention, as undoubtedly she is.

I think you would like Storrow Higginson. He seems to have very correct notions, and I found that his estimate of Mrs. Hawthorne agreed with mine— if she suspects what it is, she would not let him have Una. Not that we either of us expressed any opinion whatever of her but it is easy to guess. And he says that Julian will never be anything but a boy while he remains with his Mother. He thinks it would not be amiss for him to go alone, But he thinks it would ruin him to go to Oxford, even if he could be matriculated there, which is doubtful.[103]

—⁓—

Phillips Library
Number 68: To Maria Manning

Montserrat, July 10th [1868]

My dear Cousin,

I should have been glad to come to see you the other day, when I went to Salem, if I had had time. I was sorry to miss seeing Augusta Storey. Are you ever coming to Montserrat again? The Laurel is not yet out of bloom. I wish you would all come for a long afternoon in the woods. You know the last time you were here it rained, so that we had but a fragment of a walk.

I hope Goldylocks is well. There is a cat who lives not far from here, who looks exactly like him—just the same bright color, and the same size and shape.

I covet him, but Mrs. Cole declares she will never have another cat, and rejoices that poor Billie is not [living]; I hope she will live to want one of his race; yesterday she found a mouse in the room next to hers; she called Jane and me to assist in catching him. She took the tongs and might have caught him if she had not been so frightened. Mr. Cole came with a shovel, but they achieved nothing, except shrieks from Mrs. Cole. I Exulted, and told her so.

I am reading "All for Greed" and "Phineas Finn" to Jane, and should like the numbers of the Living Age containing them.[104] I like Phineas very much,— he is exactly the young man whom it is pleasant to meet in a novel, and I trust the Author will take good care of him and not let him come to too much grief.

I heard from Una last week. They are going to Europe, from motives of economy—to live in Dresden, where living costs less than nothing, and where the lower classes are deferential. But the house is to be sold first, and perhaps they will not go till next spring, and nothing is to be said about it.[105]

—m—

Bancroft Library
Number 69: To Una Hawthorne

[July 1868]

My dear Una,

I have been trying to think of something to say to you, but, as you know, all ideas fly away when you try to catch them. I might tell you that I have just been trying to find the chickens, in spite of Mrs. Cole's express prohibition, and that the horse came and drove them away, putting his head in my basket and devouring the food I intended for them, and then making the oddest grimaces to show that he did not think it very good. If I could but ride, as you can, I should jump upon his back, for he follows me about like a little dog, and as he does not work hard, he leaps over fences and walls, racing for amusement. Sometimes, on warm nights, he and two of his friends gallop round the neighborhood till it is time for people to get up. Then I long to join them. If you were here, it would be quite safe for you to ride, even without a saddle, upon Charlie (one horse.) He reminds me of the Arabian horses, who are brought up, it is said, in the tents of their owners with the children, and so become docile and affectionate.

My dear Una, after writing the above and reading it over, I put away pen and paper in disgust at my own folly, and at the emptiness of my mind. But after waiting three days, I do not find that anything better presents itself, and this will at least show that I think of you. And if you were well and in good spirits, I might assure you that what you say of our political condition strikes me as even more absurd. There are "folly and wickedness" everywhere, else we should need no governments, and should probably not be divided into nations; indeed, it is impossible to say what we should need: not books, or anything that implies mental effort in its production, or a strong interest to take hold of the mind. We should have nothing to struggle for, and I think we should lead an animal life, and the best of us would be more like the beasts that perish than the worst are now—not more wicked, but more hopeless. But the strife between good and evil can never lose its interest, and as to our own country, we certainly have more than the proposition of righteous men that would have saved Sodom; and men not righteous only, but strong—so that if you really have the gift of discerning the future, as I infer from your saying that you "cannot exactly see" what is to happen to us, if I were you I would not be afraid to take a good peep at coming events. For my own part, I doubt not that the same Providence that carried us successfully through the war will still preserve us— and by every trial and every struggle we become stronger.

You ask my opinion of your plan of going to Europe. I can not see, considering the expense of the voyage, how it is to be immediately economical—for a year at least, and then though your mother's friend may know what pleases her, she cannot be sure what would suit you. If you were established at Dresden, there might be circumstances that would make Dresden as distasteful to you as Concord is now, which would render another removal necessary and additional expense. Indeed, every scheme requires twice as much money to execute it as you at first suppose. Then I do not believe it will be beneficial to the health of any of you to live in lodgings in one of those old cities, where the atmosphere is full of the breath of countless generations;—not even to have a house to yourselves, but to inhabit the apartments of unknown predecessors whom perhaps you would shudder to think of, if you knew them. For houses do not burn down, as they do in this country, and I fear are not even renovated and refurbished, as Hotels and other places of public resort are annually among us. You have to tread on the same carpets and continually to track the same articles of furniture that were used and robbed of their freshness by remote generations of people, to say nothing of those who may be polluting the air now under the same roof with you; for how can it be possible to guard against contagion, if it exists, as it frequently must, in the form of fever if nothing worse, in a large lodging house? Besides, the political condition of every part of Germany is very precarious. War seems to be the one thing that is prepared for, and if it should come, though as Americans you would be protected from danger, you could not be from inconvenience.[106] In former wars between Prussia and Austria, Dresden suffered greatly, and for a long time, and there is no reason why it should not again. At any rate, I rejoice that you are not likely to go at present. The plan of living in Salem I think is a good one.

Do write soon, my dear child. I wish you could come to see me.

EMH.[107]

—⁄w—

Phillips Library
Number 70: To Maria Manning

Beverly Feb. 20th 1868

My dear Maria

I was very glad to hear from you, and I hope you will soon be able to come to Montserrat. I have written to Mrs. Dike, and I suppose she will show you the letter. I do not go down stairs yet, because I should be obliged to leave off so many sacks and other comfortable articles of attire that Mrs. Cole fears I should renew my cold. But I have passed a much pleasanter winter in consequence of this seclusion, from the beginning of January until last Thursday, when Julian came and said that he must see me, having a message for me, and his Mother was very low and Una had a heart complaint. So I had to go down and he said Una had sent him to bring me to Concord for a visit of two or three months. He said Una only expected to live a year or a year and a half—she had had the heart complaint in England and ever since. And Storrow Higginson does not believe in marriage, so she had written him a letter breaking off the engagement. He says Storrow's principles were always the same, but he was very much in love with Una and forgot them just then. But now he has "got into his old groove", and Julian thinks he is too old to change, being twenty six; He admires Shelley; I always supposed it was only Shelley's poetry, but it seems that was not all. I am glad Una has given him up. Julian has talked with Mrs. Higginson, (Storrow's Mother), who admits that the marriage is not to be thought of. It is a pity that some of the Higginsons did not tell Una in the beginning, but perhaps they thought he would be reclaimed by an engagement. Julian says they have always been as much shocked as any body could be at his notions, and that they are all very nice people. Una read some of his letters to me (I forgot to tell you that she came to see me on the 17th of January), and I thought them charming,—readable, even if they were love-letters. He seemed to be in [the] happiest and most tranquil and admirable frame of mind, and described what was passing before him in the most taking way. The only fault that suggested itself to me was that he was less intent upon making money than benefitted a young man who had none, and that Una was going to marry a person who would help perpetuate the poverty of our family. But Julian says he has three thousand dollars a year, as a professor in a college, and is in a way to qualify himself for a professorship at home, as he has excellent opportunities to become familiar with most modern languages, therefore so many people of all nations in Buenos Ayres, where, besides living is not so high but that he might lay up a good deal. Julian has the highest opinion of his talents, and of his integrity as far as adherence to his principles goes, but then, he says they are very bad principles. I am going to write to Robert.

> Your affectionate Cousin
> EMH[108]

—⁂—

Phillips Library
Number 71: To Rebecca Manning

Montserrat, February 23 [1868]

My dear Cousin,

This is a sort of continuation of my letter to Maria, which you must read first. About Storrow Higginson,—Una was evidently dissatisfied with his letters, but she did not tell me what was the particular fault. After she had read part of them to me, she said the rest was political and would not interest me, but I told her that was just what I should like best and that she was a Copperhead, if she differed from him.[109] She said no, but he thought Negroes were very superior to white people; she knew that they must be allowed to vote, whether they were fit or not. Then she read what would have done very well in a Fourth of July Oration, about the progress of freedom, &.c. but all admirably expressed, the language not high-flown, if the sentiments were. She said she knew all that before, and what was the use of his writing it? And she said that she thought he went out there to make money, whereas he said now it was because he could perfect himself in the modern languages.—I do not know whether it is right to tell you that I should like to have both these letters burned when you have all read them. Of course it troubled me very much when Julian said that Una's life was likely to be so short, but Mrs. Cole would not believe it and assured me that Una would be well enough to come see me before I was able to go out and that I should find that she had not the heart complaint at all, more than people are apt to have it after a disappointment of this kind. And she was right, for on Monday I received a letter from Una, in which she said her complaint was nervous, caused by anxiety, and that the Doctor said she would soon be well, and insisting upon my coming there to live, my society being necessary to her comfort, as, of course she was not happy, and anticipating great pleasure in reading[,] walking and talking with me, for she always said that her Mother would be utterly astounded at the things she was in the habit of saying to me, and now her Mother is frequently sick, which is depressing to the spirits of both the girls. The invitation is given in such a way that it seems impossible to decline it—but for the first few days I could not speak nor think of leaving Beverly without crying, and Mrs. Cole would come up and cry too. You would have laughed to see us. I always liked Mrs. Cole, there is something brisk and cheering in the tones of her voice, especially when she comes into my room in the morning and berates me for not getting up. And it is like a fresh breeze to hear her when she is angry, as she occasionally is at my proceedings. I don't know how I can endure to live with people whose voices never vary when they are angry, as every body must be sometimes. And besides, I love Beverly as I never did any other place, and I hate Concord, where the air is not good, nor the water, and where people get worn down with doing nothing just as they do in other places with hard work, and have to go away to get recruited.[110]

—m—

Phillips Library
Number 72: To Rebecca Manning

Montserrat April 9th [1868]

My dear Rebecca,

I have delayed writing as long as possible, in hopes some of you would come over, as it is now pleasant and the walking is not very bad. I enclose ten dollars; I will pay for the Living Age this year, and when I wrote last I forgot all about the collar you bought for me; it is very pretty indeed, and Mrs. Cole wants one just like it. When you happen to be in Boston again, if you can without trouble will you buy her one? but do not go out of your way for it. My old shaker bonnet is in ruins,—what do you advise me to have in its place? Little Abbie, when she saw its condition, said I ought to buy a hat of anti-slavery straw, with not much crown, but a broad trim. Una says that women of all ages wear hats, and nothing else, in the country.[111] What do you say about it?

I think you will have something to say when you read Una's letter, which I send to Mrs. Dike. They are all going to Germany in October. Julian is going to study, and the rest to keep him from feeling homesick in a strange land. He is also, as you will see, going to Paris to row. I have been afraid that he would. Considering that he is supposed never to have opened a book with a dubious word in it, think of allowing him to live without control in Paris, a place where vice is not even disreputable, for four months, for he is to go in June, and they are to join him there in October, or on their arrival. But if I say any of this to his Mother, she would think me utterly corrupt, to fancy that one so pure could be liable to temptation. When Una wrote before, she said that Julian had taken possession of his father's study, and—but I will send her letter.—I am more obliged to Richard than I can express, for his kind care of what Uncle William left.

EMH[112]

—⟋⟋⟋—

Phillips Library
Number 73: To Rebecca Manning

Montserrat, April 26th [1868]

My dear Rebecca,

One reason why I have not written to you is that I hoped you would come to see me, and that I should be able to go to Salem some afternoon—but the unfavorable weather has rendered both these visits impossible. I want several things, especially a pair of gloves, do you think you can get me a pair in Salem—kid, of suitable colour. I have had them too large lately. I have an old black kid glove of just the right size, if I could but send it to you; some shade of gray I should like best. I do not like to trouble you about so many things, but you are so kind as to execute all commissions with apparent willingness. I want your advice about a bonnet, too. Do you think the one I wore last summer will do with a new ruche?—Jane says I shall never like the new fashions. I can send it to the woman [who] made my winter bonnet. Winter and spring come very often indeed. Don't you think a whole year of one and then a whole year of the other would make some things easier? I am not impatient for warm weather; it is pleasant to have a little fire to sit by. I am sorry you have had such colds, and glad that Mr. and Mrs. Dike are comfortable, but when I write to her will it be safe to say so, or must I assume that she is in her normal state of suffering? It is difficult to communicate by letter with one so entirely "out of my sphere", as she is. Mere talking may be forgotten, but I believe she reads a letter over and over. There is a happy art, if I could but attain it of filling sheets of paper with meaningless words,—long words are the best. Then, if there are no blots, which I believe she disapproves of more than she would errors in grammar, all is done that can be done. Ideas are perilous.

I have promised, and hither to kept my promise, to write to Una every week. She says my letters are delightful—indispensable indeed to her comfort. She says that she finds she never loved Storrow Higginson, and that all of her relatives and friends tell her that they never approved of the engagement and are rejoiced that it is broken off. Why cannot people say what they think at the right moment and not wait until it is useless to speak at all? I like to know the opinion of my friends, especially when I ask it—but perhaps Una did not ask any one's counsel. I agree with you some of the innumerable Higginsons might have told Mrs. Hawthorne a little about Storrow. Col. T. W. Higginson made Una a visit of a day or two and ought to have warned her. But now she tells me that she feels inexpressibly relieved, and is growing happier every day. I hope she will never be engaged again, for the affair seemed, for half the winter to unsettle every thing. When I first spoke of going to Concord, Mrs. Cole said that she never should have turned me away; but she soon became accustomed to think of my going, and told me that at any rate she could not keep me another winter, as Mr. Cole's health was failing, and her own not very good. By that time I had resolved not to go to Concord, so I wrote to you to ask if you thought I could get two comfortable rooms in Salem, where I could buy my dinners and provide tea for myself—for I cannot think of going into another family as a boarder, and exerting myself to be agreeable, as I have done here. I was then quite uprooted from the soil of Beverly, and willing to go any where except to Concord. But Jane, who had never believed that I should go to Concord, persuaded me not to send the letter I had written to you, but to wait until Spring; and Mrs. Cole told me soon afterwards that Jane could not bear to be left alone, with no one to speak to, and that I should stay as long as she could make me comfortable. But you see I was kept in a state of perplexity for months, and all through Storrow Higginson's perversity, and Una's not knowing her own mind. Una asks me now if I liked Storrow, if I felt as her other friends did about her engagement. I did like him, because he had fought in the war, and on the return of peace was going to work. "Sober to toil, and valiant to fight", I supposed him to be,—handsome or elegant I saw that he was not;

but yet he was agreeable.[113] On the whole I am rather surprised that Una did not love him. Mrs. Hawthorne has been sick all winter—Una said in her letter last week that she had only been down stairs once, for a few minutes, and with her assistance. Una must have a dull time.

I think you will not wish to hear from me very soon again—This old glove is for measure. Richard has the money sent me from Concord in February. Will you ask him for it, and take what is necessary for the gloves and to pay for the Living Age? Please to select bills of Western and New York banks, which I fear are suspicious. I cannot even go to the Library for want of gloves. I ought to have attended to it before.

I send Goldylocks some Catnip, with which I beg you will allow him to hold a regular wake, in remembrance of his departed friend Billy. But I forget whether you know that Billy is dead. I wrote you word, but [it] may have been in the letter I did not send. He died during the cold weather in February. He had been hurt, in fighting, several times, and would never stay in the house long enough to recover entirely, and at last he became sick, and refused to eat, and thus we lost him. Mrs. Cole says it is a great relief to her and she will never have another cat.—Did Maria go to Lawrence, with Mrs. Blaisdale's pupils? I had not heard of Mrs. Story's death, Ellen Jewett's name was in the list of wounded, in the first paper I saw after the disaster, but not in the later papers.[114]

—⁂—

Bancroft Library
Number 74: To Una Hawthorne

Montserrat, Feb. 14. 1869

My dear Una

There is a girl in the neighborhood who goes to the village every day, and is so obliging as to bring me my letters regularly. The foreign postage stamps are mysterious to everyone who sees them, and the idea of such a constant corre-spondence to which I am a party gives me, I fancy, an importance I should not otherwise enjoy. I have just begun to read in the Living Age, (almost the only new book I see, in winter) a story from the German, The Country House on the Rhine, by Berthold Auerbach. It does not compare favorably with English tales of equally high reputation. Very likely the translator is in fault. I like to have a translation read like an original work but this does not. I dare say it may be accurate, but the style is neither vivid nor flexible. A novel, I think, must be far more difficult to render than a history, or any work of mere utility. Indeed, the translator of a history may often be very sure of approaching as nearly to the author's meaning as the author does to the truth. But in a good novel there are subtle and delicate shades of signification which it is hard to catch. And in German there are so many adverbs and other words that seem made only to puzzle people, just like go-betweens and busy-bodies in society, perverting everybody's meaning, that the difficulty is greatly increased. And the translator of this Country House seems to me not quite familiar with the language, especially with these little perplexing appendages. In some of the English magazines there are amusing stories of German tables d'hôte, and of the atrocities there committed—of ladies who drink the gravy out of their plates, using their knives as shovels to hasten the operation—and other similar proceedings. Have you observed anything like that? What you say of the Germans' neglect of personal cleanliness, reminds me of an anecdote of Madame Sontag.[115] When the streets were muddy, some gentlemen made a sort of bridge of their hands for her to walk over, either to or from her carriage, and an English lady who heard of it said that if the hands were like those of the German gentlemen she had seen, Madame Sontag might still have to pick her way.

EMH.

—⚍—

Bancroft Library
Number 75: To Una Hawthorne

Montserrat, Feb^ry 17. 1869

My dear Una

It has been so sunny and pleasant for the last month nearly all the time that I have felt as if I ought to go out. But once in a while it snows for a few hours and spoils the walking, though Jane walks down to the village very often—she is gone now—and thinks I might go with her. But it is a walk in the woods that I am wishing for. There are beautiful things, bright green ferns, and the loveliest mosses, and crimson berries to be found in moist places in mild winters, that one quite overlooks until the taller plants are dead. Just before Christmas I was much annoyed by persons who came for me to show them such spots. When I was reading comfortably with a good fire, was it not provoking to be dragged out into the cold? But Mrs. Cole was a useful ally then, declaring vehemently that I should not go, that I should get cold and be as ill as I was last winter. I always make a merit of taking her advice when it suits me, so I usually staid in the house, ill-naturedly, as I was conscious, declining to assist in such expeditions.

If the Forresters go to Dresden, what claims have they upon you?[116] A relationship that is no nearer than a second cousinship may be recognised or ignored, Just as personal qualities render it expedient. I once said something like
that to Mrs. Dike, and she professed to be indignant, though it is a principle
she always acts upon. Is it not strange that it should be more pardonable to do
than to say? as I think it is with most people. But these are things more shocking to Mrs. Dike than any I am likely to say—such blots, I mean, as deface the
sheet. To please her, a letter must above all be neat. She has sometimes called
upon me to admire a note that said nothing at all, but was written in a labori-
ous hand, like that of persons who are just able to send love and enquire about
health. I do not know whether my letters ever meet her approbation. I always
take pains to write them handsomely, and fill them with platitudes—in general,
to say exactly what I do not think, using as long words to cover more paper, as
the subject will permit. Be thankful that you have an Aunt to whom you may
write without hiding away your intellect; or rather, to whom you may safely
disclose your follies. Before I forget it, I must account for the blots upon these
sheets: I have a new bottle of ink, larger than I have been used to, and I am apt
to dip my pen into it too deeply. Of ink and pens and paper I use unprece-
dented quantities now, but I am well supplied with them all.

You must not call Boswell's Johnson prosy. A more entertaining book, by
universal consent, does not exist. And I do not believe there ever was a man
better endowed with the wisdom of everyday life than Dr. Johnson.

Yours affectionately,

EMH.

—⁊⁊⁊—

Bancroft Library
Number 76: To Una Hawthorne

Montserrat, March 4. 1869

My dear Una:

This day President Grant had been inaugurated (it is now evening) It is said
that Andrew Johnson after a short visit to [Tennessee], is going to sail for
Europe in one of the German steamers. As everybody goes to Dresden, perhaps
you will see him there. A more forlorn and miserable creature than he must be,
if he is not blinded to his own wretchedness, I cannot imagine. And I hope you
feel and exult in the happiness of the country in being rid of him, without
having sustained essential injury, and in the bright future that we have a right
to anticipate under the guidance of a man so entirely unlike him as Grant.

Mrs. Grant is said to be a very estimable, sensible, and unpretending woman. Not by any means handsome, for she squints with both eyes. She has been advised by her friends to have her eyes straightened, but she says that "Mr. Grant has liked her ever since she was a little girl with her eyes crossed, and he says he should not think it was she if they were made straight." I would let them alone if I was she—he will have perplexities enough without doubting the identity of his wife.

I was afraid you had changed your mind about the Episcopal Church—you remember that you mentioned your intention to me. I heartily approve of your being confirmed, and agree with you that there is nothing objectionable, or I should rather say, that there is everything comforting and good in the Liturgy; and it is, I suppose, rather in the Liturgy than in the Articles that the faith of its most intelligent members is reposed. The Articles are, as some of its most eminent clergymen pronounce them, "Articles of Peace," to which all can subscribe for the sake of union, and which admit, as everything transmitted from the age in which they were agreed upon does admit, of much liberality of interpretation. If Sidney Smith and Archbishop Whately could sign them, and find them no hindrance to the free movement of their minds, I think no one need scruple to do likewise.[117] And certainly the world has never seen better men, nor men of greater intellect than many who have lived in the faith of the Church of England. We cannot estimate the good influence it has exerted upon English literature, and through that, upon everything that is best among ourselves. What should we have done if our minds had been nurtured upon the literature of any other European country? In France even now, I fancy all religion is more than half superstition. The letters of Eugenie de Guérin, and another book about the Ferrmaye family, convey that impression.[118]

EMH.[119]

Bancroft Library
Number 77: To Una Hawthorne

Montserrat. September 1st. 1869

My dear Una:

I had begun to fancy that my political utterances were so shocking to you, with your English prepossessions, that you were willing to wait for another letter until I could write in a different mood.

I enclose Miss Amelung's photograph, but with reluctance.[120] Julian promised to send me one when he could get a good likeness. She has a very sweet countenance. When you told me that there was a lovely daughter, and that Julian had known the family a good while, I foresaw what was to follow. I trust they will be very happy together. You do not tell me in what part of America she lives. I shall keep the secret out of curiosity to know how long it will remain undisclosed. I have not hinted it to the Mannings, though when I saw them they were talking of Julian's two sonnets in Putnam's Magazine, and I said that Mrs Russel remarked that she did not see how he <u>could</u> have written them unless he had an attachment, and if he had one, she should not have thought he <u>would.</u> Just what has been said about some famous Italian sonnets. I think them extremely beautiful; perhaps Julian will supply the want which some critics find in the poetry of the present day—that of an impassioned expression of love.

A week or two ago I received a note from a relative of ours, Mrs Condit of New Jersey, formerly Elinor Barstow. She asked whether I would see her, and when she could call. I replied that I should be glad to see her any afternoon. So she came once in Salem, and afterwards here. We went into the woods and sat down, as you and I used to do, and talked as if we had been intimate all our lives, though I have not seen her before since she was a child. We talked of your father, who was very fond of her, and she told me a great deal that he said to her. She wrote to him once after he lived at Concord, and he answered her letter very affectionately, and urged her to come and see him when she next went to Boston; but she did not go thither again, after that, till the present summer. I find that all our relations on the Hawthorne side are proud of your father's fame. Elinor said that Gordon Coit, another cousin, was travelling in England, and visited Stratford, and Shakespeare's house. He happened to sit down, and the woman in attendance exclaimed, "Do you know where you are sitting? The great American author, Mr Hawthorne, sat down in that chair, putting his hand over his eyes, and never moved for two hours." Gordon Coit then told her that he was a kinsman of the great author. Mrs Coit, his mother, is the wife of an Episcopal clergyman, I think in Connecticut. Soon after the Scarlet letter was published Bishop Clark reviewed it unfavorably, censuring it as immoral. Mrs. Coit was exceedingly angry, and scolded the Bishop. He apologised, and said that if he had been aware that the author was a kinsman of her he would not have written in that manner. Then she told him that his conduct was the more despicable, if he could be biased by such a consideration as that. Her husband, Dr. Coit, wrote a book twenty years ago or more, called "Puritanism" in which he spoke of the Puritans as Episcopalians are apt to do, but she insisted on his omitting all irreverent notice of her forefathers.[121] I do not suppose either the Bishop or her husband cared for her remarks, except for the sake of peace; she is not uncommonly intellectual, though not at all deficient. She has been a great reader, however, and she ought to have remembered that Walter Scott was glad to have his ancestors' importance recognised in any way. I am trying to write, but Hannah (the blind woman) is talking to me so stupidly that she makes me stupid. But something has happened since I began this letter which you will be interested to know. Mr Cole is dead, after much suffering. Mrs. Cole is glad to have me here she says, for company; indeed she is unwilling to spare me, even for a day, and I am well pleased to be able to give a reason for declining to go to Salem. I only wish you could transport yourself hither two or three times a week, for the weather and the walks are so charming, and the nights are so clear, and the air so full of fragrance, that you would enjoy the mere seeing and breathing, I daresay, much more than I can imagine, for I am grown dull and stupid.

I suppose you have heard of Mrs Stowe's article upon Lord Byron—perhaps you have read it.[122] I do not believe her accusations, and never having been able to read her books, I was not aware, until I looked over this production, how wretched her style is. It is so weak, and so overladen with commonplace epithets that it betrays a corresponding weakness of mind. Besides, if all she says were true, it would be injudicious to tell it. One noticeable result is already apparent; all the young girls, it is said, are reading Don Juan, and older people are applying themselves to Moore's Life and Correspondence of the Author. This is what I mean to do myself. It is evident from the tone of the periodicals that the Episcopal Church is losing its hold upon the nation—the English nation, I mean. It seems to be supported as a political institution, and to be tottering, like many other remains of a less investigating age. I daresay most of the people prefer it for various reasons to any other mode of worship, but those who know best how to express their opinions probably believe no more in its divine origin than in the divine right of the Queen; it rests upon expediency, which is but a weak substitute for faith in religious concerns. They are trying in England to "put new wine into old bottles." I wonder what kind of people they will be when important changes have been made in their government. I should like to outlive Queen Victoria, out of curiosity, rather than from a wish to see the evil doings that may come to them when that scampish Prince of Wales ascends the throne. When they have a monarch whom they cannot respect in his character, will they respect his office? You will probably see this question answered by events, but the Queen may live as long as her grandfather, so that I am not likely to witness the reign of her successor. It is a melancholy consideration, for the future of nations has an exceeding interest for me. As to what is going on now, and in this country, everything appears to be quiet; we do not think so much of Mr Sumner's speech as they appear to do in England, and it is said that the President has in no way expressed any concurrence with his views.[123] But then the President never expresses anything. It is said that Summer has begun to find fault with the administration. You desired me to tell you a little about American politics; a very little I suppose will satisfy you. I advise you to read all the newspapers that come in your way, for the course of public affairs will furnish an unfailing subject of interest, which—relieved by poetry and a little fiction—fiction, I mean, of a different sort from that inseparable from politics, will at all events save you from ennui. I must not forget to tell you that whereas Grant is said in European journals, German ones among others, to have a sort of mania for annexation, to be a filibuster at heart, no such propensity is apparent at home. As he is no talker, he must be judged by his actions, which as yet have not been aggressive.

You say that you have taken my advice about reading Boswell; but have you gone through the whole book? It is the middle part, Johnson's London life, that is so good; it places us among the prominent people of that time, and gives us Johnson's opinions on so many topics, and shows him to us in so many peculiar ways, that I do not understand how you can say that you have read it. It is a book to be taken up every day and never to be finished and done with. There are some literary men who it seems to me ought to live till the end of the world, they have such an insight into its affairs, and the daily occurrences of life; they have not the wisdom that may be bottled up and preserved for posterity; it should be taken fast, just like the water that we drink—and Johnson was one of these. From some articles in English magazines, I suspect that he is beginning to be forgotten in England; he is evidently not understood as he once was.

EMH.

—〰—

Phillips Library
Number 78: To Rebecca Manning

Montserrat October 11th [1869]

My dear Rebecca

With great labour I have succeeded in digging up the fern-roots for which you asked me. I am afraid the largest one will not live, for I was obliged to tear away the fibres of the roots, which seemed to extend for half a yard round. One of the others came up easily enough, as it grew upon a rock that formed the roof of the abode of some wild animal, whom I expected to see come out of his hole to ask what I was about. The one with broad leaves is the Royal Flowering Fern. Wordsworth calls it the Queen Osmunda. It has tall brown blossoms, and in the Spring the young leaves are very pretty. To accomplish this work, which was harder than you can imagine, I took the large iron spoon with which Mrs. Cole mixes bread and cake,—without asking her, for she had company,—and it bent itself almost double, which, however was better than breaking, and muddied itself. I took it upstairs, and stood upon the handle to straighten it out, and washed it as well as I could in cold water, but if the next batch of bread had had a flavour of the soil I should have known the reason why. Thus I corrected its perversity, then restored it to its original shape, and replaced it in the closet whence I took it. You must set the roots in a moist place, and put in all the dead leaves and stalks, to make the earth as much as possible like that from which it was taken. There is a little three-cornered fern among the rest and some golden thread which has pretty green leaves.

Miss Larcom was in the car, the other evening, which was very pleasant, for we were a long time on the way, stopping once or twice; and once we had to get out and go round a corner where the streets were dug up, to another car. That same evening a woman fell into a pit, as she was leaving the car, and broke her arm. The clock struck seven when I was hardly out of town so that I had a long walk alone in the dark; but there is never any danger on that road. I do not know whether I shall go to Salem this week. We want to go to the Museum, with Abbie, perhaps on Saturday afternoon. Will you go?

In Trelawney's "Recollections of [Byron] and Shelley" there is an unfinished letter to Mrs. Leigh, which Trelawney found among Byron's papers after his death. The letter is entirely inconsistent with Mrs. Stowe's story. I think it could not possibly have been written if what Mrs. Stowe says had been true. Mrs. Leigh seems to have been the medium of communication between Byron and his wife. Mrs. Stowe is an author by profession, therefore the plain truth is not to be looked for from her. She must write what people will read, and in her own mind habitually mixes up fact and fiction. I dare say she does not know them apart. All the time she was in England she was thinking of making a book, or as many books as she could. Then she has never followed Dr. Johnson's advice, perhaps never heard it. "clear your mind of [cant]" Her [Byron] article is full of [cant], and [cant] blinds the eyes, like dust, and, besides all the rest, she is a Beecher, and what Beecher can live without excitement,—without creating a sensation? As to Lady [Byron], she appears to be one of those people who cannot discriminate between sins, but think one as likely to be committed as another—or rather, who thinks every departure from their own particular rule of right is a sin so enormous that the person guilty of it would hesitate at nothing. Even in my extremely limited sphere of observation I have seen such persons. Lord [Byron] said that his wife "could reason a great deal without being reasonable". I have also known persons who could do that. No expenditure of words could convince them; the truth lies deeper down than they are able to go; it would be harder to bring it up to their comprehension than to dig roots out of a swamp. It is strange how persons who have very little imagination contrive to delude themselves. One would suppose that matter of fact minds would be free from idle fancies, whereas they seem to be full of them, and always of an annoying nature.

I see by the papers that one of Dr. Holmes's sons is Private Secretary to Mr. Sumner. Has Moorfield Storey resigned, or how many Private Secretaries does Sumner employ?

I am afraid it would agitate Mrs. Dike as much to write to her—especially if I wrote as I do to you—as to talk with her. So, when you see her you can give my love and say that I want to hear how she does.

EMH[124]

—∿—

Bancroft Library
Number 79: To Una Hawthorne

Montserrat, Nov. 15th. 1869

My dear Una

I had an odd volume of Frazer's Magazine for the year 1859, last week, and thought it better than anything I had read lately. There were two articles upon Mr Gladstone's "Homeric Studies" then just published, which interested me. They were written by Mr Barham Zincke, who maintains, contrary to the general opinion of learned men now, that the Greeks were not of Oriental origin, or if they were, that in Homer's day as much time had elapsed since they diverged from the parent stock, as has sufficed to develop the different races of mankind, such as negroes, American Indians, &c. He speaks of the Iliad and Odyssey as works to be relied upon as good authority for what they depict in scenery and manners; and points out many resemblances between the ancient Greeks and the modern Europeans, or rather, it seems, to the English: for instance the way in which every subject of public importance is discussed in an open assembly, where all the people are as free to listen as they are now to read the Parliamentary debates, and of the universal love of conversation, and of the liberty of the women, and the respect paid to them; and especially the circumstance that every Greek hero has but one wife. The Trojans were partly Asiatic, and this writer observes that Priam, when asked how many children he had, tells the number of his sons, but does not mention his daughters, which is exactly what an Oriental Chieftain would do now. He also mentions Ulysses' dog, as indicative of a taste quite at variance with that of all Eastern nations, among whom dogs are detested. he says, too, that the Greeks were not the slaves of systems of belief or of custom, as Asiatics are. In the hands of the Greeks everything was plastic. And the Greek priests had few functions but the performance of certain ceremonies. They were not the guardians of religious belief. The notions of morality entertained by the people were instinctive; and their gods were human, the creations of the popular mind. If I dwell any longer upon this subject, upon which you will not be offended if I assume that you are as ignorant as I am, I shall have neither space nor time to say anything else.

You have read Trelawney's "Recollections of Byron and Shelley." Read the letter to Mrs Leigh which Trelawney found among Byron's papers after his death, and see how utterly irreconcilable it is with Mrs Stowe's story. I believe Mrs. Stowe's theory is, that lady Byron's superhuman virtue converted Mrs Leigh; whenever anything is published in her favor, the public is requested to suspend its judgement until Mrs Stowe has received certain documents which will enable her to place every circumstance in its proper chronological order. Nothing can be more absurd than the idea of vindicating Lady Byron's memory. What does Lady Byron's memory, or what did her existence, signify to the world? She was Byron's wife; except in her relations to him, she was nobody. Mrs Stowe was so dazzled by her acquaintance with people of rank, that she forgets that it is only genius that can interest posterity. Think besides, of the countless numbers of miserable wives who have not the means of living apart from their husbands. They are the true objects of pity. It never surprises me when married people part, and I do not at all blame Lady Byron for leaving her husband; but I think there are very few women who would not have been proud of him, and have loved him—at a distance.

EMH.

Bancroft Library
Number 80: To Una Hawthorne

Montserrat. Jan. 2nd. 1870

My dear Una,

I wish you all many happy New Years. To me, the year opens sadly. Mrs. Manning of North Salem is dead of lung fever, of which Maria and Rebecca are both sick, though now recovering.[125] I went to the funeral, which took place on Sunday, the day after Christmas, at nine o'clock in the morning. Richard sent, Friday afternoon, to know if I would come, and as there are very few relations left, I said that I would. So I sat up all night, sleeping as well as I could in the great chair that you gave me. Whenever I opened my eyes, I could see the clock upon the mantel piece, whereas if I had gone to bed, I must have got up many times to look at it. About seven I began to dress, and when it wanted twenty minutes to eight, Mrs Cole came up scolding because I was not ready, for they had come. "Here it is eight o'clock" she said, "you ought to have been dressed." I was nearly, and we set out before eight. I always keep my clock right by listening for the nine o'clock bell in the evening, and she lets hers run down half the time, but she is by nature in advance of the hour. It was a warm gloomy day, raining incessantly. I was glad to be early, for I had time to go up to see the poor girls, who were both in bed in adjoining chambers, so that they could speak to each other when they were able to speak, but could not see each other. It was sad to look at them, with their long black hair spread out upon the pillows, and their eyes sunk, and seeming like great black caverns. They were glad to see me, and Rebecca asked if I had been to Mrs Dike's, and said I must go. They had wished to be carried in to see their mother before she died, but she thought it would be too much for them. She said that in the morning she could be carried to them. That was Thursday evening, and that night she died. In the morning they insisted upon going in, and went supported by their brothers and the nurses to the bedside. Rebecca gave one look and begged to be taken away, but Maria stood over her mother kissing her and weeping, as long as they would allow her to. After all was prepared for the grave the coffin was carried and placed by Rebecca's bedside, and Maria came to look at it. It was a solace to them. Rebecca spoke of it to me, saying she should never forget how beautifully her mother looked. She did indeed. There was a wonderful sweetness and repose in her countenance. The coffin was decorated with wreaths of the loveliest flowers, one sent by Mr Wilder of Dorchester, with long tendrils of vine with small leaves called smilax, which also hung around the mantel piece and the other parts of the room. I remember the name smilax, because it is that of an odious running plant with terrible thorns that abounds in the woods, which Robert says is like one Dr. Livingstone found in Africa, and called "Bide a While" because it holds you fast. Mr Dike was at the funeral, looking wretchedly, poor old man. His mind is so decayed, he is little better than a child; indeed he is worse, for a child can be silenced and subdued, but a man of eighty must be treated with outward respect. Robert has been so ill as to keep his bed one day. None of them know yet what a loss they have sustained; every day they will feel it more, as they recover their strength. He said it seemed to him that he must find her in whatever room of the house he entered. She was very active, and took a constant care of everything, "looking well to the ways of her household."

But I have more melancholy news to tell. Saturday morning I received a letter from Richard to tell me that Mrs Dike was very sick. It is an attack like several she had had before. She suddenly becomes unconscious. When Mr Dike got up Monday morning, he found her upon the floor, dressed as usual, having sunk down there the night before. For more than ten years they have had separate beds, which stand parallel with each other, with just room for a chair between, else I suppose he would have found it out before. It was not a cold night, and their house is always warm; but is it not dreadful to think of? I am extremely anxious, and every vehicle I hear in the road I fancy is coming after me. I shall go if I am sent for, but besides the impossibility of walking, I am resolved not to go uncalled for. Last summer Mr Dike sent me word that his wife was not expected to live through the night—the night before. So I went over after tea, and the first thing he said was "Where do you expect to lodge tonight?" "Here," I said. "Why" said he "the house is full, there is no room for you." And though Mrs Araber the nurse was very glad to have me, and there were rooms enough, his behavior while I stayed, which was a few days until she was considered out of immediate danger, was such that even Mrs Cole does not advise me to go again.

I told you in my last letter that my gown fitted admirably. I know not whether anybody will be alive to see it, and when you come, what a change you will see.

EMH.

Phillips Library
Number 81: To Richard Manning

Montserrat Feb 23, 1870.

My dear Cousin,

   I have received three letters from you, one containing money, dated Jan. 1st. As usual, I ought to apologize for not answering them sooner. But, as long as the sleighing continued good, I was in hopes that you would drive over, with Lizzie, and then I could have told you all that I remember about the houses in which my Brother lived. He lived in the house in which he was born until the spring, I think, of 1808, then in the house in Herbert St. until October, 1818, when we went to live in Raymond; where I think, he stayed about a year, and then returned to Salem, and lived in Herbert St. again until he went to College, and during the vacations, and after he graduated, until December 1828, when as you know, we removed to North Salem, remaining there until December 1832, then going again to Herbert St. I think it was in 1838 that he went to Boston to edit a Magazine, but I have only my memory to rely upon; he burned all his own letters, whenever he came home. After a short residence in Boston he returned to the same old house; but not long after he went again to live in Boston, where he stayed until he went to Brook Farm. In October 1845, he came to Herbert St. with his Family, as borders, remaining until April 1846 when he removed to Boston, but in August, he came back to Salem and lived in a house in Chestnut Street until October 1847, when he removed to a house in Mall Street; where he lived until April, 1850, and then left Salem, for the last time as a resident.

   You are not to let this be publicized as coming from me. let whoever desires the trifling items of information I have given to you, communicate them in his own words. I have an aversion, always, to see a surviving relative of any man tell the public about him. And an author, you know, speaks for himself. You do not mention Little Dickie; but I trust that he is thriving. Next summer, he will be big enough to enjoy running about in the woods, and then you must bring him over.

I am your affectionate cousin
E. M. Hawthorne

Enclosed is a letter to Maria

—m—

Phillips Library
Number 82: To Robert Manning

Montserrat, March 6th [1870]

My dear Cousin,

I received a letter yesterday from Richard, telling me that Maria and Rebecca go out whenever the weather will permit, and that he had seen you in Boston, in good health—two very gratifying pieces of intelligence. And something else, which I am so wicked as to find agreeable, I hear from Una; it is that she is heartily tired of Dresden, the climate of which is "remarkably disagreeable, and so changeable that one can never get used to it". Every body has a cold, all the time, in winter. She is glad that they are not to spend another winter there. When people are so abject as to prefer other countries to their own, the mildest punishment they merit is to endure cold and weariness, and such disappointment as is the inevitable result of every delusion. Yet I am sorry it has fallen to the lot of poor Una; her Mother is the only really blamable person. I shall always think that my brother might have been alive and well now if she had not kept him in Rome so long. I have always thought so, and now Una says in her last letter that they have just heard of the death of a friend of theirs in England, an elderly man, who had been in poor health for several years, "ever since they went to Rome, where the climate had the same effect that it had on Papa and me". I told Una once that I thought it was living in Rome that first injured her father's constitution, but she said, as her Mother always did, that the climate of America never agreed with him. So, they were always urging him, after his return from Europe, to travel again. That was one of Mrs. Hawthorne's absurdities. After a little more experience, I hope Una's eyes will be opened, but her Mother's influence has never been otherwise than hurtful to her. I endeavored to make her promise, before they went away, never to go to Rome again, for if her Mother took a fancy to go, for her own health or pleasure, she would not be deterred by any consideration for Una. I am especially out of humor with her today, for I have just come across a note from her, written to tell me of her delight at Una's engagement to Storrow Higginson. She says, "If you could know him well, you would very much love and admire him. He is a true noble, pure soul, with a fine and cultivated intellect, and the loveliest character. My prayers for Una are answered in him, and I confide her to him without a doubt or misgiving. I did not expect to say that of any man, for I was difficult to be pleased and satisfied with any one who should ask for Una". And all the time she knew nothing about him, except that his family connections were such as appeared to her eligible. She was acquainted with many people who knew him well, but she never made a single inquiry. After the engagement was broken off, several of Una's friends told her that they were always surprised at her accepting him. I do not think he ever concealed his opinions. He was very intelligent and agreeable, and there was no doubt of his opinions. If Mrs. Hawthorne had talked with him rationally, as most Mothers would, I dare say he would have told her exactly what he thought, and Una might have been saved a great deal of unhappiness. Then, as to Julian, it was because she could not dispense with his society, because he could, Una said, [soothe] her and put her into a happy frame of mind, that he was, twice at least, called home from his studies; and then taken to Dresden, because she could not bear to be separated from him; and there he has been obliged to spend a whole year learning the language, before he could enter on the study of his profession. She had not the sense to see that he could not learn any thing else of German teachers before he had learned that. And yet, with all her love for him, she is looking forward with pleasure to his going to the west, to practice his profession. That is to be next year and she is to go to England with her daughters, to reside for an unlimited time. You see it is not even Julian that she cares about, but her own fancy of living where she thinks she shall be happy. But her position will in many respects differ from that which she occupied during her former abode in England. She goes there now to live cheaply—just what the English themselves go abroad for. And it is not likely that her society will be courted for her own fascinating qualities. Even during her husband's life she was not often tempted to go much into the world. Once, she did attend a great party in London, I saw the letter in which she described it, beginning with her dress, and ending with these words, "now behold me fairly launched upon the current of London society". She did not float long, probably, she was a great drawback to her husband. Willis says that the wives of literary men are not often invited with their husbands, being usually "unornamental". But she always would stick to him, and he, being aware that she thought her claims as good as his own, never separated himself from her. Eleanor Condit asked me last summer if I thought she appreciated him. I told her that she believed herself worthy of him; at which Eleanor was indignant. Una says that even the "crusty" Saturday Review praises her Mother's book. You know it did not heartily praise her father's [,] deeming the "Note Book" hardly worth publishing. They do not perceive (I mean Mrs. Hawthorne and Una do not) that it is her very want of discrimination, her inability to see anything but the shape of a building, and her blindness to everything significant, that entitles her to favour.

Looking at what I have written it appears to me that I have scolded enough about her; which it was not my purpose to do when I began. I meant to amuse you, as you are probably lonely, at intervals of business, in return you may disclose all [your] vexations to me. As we are neither of us married, we might safely deposit even secrets, if we had any, with one another. To Richard, who has a wife, I do not speak with the same freedom.

I did not invent that story of the Pope;[126] it was in the Traveller, a similar one is told of every distinguished man who dies unmarried—of George Peabody, of James Buchanan, of Washington Irving, whose heart was broken twice over, once by Rebecca the Jewess, suggesting to Walter Scott, when he made his confidant the character and designation of the heroine of Ivanhoe. And Scott's own heart, you know, though he was happily married, had a great crack in it, made in early life. There is another anecdote of the Pope, from the French Figaro, I believe, though I saw it in a Baptist Paper. An American lady called upon him lately with a pile of beads, which she asked him to bless. (how foolish he must have looked, doing it! I wonder she did not laugh). And then, very good naturedly, inquired if he could do any thing else to gratify her. She said yes, she wanted his photograph; he gave it, and begged to know if she had any other favour to ask. "Yes Holy Father, your Autograph, on the Carte de Visite". "Any thing else" he said, beginning to lose patience. "Yes, holy Father, the pen with which it was written". "Take it", said he, "and the penholder and the Inkstand too". She took an old Newspaper out of her Carpet Bag, wrapped them all up in it, and departed, with a sweet smile and a deep courtesy to the Pope. The newspaper gives the story such an air of truth that I cannot help believing and indeed there is nothing in it unlikely to happen. But I think the conversion of such people as the Americans must seem hopeless to the poor old man, if he views the prospect with any other than the eyes of faith. If the [women] have no more reverence than that, what can be expected from the men? If they hated him or feared him, even if they looked upon him as the Antichrist, it would be flattering and therefore encouraging, but to be a mere show, visited exactly as if Barnum had him in charge—even before being pronounced infallible, I may guess that there is a lump of irreverence, big enough to be a stumbling block in the American cranium.

I have been reading H. C. Robinson's Diary, with much delight.[127] It makes me feel as if I had been in pleasant company, among old acquaintance, because the literary people whom he knew are those who were most eminent when I was young. If you have seen the portrait in the first volume you will recognize the likeness to one of our friends. Both Mrs. Cole and Jane seeing it at different times, thought it was taken for him. But I think him one of the happiest men whose life I ever read. He never suffered a reverse of fortune and his health was almost uniformly good, he lived always in intellectual society, and possessed great intelligence without extraordinary sensibility. Not that he was deficient in feeling, for he was very benevolent, but he was not continually falling in love; his heart seems to have no crack in it. His greatest trouble was a terror or mob-rule, as it is that of so many Englishmen. When the Reform Bill passed, (the first one) he had dark forebodings, and their non-fulfillment never taught him that he was mistaken. It is the way, you know with old people; it never shall be with me. One thing, very comforting to me he said in his journal, when he was seventy years old, on his birth day; that old age was then beginning with him. I adopt his mode of computation which adds two years to middle life for me. And there is something in a letter from Coleridge, which I take to myself. Coleridge was apologizing for neglecting to write and says that a moral obligation was such a strong stimulus to him that it acted as a narcotic; stunned him so that he could not do the thing incumbent on him. I have been thus stunned many times; it is a positive inability, as permanent as the view you are taking of the duty. But if you suffer it to pass out of your mind for a time, the next aspect in which it presents itself may be quite different and not at all formidable. I dare say you are familiar with the perversity in question?

I must not forget to inquire about Goldilocks. I do not like to ask Maria or Rebecca, but do remember to tell me if [he] is safe. I received a letter from Maria yesterday. She says Mr. Dike proposes that they come to reside in his family; and she asks my "<u>unprejudiced</u>" opinion. I am not sure that I know what it is to be unprejudiced. My way is to let all prejudice meet together and have a fair fight, and then yield to the strongest. As to Mr. Dike, I know that he will be very exacting; I heard him say last summer "that he did not know but they should be obliged to hire some young woman to take care of them;" so though he likes both Maria and Rebecca, the former especially very much indeed, I am sure his motives are entirely selfish. I think he might easily [be] managed by any artful woman if he were left alone; but he will make the lives of conscientious persons miserable, as it is likely he does that of his wife. I am in doubt whether I ought to say this to Maria because I am ignorant of her reasons for asking the question. Still I need not feel much responsibility about giving advice, because nobody ever takes it from me.

May Almon brought me Mrs. Hawthorne's book to read. Una says I am to have it when the second edition comes out. It is flimsy, but if I can discover any thing to be commended I shall enlarge upon that when I write.

I have several other letters to write, else I should burn this and write you another.[128]

—ɯ—

Phillips Library
Number 83: To Rebecca Manning

Montserrat June 9th [1870]

My dear Rebecca,

I hope you have been in no particular haste for that address I promised to send you Here it is at last

Care of Francis Bennock, Esq.

No 80, Wood Street

Cheapside

London.

But I am not sure whether it is 80 or 86; if I write I shall direct it to No 80 or 86, and the name may possibly be Bennorck, but if the number of his office is right the letter will reach its destination. When I come over, as I hope to do when the weather becomes favorable I will bring you two more letters from Una.

I have been looking over Gail Hamilton's <u>Battle of the Books.</u>[129] It is smart, and I dare say true, but why should any body buy it. It might have been published, if at all, in a newspaper. Yet in newspapers we expect to find some thing of general interest. If she could have epitomized the story of her wrongs into a few pungent verses, she need have adduced no evidences; every body would have read and remembered and she would have had her revenge. Weapons of offence should be polished, and if intended for individual use and handling, should be small. Gail Hamilton speaks for Mrs. Hawthorne as well as herself; but if you saw the book, of course you observed this. Mr. Edwards must be Mr. Hillard. So sensitive as he is, I fancy he will not like to be brought in; nor will Mrs. Hawthorne, to see the remark that she is worrying the life out of him. Books given me. I shall have to buy them though the price is four dollars. I shall wait a week or two, as it is possible they may come to me.

I am afraid the Laurel will not be in bloom on the Seventeenth of June. I have never seen it earlier than the twentieth; but, as soon as the rain intermits enough for me to go out I will see how forward it is, and send you word. Do not forget that you are to come and spend a day, you and Maria. You may come at sunrise, if it will particularly gratify you to rouse me from my slumbers. I am frequently awake at that hour, "opening with haste my lids", to see the Robins and other birds upon the elm tree close to my bed, which I always keep near one of the windows for that purpose. Some of the birds are so small that a large robin might gobble them up. I go to bed earlier than I used to, for the pleasure of feeling the wind blow over me, for at daylight I am obliged to close the blinds after which I feel as if the air was close. All the cold and damp weather that we have lately had I have slept with the three windows and blinds open; it is the only way to avoid taking cold. There is a mouse in my room sometimes. I hear him nibbling crumbs that I save for the birds, and one morning I saw him. I shall not tell Mrs. Cole. She can afford to support one mouse, and this one is very pretty. I wish Robert would come over.[130]

—ᗰᗰ—

Beinecke Library
Number 84: To Una Hawthorne

Montserrat, August 5th [1870]

I have just received your letter of July 17th. It came on the accustomed day and I hope this will reach you wherever you may be, as the newspapers say that letters to Germany will go by the way of England. I am afraid you will meet with annoyances upon your journey, as I suppose there is no man upon whom you have a claim for protection, but, as Americans, I know you will be safe from any thing more serious.[131] If I were you I would wait till the crowd of foreigners had departed. Dresden will be safe for some time, probably always. It is not likely that the enemy will penetrate so far from the frontier. The French, as Mrs Cole very happily characterises them, are "Saucy Toads," and I hope will be beaten back with an ignominy that not even the Emperor's grandiloquent dispatches will be able to disguise.[132] It would delight my heart to hear of the Prussians in Paris: but the strength of the contending parties seems to be so well matched that such decisive success is, perhaps, not to be expected. Unless there is a probability of England's being drawn into the contest, within a short time, (which, for her own sake, I hope she will not be, for the disposition of the Irish, to say nothing of other causes, is enough to render a war peculiarly perilous to her,) you might go with a little inconvenience a week or two hence it appears to me, as now: for the roads must be encumbered with baggage, and every vehicle loaded, when so many people are hurrying away. But I suppose you will be in England, before you get this letter, so my counsel will be thrown away as it always is. I half envy you the opportunity you have to see, if not

great events, at least their small accompaniments. I dare say I should find Dresden a more agreeable abode now than in its days of quiet monotony—that is,
if I could see plenty of newspapers, and could read them. But I suppose German papers have not the life of ours in America, and I see that correspondents
are forbidden, by both the Prussian and the French governments, to accompany
the armies, so that one unfailing source of information and interest, letters from
the seat of war, without which it seems to me life would have been unendurable
in our rebellion, will be wanting to the people of both nations. I am aware that
these correspondents are supposed to have caused many disasters, by disclosing
what should have been kept secret, and that most of our Generals would gladly
have hanged them all, but still the fervor of the public mind was kept at the
highest point by their communications. The Emperor tells his subjects that he
himself will inform them of all that occurs,—as truthfully, no doubt as the first
Napoleon did, in his day. Napier says that in the Peninsular war, the French
Officers, when the armies were near each other, used to borrow newspapers of
their British opponents, being well aware that they could learn nothing reliable
from the Moniteur and other French organs—until at length Wellington forbade the lending of them. Our General Sheridan is going to Europe, to visit
both armies, to see what I suppose he would gladly join in; it will be very hard
if he is not permitted even to look on, but it has been said that no foreign
officers will be received by either army.

I fear I am writing what you will not care to read; you do not, like me, make
public affairs your own, though I assure you that in no other way can an un-
eventful private life be made so bright and stirring. Poetry and fiction awaken
a more refined interest, but there will be moments, or even hours, of mental
lassitude, when nothing can rouse us but a newspaper. If women in general
were aware of this I think they would be both healthier and happier. I do not
think it well for our sex to take an active part or even to express a very decided
feeling in regard to political events, but still we may ponder them in our hearts.
I generally have a preference for one statesman over another, English as well as
American, and I am afraid I like D'Israeli better than Gladstone, though he
seems rather lacking in conscience. I think there are not many things that
he would not do. But then Gladstone, though he has plenty of conscience, he
appears indeed to be always burthened with it, never makes it available at the
critical moment. I fear he would, and will do as many exceptionable things as
his rival. Then he is sensitive and irritable, and when he is anxious, he lets it be
seen; in the recent war debates in Parliament he "spoke with a pale face and
hesitating lips." Above all things, a leader should be bold. Do you remember
the reiterated injunction of God to Joshua, as related in the Bible, "Be strong,

and of good courage." It seems to me that Mr Gladstone might profitably re-member this. I meant to write to you while you were in England, and if I had you would have been spared this rigmarole. But I knew you would be too agreeably occupied not to excuse my delinquency. If you had but been here this summer, which is almost tropical, in its heat and occasionally in its tempests, I should have enjoyed your society particularly, because you would have sat quietly at home, or in the woods, where the fragrance of the pines, and of the sweet fern, and other shrubs is delicious; if you could but inhale it, which I think you never did, in perfection, because you have hardly been here at the right season, you would more be more invigorated than by any breeze that blows in England. When you come next summer, cannot Rose accompany you? It would be so delightful to me to see her! I am in hopes, however, that you will, after all, conclude, to return home. If England is involved in the war, living will be more expensive there than here. And no one can predict the effect upon the social condition of the country. I am glad that Julian had left Germany before the outbreak; and, though this is strictly between ourselves, I rejoice that Minnie is prevented from going again to Dresden. I have not quite so high an opinion of Mrs Amelung as I might have had if she had not proposed to take her daughter across the Atlantic merely to be with Julian. being together would not have conduced much to their happiness unless they could be married. And though I am ignorant of his prospects, it appears to me that if he is in a situa-tion to support a family in a style that he would find comfortable and easy by the time he is thirty, he may be deemed successful. I agree with you that he grows handsomer and nobler in his appearance. I am infinitely obliged to you for his photograph, which I am proud to show all my friends. <u>All</u>—how few they are.—I shall hope, now that he is to remain at home, that he will come to see me. And perhaps I may see Minnie too, by some good fortune. Now, pos-sessing your photograph and Julian's, I only want that of Rose.

I must stop now, for I have an opportunity to send my letter. I have not told you how much I love you all, and how grateful I am to you for loving me.

your Aunt
EMH.

After all I could not send my letter then, for I found my postage stamps, being folded with the gummed side in, stuck together, and it took five minutes to get them apart and put them on. I shall be anxious to hear of your safe transit from Germany to England. I depend upon you to write immediately. I am afraid your Mother will suffer from care, and fatigue. The newspapers say that the weather in Europe, like our own, is unusually warm, very pleasant, I think, to sit still in, but the thought of a journey would be appalling to me. For two or three weeks people seem to have done nothing but go to Pic-Nics. Every religious society, and every association, such as the Odd Fellows, &c has one, and a great many pass by here, many with bands of music, and all singing on their way to some Lakes in Chebacco. It is so all over New England. Notices are given in the Newspapers. Then there are Camp Meetings with preaching for those who like it, and Croquet and other amusements for lovers of pleasure. All sorts of people meet together on these occasions. Some of the preaching, especially that of Ministers, from the west, whose voices are incredibly powerful, and the hymns that they sing, must be worth hearing from their oddity. And next summer I propose that you and I go. The Cars will take us thither at any hour; the grounds are well arranged and everything is decorous and convenient.

When you write, tell me whether any of your valuables are lost on their way from Dresden. There is nothing that I particularly care about except my Father's Miniature. I should be sorry to hear that that was missing. Do not forget to mention it when you write.

The Book-Mark that Rose sent me has been copied by one or two persons. I think it very beautiful.

Rebecca told me that she had written to you. Her health is far from good; I cannot help feeling some anxiety about her. I have been to Salem but twice this season.

Have you read Leigh Hunt's Day by the Fire? He is the most appreciative critic of English Poetry with whose writings I am acquainted. He never misses seeing a beauty.

EMH[133]

Phillips Library
Number 85: To Maria Manning

Sunday August 15th [1869]

My dear Maria,

Mr. Dike sent me word yesterday, by Mrs. Burchstead, that Mrs. Dike was not expected to live through Friday night, but was then, (Saturday), a little more comfortable. Will you be so kind, you or Rebecca, as to write and tell me how much truth there is in this information, because if she is dangerously ill, I suppose I ought to go see her, though he said nothing about that, and probably would rather I did not come, unless I could save him some expense by acting as nurse, for which office I do not feel myself competent. You know that if their reports concerning each other are to be relied upon, one of them is always going to die without delay. Mr. Dike did not say what was the matter. The girl in the kitchen told Mrs. Burchstead that Eunice would probably come to live there when she returned to Salem, One day about a fortnight ago, when I was not at home, when nobody was at home but Hannah, somebody, whom I presume to have been Eunice, with another woman, called to see me. Hannah did not hear them knock, but one of the neighbors spoke to them and learned that it was me whom they wanted. I should have been very glad to see Eunice. I dare say that both Mrs. Dike and she commend themselves for the forgiving dispositions they manifest towards each other, in consenting to live together again, but to me it is plain that they feel no reluctance to lead a life of combat, indeed that they have a decided preference for being in hot water, for into hot water they are plunging, you know, when they put themselves within the possibilities of meeting in their old relations.

I should have come to Salem last week, if it had not been so dusty,—that was the reason I did not answer [your] note. I am glad little Dicky was so good and so happy at your house. Have his Father and Mother returned? Una says that when Mr. Hillard wrote to them last he was just recovering from a serious illness. She wants me to tell her whether he sent what will be due this month, as well as that for May. I hope you will all come to see me very soon, but I am not in want of Money. If I do not come to Salem to spend some, what I have now will last until about the end of September. I am very anxious to hear about Mrs. Dike. Mrs. Cole always tells me, at such times, that there must be a last illness, and that I ought to go immediately to her, but when I am really wanted I Think they might send for me; certainly they might afford the cost of the especial conveyance, when it was to be one of the last of their earthly expenditures. If you will write the word <u>important,</u> on one corner of the back of your letter perhaps the postmaster, who is apt to be negligent, would send it to me immediately, then if there is a pressing necessity, I will try to come over.

EMH[134]

———ɯ———

Phillips Library
Number 86: To Richard Manning

Beverly, Nov. 11th 1870

Dear Cousin,

I have my Wood-Bill to pay, and you know I have not received the interest, or whatever it is, due in July, I believe. I have not wanted it until now, and have never thought of it when I saw you. I should think it would be safe to send it by mail, if you would be so kind as to do so, on Monday. There are too many people at Mrs. Dike's and no one to take any care, that perhaps it is better not to have it left there; besides, there might be no opportunity to send it to me, as Mrs. Burchstead seldom calls. But, upon consideration, I think twenty dollars will be all that I shall require just at present.

I have news to tell you which I do not like to call bad. [It] may be, however, that it has been notified to you as it was to me, Julian is going to be married next week, Tuesday afternoon, Nov. 15ᵗʰ, at two o'clock. Cards for Mr and Mrs. Dike came with mine last Saturday, and I carried them over, in my Carpet Bag when I went to Salem on Monday and forgot to take them out, when Una's last letter, dated October 23ʳᵈ was written they knew nothing of it and I do not believe it will be an agreeable surprise to them. Julian said that he had several offers of employment—he said so, that is, when he came to see me, for no letter came with the invitation. He seemed quite awake to the necessity of earning money, and his disposition is naturally active, rather than meditative, his habits are good and he is very strong, so that I hope he will do very well. You sometimes go to New York, and perhaps you could without much trouble find out something about the Amelungs, J A Amelung and Sons is their business address. Minnie is evidently a very nice girl—amiable and artless, I should think; but I suspect her mother to be a fool. If she were a scheming woman she would have aimed at a different object.

Your cousin
EMH[135]

—〰—

Boston Public Library
Number 87: To James T. Fields

[December 1870]

My dear Mr. Fields,

The reason I did not write to you immediately, is that I sprained my right wrist a fortnight ago, in getting out of a wagon in the evening: I can hardly hold a pen yet.

In some Portland newspapers, within a year some communications, relative to my brother and purporting to be written by friends of his, have appeared.[136] I have not seen any of them, therefore I do not know how much credit they are entitled to; but my cousin Richard Manning told me some things that were in them which had been told to him for he had not seen them himself. One was a letter from an early acquaintance, who had been my brother's companion in many rambles and fishing expeditions, and afterwards met him in Europe, where my brother said that he had hardly been more charmed when, so many years ago, they sat "looking over the pond at the slopes of Rattlesnake Mountain", or something to that effect. I believe that to be true, because I remember the place, which was one of his favorites. Perhaps you have seen those newspapers. You know my brother was once an inhabitant of Maine, though but for a short time, except as a student. We lived in Raymond, on the side of the Sebago, then a Pond, now a Lake. We spent one summer there when he was twelve years old, and became permanent residents two years after. It did him a great deal of good, in many ways. It was a new place, with few inhabitants, <u>far away</u> "from churches and schools", so of course he was taught nothing; but he became a good shot and an excellent fisherman, and grew tall and strong. His imagination was stimulated, too, by the scenery and by the strangeness of the people, and by the absolute freedom he enjoyed. One of those newspaper writers says that he was very strictly brought up, and not allowed to form many acquaintances; but I do not remember much constraint, except that we were required to pay some regard to Sunday, which was a day of amusement to most of the people. On Sundays my Mother was unwilling to have us read any but religious books, but, as we grew up, that prohibition was sometimes disregarded. We always had books, perhaps full enough. As soon as we could read with ease, we began to read Shakespeare, which perhaps we should not have done if books of mere entertainment had been as plentiful as they are now. My brother studied Shakespeare, Milton, Pope, and Thomson. The Castle of Indolence he especially admired. As soon as he was old enough to buy books for himself, he purchased Spenser's Faery Queen. My Uncle Robert was always buying books. I ought to have said in the beginning, that our father died when Nathaniel was four years old, and from that time Uncle Robert took charge of his education, sent him always to the best schools in Salem, and afterwards to College. After the loss of our Father, we lived with our Grandfather and Grandmother Manning, where there were four Uncles and four Aunts, all, for many years, unmarried so that we were welcome in the family.[137] Nathaniel was particularly petted, the more because his health was then delicate and he had frequent illnesses.

When he was, I think, about nine years old he hurt his foot playing bat and ball at school, and was lame for more than a year. No injury was discernable, but in a little while his foot ceased to grow like the other. All the Doctors, far and near, were brought to look at it. Dr. Smith of Hanover, then very famous, happening to come to Salem, saw it, among the rest, and he said that Doctor Time would probably help him more than any other. He used two crutches and wore a wadded boot to sustain the ankle, but it was Doctor Time who cured him at last, and at twelve years old he was perfectly well. People who saw him then asked if this was the little lame boy. Mr. Worcester, the author of the Dictionary, taught a school in Salem when Nathaniel was hurt, and he was one of his pupils. Mr. Worcester was extremely kind, offering to come every day to hear his lessons, so that my brother lost nothing in his studies. He used to lie upon the carpet and read; his chief amusement was playing with kittens of whom he had always been very fond. he would build houses and covered avenues with books, for the kittens to run through. Of course everything was done that could be thought of for his entertainment, for it was feared that he would always be lame. it was then that he acquired the habit of constant reading. Indeed, all through his boyhood, everything seemed to conspire to unfit him for a life of business, for after he had recovered from his lameness, he had another illness, seeming to lose the use of his limbs, obliged to resort again to his old crutches, which were pieced at the ends to make them longer. he said, after he begun to write, that he had not expected to live to be twenty-five. But at seventeen he was perfectly well and entered college, and after that his health never failed until his long stay in Rome, which I think caused his death.

He was a very handsome child, the finest boy, many strangers observed, whom they had ever seen. When he was well, Uncle Robert frequently took him in to the country, and once, at some place in New Hampshire, they met a gentleman and lady, who seemed much pleased with him and offered him money, which he refused, because, he said, he could not spend it there, there were no shops. Another time, in Salem, an old gentleman, a connection of ours, but one whom my brother seldom saw, stopped him in the street and, after talking with him a little while, offered him a ten-dollar bill, which he also declined to accept, I believe without assigning any reason. The old gentleman was not well pleased, and spoke of it to one of his uncles, apparently thinking it implied an unfriendly feeling towards himself. My Uncle apologized as well as he could, by saying that his Mother disapproved of his having much spending-money. I dare say he would have liked the money, in both instances, if it had come from anyone, whom he thought nearly enough related to have a right to bestow it.

I cannot write more now, but tomorrow, when I hope my hand will be stronger, will begin again. I depend upon your assurance that no one shall know that I write this. if you think it too trivial to be of use, pray let me know.

Yours,

E. M. Hawthorne[138]

—⁂—

Dec. 13, 1870

All the anecdotes that I can remember are too trifling to be told; for instance, he once kicked a little dog that he was fond of, and, on being told that the dog would not love him if he treated it so, he said, "Oh, he'll think it is Grand-mother", who hated a dog, though she would not have kicked it. When he could not speak quite plainly, he used to repeat, with vehement emphasis and gesture, this line, which somebody had taught him, from Richard Third;

"My Lord stand back, and let the coffin pass". It is where Gloster meets the funeral of King Henry the Sixth.

Pilgrim's Progress was a favorite book of his at six years old. When he went to see his Grand-mother Hawthorne, he used to sit in a large chair in the corner of the room, near a window, and read it, half the afternoon, without speaking. No one ever thought of asking how much of it he understood. I think it one of the happiest circumstances of his training that nothing was ever explained to him, and that there was no professedly intellectual person in the family to usurp the place of Providence, and supplement its shortcomings, in order to make him what he was never intended to be. His mind developed itself; intentional cultivation would have spoiled it. he used to invent long stories, wild and fanciful, and to tell where he was going when he grew up, and of wonderful adventures he was to meet with, always ending with: "And I'm never coming back again". That, perhaps, he said, that we might value him the more while he stayed with us.

He inherited much of his temperament, his sensitiveness, and his capacity for placid enjoyment, from his mother, and he looked like her.

There was one boy at school with whom he had a regular fight every little while. He said the boy was overbearing and quarrelsome, being a little older than himself. He often took long walks alone, both before and after his lameness. When we lived in Raymond, I generally went with him, and one cold winter evening when the moon was full, we walked out on the frozen Sebago to a point which we were afterwards told was quite three miles from our starting place, and that we were in danger from wild animals. Perhaps we were, for bears were occasionally seen in that vicinity. But Nathaniel said that we would go again the next evening and he would carry his gun. The next evening it fortunately snowed; for we should not have been allowed to go, and there would have been a struggle for liberty. Soon after that he went back to Salem, to go to school. The walks by the Sebago were delightful, especially in a dry season, when the pond was low and we could follow, as we once did, the soundings of the shore, climbing over the rocks until we reached a projecting point, from which there was no resisting the temptation to go on to another, and then still further, until we were stopped by a deep brook impossible to be crossed, though he could swim, but I could not, and he would not desert me. He went for a few months to a school in a neighboring town, of which I have forgotten the name. It was kept by the Rev. Mr. Bradley, in whose family he boarded. I do not know whether he learned much, but he had a good time, one night especially when the barn, close to the house, caught fire, for all his life he enjoyed a fire. On this occasion he said that he had helped to dress the children, but there was a complaint made that he snatched up one of them, with a heap of clothes that did not belong to it, and ran to a spot where he could look at the fire; there he put the poor little thing into the trousers of an older boy, and contrived to fasten them around its neck, and supposed that he had done all that was incumbent upon him. Mrs. Bradley said that the child caught a cold, and that Nathaniel was a shockingly awkward boy. In Salem, he always went out when there was a fire; once or twice he was deceived by a false alarm; and after that he used to send me to the top of the house to see if there really was a fire and if it was well under weigh, before he got up. He said that once an old woman, who saw him looking up at a great fire, scolded him in threatening terms, though she forbore from actual violence, in her indignation "at a strong young man's not going to work as other people did". But there was seldom any derangement of the usual routine of things in Salem, and the more people were in any way stirred up the better he would be pleased.

I cannot write much yet, and I am advised not to write at all for the present, so I send you two letters, written in two separate years. The uncle with whom he journeyed was an invalid and also a Stage Proprietor, travelling at once for health and business. There is nothing remarkable in the letters, but they will show you that he was essentially the same in earlier life as when you knew him.

The reason that I have no other letters of his is, that he always, when he came home, burned all he had written.

Tomorrow I hope I shall be able to write more legibly.

You sent me the American Notes—you were so kind as to give me a complete set of his works—but not the English Notes. I shall like them very much.

Yours,
E. M. Hawthorne.

—m—

Number 89: To James T. Fields

Dec. 16th [1870]

I have just received your note written on the 13th. Please to direct to the care of Mrs. Samuel Cole, Beverly. Anything so directed will be brought to me immediately.

I shall be very much obliged to you for the Atlantic Monthly. Living, as I do, far from all society, a new magazine will be always welcome; and I want to read your Recollections of Thackeray, whom I prefer to Dickens. I fear that I shall be sometimes tempted to ask for a new book, though perhaps I ought not to do so. The English Notes had better be addressed to the care of R. C. Manning, Salem.

Soon after Nathaniel left College, he wrote some tales—"Seven Tales of My Native Land", with the motto from Wordsworth—"We are Seven". I think it was before Wordsworth's Poems were republished here. I read the tales in Manuscript, some of them were very striking, particularly one or two Witch Stories. I will tell you more about them.[139]

—m—

Number 90: To James T. Fields

Monday, Dec. 26, 1870

When my brother was about fourteen, he wrote me a list of the books he had been reading. There were a good many of them; but I only remember such of the Waverley Novels as he had not previously read, and as were then published, and Rousseau's Heloise and his Confessions, (both of which were con-

sidered by his friends extremely improper) and the Newgate Calendar, which
he persisted in going through to the end, (though I believe there are several
volumes) in spite of serious remonstrances. But every book he read was good
for him, whatever it would have been for other boys. I do not think he ever
opened one, except in the course of his education, because it was recommended
as useful, and to be true was sometimes an objection in his eyes. In one of Miss
Edgeworth's Tales, a novel written by Bishop Berkeley—<u>Gaudentio di Lucca</u>—
is mentioned; and, as it happened to be in a Circulating Library, I got it for
him to read; but he said that it was <u>true,</u> and he would not even look it over.
The printing and binding were unlike those of novels, and it was not particularly entertaining, but there was much in it that would have suited him. After
he left College, he depended for books principally upon the Salem Athenaeum
and a circulating library, the latter of which supplied him with most of the
novels then published. The Athenaeum was very defective; and it was one of
my brother's peculiarities that he never would visit it himself, nor look over the
catalogue to select a book, nor indeed do anything but find fault with it; so that
it was left entirely to me to provide him with reading, and I am sure nobody
else would have got half so much out of such a dreary old library as I did. There
were some valuable works; The Gentleman's Magazine, from the beginning of
its publication, containing many curious things, and 6 vols., folio, of Howell's
State Trials, he preferred to any others. There was also much that related to the
early history of New England, with which I think he became pretty well acquainted, aided, no doubt, by the Puritan instinct that was in him. He was not
very fond of history in general. He read Froissart with interest, and his love of
Scott's novels led him, when very young, to read Clarendon, and other English
histories of that period, and earlier, of which there were several very curious
ones in the Athenaeum. He said that he did not care much for the world before
the fourteenth century. He read such French books as the Library contained,
there were not many except Voltaire's and Rousseau's. There was one long series
of Volumes, the Records of some learned society, the Academie des Inscriptions,
I think, which contained a good deal that was readable. It was his custom to
write in the forenoon, unless the weather was especially fine, when he often
took a long walk; but the evenings he spent in reading, going out for about
half an hour, however, after tea. If there was any gathering of people in the
town he always went out; he liked a crowd. When General Jackson, of whom
he professed himself a partisan, visited Salem, in 1833, he walked out to the
boundaries of the town to meet him, not to speak to him, only to look at him;
and found only a few men and boys collected, not enough, without the assis-

tance that he rendered, to welcome the general with a good cheer. It is hard to fancy him doing such a thing as shouting.

When he was a boy of fifteen he was not so very shy; he was too young to go into society, but he went to dancing-school balls, for he was a good dancer, and he never avoided company, and talked as much as others of his age. I think, too, that his boyhood was very happy, for his imagination was agreeably occupied, and his feelings were in all things considered, and, though he was lame and sometimes otherwise ill, he suffered but little actual pain. And I know his college life was pleasant, and that he had many friends. it was only after his return to Salem, and when he felt as if he could not get away from there, and yet was conscious of being utterly unlike everyone else in the place, that he began to withdraw into himself; though even then, when there were visitors in the family, he was always social. But he never liked to have his writings spoken of; he knew their merit, and was weary of obscurity, but yet he shrank from observation. Once in a while, every summer if he could, he went out of town for four or five weeks; he went to Niagara, to Nantucket, and Martha's Vineyard, and other places. Once he spent two months at Swampscot. You remember Susan in The Village Uncle, one of the Twice-Told Tales. She was not quite the creation of fancy. He called her the Mermaid, and was perpetually telling us how charming she was. He said she had a great deal of what the French call espieglerie, describing her just as she is represented in the Village Uncle. She kept a little shop, too, and her father was a fisherman, who brought fish to Salem to sell. I should have feared that he was really in love with her, if he had not talked so much about her; and besides, she was not the first one of whom I had heard. There was a girl in the interior of Massachusetts, as captivating, in a different style, as the Mermaid. In his youth, beauty was the great attraction to him, and one which he declared he never could dispose with in a wife. Where there was beauty, he fancied other good gifts. In his childhood homeliness was repulsive to him. While he was lame, a good, kind-hearted woman used to come to see him, and wanted to carry him about in her arms, as he was fond of being carried; but he seemed to feel as if she were an ogress, and hated to have her look at him, only because she was ugly, and fat, and had a hard voice. The woman who made his clothes, before his lameness, was also extremely plain, and it was very difficult to persuade him to go to her to be measured. As to clothes, it was one of his whims to dislike to put on new ones.

When the Exploring Expedition, under Commodore Wilkes, was sent out, he endeavored, through Franklin Pierce and others of his political friends, to obtain the office of Historiographer. On some accounts it would have been a good thing for him, but he never would have written The Scarlet Letter, if he had succeeded in getting that appointment. If he had gone out into the world, he would have hardened his heart, as I suppose most men do, and his novels are the result of the most exquisite susceptibility. And if he had been happily married in his early manhood it would not have been so well for the world. The mingling of another mind with his, would have spoiled the flavor of his genius. (This is your remark, Mr. Fields, nobody's else, certainly not mine; it is something that the keenness of your insight shows you, and you will never discern a more absolute truth.) Goethe said, in reference to Byron, that ennui was the true source of inspiration. Ennui may perhaps be defined as the feeling that a square peg has, when he is put into, and kept in, the round hole. There, if this peg could relate its feelings and its thoughts, they would be better worth hearing than any it would have in a more congenial position. Now my brother was all his life just so misplaced, as far as his inclinations were concerned. he wished to travel, and he desired every advantage that prosperity can bestow. One old, but characteristic notion of his was that he should like a competent income that would neither increase nor diminish. I said, that it might be well to have it increase, but he replied, "No, because then it would engross too much of his attention". Afterwards, when he lived more in the world, he must have felt that an increasing income could in no circumstances be objectionable. There is a little poem of Lord Surrey's, called "The means to attain happy Life", which expresses what my brother's ideas of happiness were; probably he had never read it, at that time; but the Author must have been of a mind kindred with his.

In 1836, I think, he went to Boston to edit the American Magazine of useful Knowledge. he was to be paid $600 a year, but probably he was not paid anything; for the proprietors became insolvent, or were already so before they engaged him, when a few numbers had appeared, I believe Mr. Alden Bradford had been the Editor, and Nathaniel did not change the plan that he had pursued, admitting no fiction into its pages. It was printed on coarse paper, with wood engravings that it was a pain to look at. There were no contributors; he had to write it all himself, and he was furnished with no facilities for collecting the useful knowledge that it was his business to send forth to the world. He wrote short biographical sketches of eminent men, and other articles of a similar kind; and when I met with anything that might pass for <u>useful,</u> I copied it and sent him,—extracts from books such as people who subscribed for that Magazine would be likely to comprehend. He wrote a narrative of Mrs. Dunstan's Captivity—you know she was carried off by the Indians—in which he does not much commiserate the hardships that Mrs. Dunstan endured, but reserves his sympathy for her husband, who suffered nothing at all, who was not carried captive; but who, he says, was a tender-hearted man, who took care of the children, and probably knew that his wife would be a match for a whole tribe of Indians. Mrs. Dunstan, when she escaped killed as many of her captors as she could, boys among others, which seemed unfeminine to my brother. It was told in a very entertaining manner, and the narrative ought not to be lost; indeed all that he wrote for the magazine did him great credit, evincing, not only, much miscellaneous information, but a power of adaptability himself to the minds of others whose culture and pursuits were unlike his own.

He wrote a good deal for the Token,—some Tales which I believe were not published besides the "Seven Tales of My Native Land," which he ought not to have burned; I should have been very glad to have them now.

When the Rev. Mr. Cheever, who was in College at the same time with my brother though not in the same class, nor the same set, was knocked down and flogged in the streets in Salem, and then imprisoned, Nathaniel visited him in jail; this showed great sympathy and strong indignation.

I am sorry that I have had nothing more important to tell you, his life was so monotonous that if I could recall every event of it, I could hardly record more than a list of the books that he read.

If my hand were not lame I would not send you such an illegible scrawl; but it has been so painful for a week as to unfit me for everything. This is the first day that I have been able to write, and I will not delay any longer in order to correct what I have written, but will send it off at once.

I am very much obliged for the beautiful books that you sent me, and for the magazines. I do not often see new books. The future numbers of the magazine can be sent to me at Beverly.

I have just received a letter from a gentleman who wishes to prepare something about my brother for publication. I have had many such applications, but I have always declined supplying more than dates and places of residence, and I shall of course decline now, because I have told you all there is to be told.

Will you oblige me by burning what I have written when you have done with it.

Yours &c
E. M. H.

Say that you had your information from a friend of his, older than himself, who had known him all his life.

—w—

Phillips Library
Number 91: To Richard Manning

Montserrat Dec 31[1870]

Dear Cousin,

I would prefer that Dr. Wheatland should send me the questions that he wishes to ask in writing; I can reply to them much more accurately if they are made in that way. I shall want time to recall things that occurred so long ago, and I have naturally a poor memory for dates and for such items of information as he probably requires. I shall be glad to assist him if I can. You know that it was my brother's especial injunction that no biography of him should be written; and even if he had not expressed such a decided feeling upon that point, there is really very little that I could tell. Perhaps there would be nothing objectionable in publishing a record of his places of residence. I have a lame wrist, so that I can write but a few sentences without pain, and I have been lately unfitted for all exertion in consequence. It has deprived me of sleep, and I cannot comb my hair or put on a tight dress, or indeed use my right hand at all comfortably.

I hope Lizzie is better. You must be careful of little Dickie if he has a croupy cough, which Mrs. Cole says should never be neglected for an instant. She has seen a good deal of the croup, and she says you should always have proper remedies at hand.

I wish it were possible for the girls to come and see me. Julian's mother and sisters were made perfectly happy by his marriage.

Yours,
EMH

I wish you all a happy new year[140]

—w—

Boston Public Library
Number 92: To James T. Fields

Montserrat, Jan. 4, 1871.

My dear Sir,

I ought to have told you, though I daresay that you already know it, that my brother published a Tale called Fanshawe, about the year 1829, I think, of which he afterwards destroyed all the copies he could find. But I know of two still extant. Una has one, given her by one of her father's friends, who purchased it from a circulating Library. As far as I can remember, for it is forty years and more since I read it, there was not much in it characteristic of its author. it was written soon after he left college; before he began to feel that disgust with his lot in life, which at least shielded him from all prosaic influences. Yet, after all, I suppose he was as happy as most people; and I do not think that any other place would have suited him better than Salem.

He also wrote, for Mr. Goodrich, Peter Parley's Common School History, the only one of his early works, of which he was not ashamed. Even at the beginning of his authorship he never revised any of his writings; that is he wrote exactly as if he were writing a letter. Miss Mitford says she wrote everything three times over, which must have been very tiresome.[141] My brother always said that he ought to have been a Painter instead of an Author. It is certainly true that whatever he knew, he knew by sight, never by reasoning; and no argument ever convinced him of anything; it must be shown him. I often told him so, and he acquiesced. The difficulty was to make him look, for whatever he looked at he saw at once in all its striking aspects. He speaks of "the one grain of hard common sense" in his mind. His mind seemed to me to be all made up of common sense, that is of intuition. But on many subjects he felt no interest. He knew but little of science. When he was a mere boy, he wrote for a newspaper, some verses, of which I only remember the first:

The ocean hath its silent caves,
        Deep, quiet and alone.
Above them there are troubled waves,
        Beneath them there are none.

I was amused, when the Atlantic Cable was about to be laid, to hear a person, quote those lines in confirmation of the opinion, that there was calmness enough in the depths of the ocean to render the undertaking practicable. I told him of it; he laughed and said he knew as much as anybody about it.

I used to think that he was in love with Perdita, in the Winter's Tale. He said she was the sweetest of all Shakespeare's heroines. He said he thought Polonius was a man of great worldly wisdom, but rather superannuated. It was his own opinion, for he was not in the habit of reading criticism.

The Seven Vagabonds; one of the Twice-Told Tales, first published I believe in the New England Magazine, he was very unwilling to have inserted among the others, when they were collected. He seemed to dislike it. He made one alteration in it, too, which he ought not to. As it was first printed, he offers the old beggar a bill of the United States' Bank, but as reprinted, it is a bill of the Suffolk Bank. As it stood at first, it gave a date to the story, putting it several years further back than one would ascribe to it as it is now. Now in Dickens' Old Curiosity Shop there is Mrs. Jarley's wagon, which goes about something like the Showman's in the Seven Vagabonds, and it may be supposed that my brother had stolen the idea of it; whereas his story was published many years before we had ever heard of Dickens.

It was true that the old beggar, or fortune-teller did, as he relates it in the story, tell him of a past event in his life and also predict a future destiny for him; he never told me what they were, but as he says that the destiny is one "which time seems loath to make good", I have made up my mind that it was the one I have seen accomplished. It was at college that it was foretold, with the fortunes of several other students.

I have been told that the authorities of Bowdoin College had at first high hopes of my brother, as it regards scholarship; but when he graduated, it was only with the reputation of ability, not of performance.

I beg you to remember that it would be unbecoming in his sister to come forward and gossip in this way about him. If you can make use of anything I have said, I shall be glad, but it will be unnecessary to give any authority; say it all as if it were of your own knowledge. I have written freely in order to show him to you as he appeared to me; it is for you to present him to the public.

I need not tell you that after his marriage he did not, even during his abode in Salem, live a secluded life.

E. M. H.

—⚮—

Boston Public Library
Number 93: To James T. Fields

Beverly Jan. 28th. 1871

My dear Mr. Fields.

I receive the Atlantic Monthly and read it with much pleasure. I am quite satisfied with what you say about my brother, which I have never seen before, with any thing that I have read about him. You ask me if there is any thing to correct; except that Fanshawe was published at least four years before 1832, I observe nothing. Before 1832 he had become thoroughly ashamed of it. Perhaps

I made the mistake when I wrote to you, but I am sure that I am right now, because I remember the date of the occasion on which my copy of the book fell into his hands, and I never saw it again; it was in Dec. 1832—and I think it was published in 1828.

Will you tell me who the old lady is who remembered my brother in his cradle? Most of the families who lived in that neighborhood then were fixtures, and I recollect them twenty years after. There is, (if she is living now) a Mrs. Oliver, who was a Miss Braggs; if it is not she I am at a loss to guess who it can be. Or it might be Mrs. Barstow, my father's niece; but she was not exactly a neighbor. It is her daughter Elinor, now Mrs. Condit, who was the original little Annie; my brother was fond of her. He liked little girls, but he said he did not think boys worth raising. Elinor was a very affectionate child. She was almost the only person out of his immediate family who knew my brother; and I believe people liked to tease her about him—to say something to his disadvantage, in order to see her kindle into wrath in his defense, She told me about it last time I saw her. She said that she was a perfect little tempest. Once she came to him, crying, because somebody had told her that he was an infidel—he must be, as he never went to church.—He took her on his knee, and comforted her.—told her he was not an infidel, and that he did go to church whenever he happened to be elsewhere than in Salem, on a Sunday. Then he talked very seriously with her, she asking of The Scarlet Letter, she said that he must have intended to represent Hester as unrepentant: else her peace of mind would have been restored, and above all, she would not have been ready to fall into the same sin again.

I think if you looked over a file of old Colonial Newspapers you would not be surprised at the fascination my brother found in them. There were a few volumes in the Salem Athenaeum: he always complained because there were no more. Cookery-Books, especially old ones, were another odd fancy of his. He sometimes talked of compiling one:—not for the concoction of luxurious dishes, but of the homely New England dainties to which he had been accustomed in his childhood.—Not even dainties, indeed, but such plain things as Apple Dumpling, of which he was fond all his life; and Squash Pies and such Indian Cakes as Phoebe made, in the House of the Seven Gables. He said he thought all the old New England dishes were good, but that a professional cook always spoiled them.

Una has written to ask me if I have any articles of his in any old Magazines which might be inserted in a new edition of his works. I have nothing at all, no Magazines—though I think that there must be papers of his in some Magazines or Annuals, for I remember tales which I thought admirable; but it may be that they were never published; for he was very impatient and if there was any delay, he would have them returned to him if he could, and I suppose put them into the fire. He wrote two or three New Years' Addresses for the Salem Gazette. In the Twice Told Tales there is only one republished—The Sister Years, I suppose the others might be found. For the Democratic Review he wrote a biography of Cilley, who was killed in a duel: it was quite long and would help to fill up the volume, but it was mostly political. Some portion of it, however, might be worth republishing. There was, in The New England Magazine, I think, an article called "My Visit to Niagara." I do not know why that was not inserted in the complete edition. He wrote several things for the Knickerbocker Magazine, which was sent to him for three years. It was among his books in Concord. If Mrs. Hawthorne has it in England, perhaps she will find something there.

When my brother was young he covered the margins and the fly leaves of every book in the house with lines of poetry and other quotations, and with his own name, and other names. Nothing brings him back to me so vividly as looking at those old books.

I did not [think] of writing so long a scrawl when I began. You must excuse the writing, for my hand is still lame.

Yours,
EMH[142]

—⁂—

Huntington Library
Number 94: To Una Hawthorne

Montserrat. Jan. 28th [1871]

My dear Una,

I am not quite so much to blame as you suppose, for it is nearly three months since I was able to write without pain. I went to Salem early in November, and when I came home it rained fast; so, as there is a stable close to the termination of the Horse railroad I thought it best to be brought up: especially as it was growing dark, and I had several packages. I had a nice covered wagon, one of the Beach Wagons as they are called, and I considered myself very fortunate until it was necessary to get out. I asked the driver to hold the umbrella over me, and told him I could get out alone, but these wagons are high from the ground, and in the dark I could not find the step with my foot, and, in short,

I fell out, coming with my whole weight on my right wrist, spraining it badly. The ground was soft; if it had been frozen I would have been half killed, and if it had happened anywhere but just at our own door, I do not know what would have become of me. But Mrs. Cole is better than a doctor in such cases, and she washed and bathed it in hot vinegar and salt, and rubbed it with Arnica, and then with some ointment, and treated it so successfully that it is now nearly well. She says it was the worst sprain she ever saw, and that she did not think it would be so well all winter, if it ever was. The cords were drawn up into a knot, and the hand was a good deal worse than useless. I counsel you to learn to use your left hand, that you may not be so utterly helpless in case of any accident to the right. But I own that I do not practice what I recommend, but on the contrary, I quite despise my left hand for availing me so little, and take no pains to educate it into usefulness, as I probably might do.

My dear child, I cannot possibly go to England: I never should recover from the discomforts of the voyage, which, combined with the change of climate would kill me; or at least turn me into a decrepit old woman. Next March I shall be sixty nine years old. I am well now, and can walk about just as I always could; but if I go even to Salem to stay all night it hurts me. I do not feel so well any where else as I do here; and to go from these fine woods to London would be great folly. You will stay here, I hope, two or three months, and we will be happy together; and I know that you will come again in a year or two, even if you don't return for a permanent residence.[143]

—⁓⁓—

Phillips Library
Number 95: To Rebecca Manning

Montserrat, Feb. 1ˢᵗ 1871

My dear Rebecca

I have just received Maria's letter and your note. First of all I must express my indignation at the treatment poor Goldie received from Robert, whom I thought incapable of such barbarity. Next, I must charge you not to let Mr[s]. Dike know that I can write. Indeed I can not write such a nice looking epistle as she likes, and you know there is but little to be said to her—nothing that would please her. I send you a letter from Una. I am glad you have written to her, and I hope you enlarged upon the impossibility of my going to England, for in her last letter she urges it strongly. I wrote to her on Monday, and told her that I could not go, but she will not [believe] me unless somebody else says so.

I thank Robert for buying the Book for me. It is so much cheaper than I expected that I can afford to give you one, which you must buy with the remainder of the money. I shall be very glad if you will send the package by the Horse Railroad. They bring packages. Or if it is more convenient to you to send it by the express, it will do just as well and be quite as safe. Please to pay for the bringing.

I certainly do not like to have much company in winter, because whoever comes must be received in the kitchen, but you and Maria and Robert will not mind that, and so I am always glad to see you.

When you see Richard tell him that at first I thought that Diary could not have got back to Uncle Richard's house: but now I remember that though Mother left Raymond in 1822, her furniture remained in the house till 1824; and as she came away in a hurry, and as I suppose Nathaniel had been spending the vacation there, it is very likely the book was left lying about. What there is in the Portland Transcript is absurd; especially when this unknown person says that Mother was superstitious. I never [saw] anybody less so. She not only did not believe in the supernatural, she never thought of it, and had no taste for ghost stories, or any thing of the sort. None of Grandmother's children ever had. I will send the Paper back when I have the opportunity. But I want to see the other communications to the Portland papers. I recollect that Fast Day of which one of them tells the story.

I remember Jacob Dingley very well; He was about Nathaniel's age. I have no doubt that he may be relied upon.

I shall expect to see you all one of these days, when the walking is good. I have another Times and a Punch and Pall Mall Gazettes &.c. Do you want them?

EMH[144]

—⁂—

New York Public Library
Number 96: To Una and Rose Hawthorne

Montserrat, March 2nd [1871]

My poor children,

I have just read the notice of your bereavement in the paper.[145] My heart aches for you. If you were but at home, I feel as if I could take care of you: at least as it regards your health; but it is dreadful to think of you, two young girls, alone in a strange land. The grief would be the same, wherever you might be, but the feeling of desolation could not be so deep if you were among those upon whom you have a natural claim. I know that you have many kind and attached friends in England, and I trust that they are near enough to you to comfort you. I shall suffer the most intense anxiety until I hear from you. I fear that sorrow, and perhaps fatigue and exhaustion will make you ill. I have seen only the bare announcement of her death: I know that she could not have been long ill, because in your letter dated the 12th you say that "last evening Mama took tea at Mr Hughes'," —and I have supposed, from her going out so much this winter, that she was pretty well. But probably early spring in London is very trying to the lungs. There were many who knew and loved her there, and I hope they will watch over you.

I was relieved from some anxiety by the information that you had both been vaccinated, for the newspapers say that small pox is an epidemic in London. Have you ever had the measles? if you have, you are to be congratulated, for to me the measles have all my life been a terror. I would prefer to be exposed to the infection of small pox, from which probably I am sufficiently protected by two vaccinations.

How Julian must feel, not to have had an opportunity to see his mother in her illness. I know how to sympathize with you all, for I have suffered the like affliction. It seems to me that there can be no such bereavement as the loss of a parent. But remember my dear child, that as much as any one not your mother can, I love you, both of you, and let me hear from you as soon as possible. I hope this will reach the mail in time to go by the next steamer.

EMH[146]

—〰—

The Letters

The third and last group of letters, twenty-one of them, spans the last twelve years of Elizabeth's life. By this time, only the Manning cousins and the adult Hawthorne children, Una, Julian, and Rose, survived. Like her brother the year before, Rose married, living in the United States and traveling to England, where Una, still Elizabeth's principal Hawthorne correspondent, also lived.

In letters broaching a range of political and literary topics, Elizabeth writes disdainfully of Charles Sumner, a wartime opponent of slavery and a champion of freed people's rights. She expresses a similar attitude toward the controversial and daring George Eliot, who, like Elizabeth herself, was approaching the end of her life. Elizabeth shows the most passion, however, in reacting to the biographical work published by Rose's husband, George Parsons Lathrop, who used some of Nathaniel's own letters. Angered by George's attempt to write a biography despite Nathaniel's objection, burned by her own unwitting complicity, and ironically adamant that any biography written should come from a Hawthorne, specifically Julian, Elizabeth embroiled herself in the family dispute involving the Mannings, the Lathrops, Una, Julian, and their attorneys. As the letters record, the quarrel eventually died down.

Una, Elizabeth's favorite of the children, lived with Julian in England and worked at an orphanage. Her second engagement, this one to Albert Webster, ended with the death of her fiancé. Una herself died shortly afterward in 1877. The letters make only a single, incidental reference to her death, the last great loss in Elizabeth's life. Harriet Cole, Elizabeth's landlady, died in 1876, and the Appleton family bought the farmhouse where Elizabeth had boarded for twenty-five years with the Coles. She stayed in the Appleton home until her own death in 1883, apparently of measles.

Phillips Library
Number 97: To Rebecca Manning

Montserrat, May 11th [1871]

My dear Rebecca

(Here several lines cut out by RBM)[147]

ones, two kinds of violets, three kinds white and purple,—with other flowers. If you will come on Saturday I shall be glad. I have never thought before that the season was early, fancying that it was the reverse, from my own observation; but these flowers have certainly come sooner than usual.

(Here the reverse of the lines cut out)

I send you a letter from Una—you can use your discretion about showing it. It came a week ago. Do not tell any one that I write to you, for I am not equal to writing to any body else, except to Robert, which I shall do soon. I owe six letters, and am so oppressed with the weight of my liabilities, that I do not think of discharging them. I am determined to write to Una, in order to counsel her upon certain subjects. One admonition I must give her—She calls Rose "that child" and speaks of herself as if she were at least as old as I am—or, certainly as old as I feel. Then they have sent out Cards to twenty-five select friends "at home on Wednesday afternoons, &.c" I will give you the Card that she sent me, when I see you. Do you think that quite proper for two young ladies? If I were with them we should live in an endless dispute, for I have no patience with any follies but my own, which I flatter myself have the negative merit of being only passive, merely shortcomings in wisdom. Mrs. Loring and May Almon called the other day to ask to see some of Una's letters. I do most earnestly hope that I [showed] them none which I ought not to, but so many of them have objectionable sentences relating to the Peabodys, and when you are in a hurry it is hard to be sure which to choose, so that I cannot be certain. I told Mrs. Loring what I feared, and Miss Almon said that if I had they must forget it.

I have not seen Mrs. Hawthorne's likeness; they said that it was frightful, and not in the least like her.

EMH

You can ascertain whether this old postage stamp is good and use it if it is, when you write to Una.[148]

—⁂—

Phillips Library
Number 98: To Robert Manning

Montserrat, June 30th [1871]

My dear Cousin,

I must not forget to tell you that the name of Montserrat has been changed to Centreville; we were formerly, to the great disgust of all dwellers of the region, except myself, called Ratters; now we are Villens—Centrevillens; an appellation full good enough for people who are so wanting in taste and ingenuity as to be dissatisfied with a good old name, and yet unable to find a tolerable new one.

I hope you will come with the girls—your sisters and as many more as you can muster—on the Fourth of July. If Mary Shepard is in Salem I shall be particularly pleased to see her. I am afraid the Laurel is out of bloom; all kinds of flowers have come and gone earlier than usual this year, but the trees and the rocks remain to delight our eyes. I do not know whether you like such cool weather as we have had during the greater part of this month. For my part I have suffered more with the cold than I did last winter. Then I could have a fire, which is hardly possible now, for the wind blows the smoke out in a very unpleasant way,—putting out my eyes and stopping my breath. For every thing out of doors is so beautiful that I cannot refrain from keeping the windows open and sitting by them to behold what will so soon pass away, to be replaced by the season when all the attractions are within the shelter of the house. During at least half my life I have reflected, every summer, that it might be the last I should ever see, or at least, ever be well enough to enjoy—for so many people are sick and miserable—and therefore I have always endeavored to get as much pleasure out of the present as I conveniently [could]; but it is quite a drawback to be continually petrified with cold.

Una has sent me an Astrachan Jacket which she says will keep me warm next winter. Her mother, and she and Rose each had one in Dresden; [this] is hers; she has taken her Mother's. I am no judge of such things, but Jane says it is a very handsome one, and would cost a good deal of money here. I shall lend it to Rebecca next winter, or to Maria, as I never go out in cold weather. But was it not extremely kind in Una? I think she is the best person of the name—born to the name, I mean, that I ever knew; for I cannot claim the merit of such amiability for the [Hawthornes], as a race. She has also sent me a large Photograph of herself and Rose, and a small one of herself; and I have received a letter from Rose, who, Una says, is making unusually rapid progress in the art, (drawing) to which she has devoted her self. Julian says that Rose is the only one of them who has any constructive genius, and I believe her Father thought so too. But Julian also says that he does not think she will ever accomplish much, and there I hope he is mistaken. He says it is ruinous to the health to frequent picture galleries, as Rose does, and that she requires as much exercise as he does. And he thinks she does not put herself forward as she ought, and that she does not choose the right kind of friends; going he says to drink tea with elderly women who are quite insignificant in social position; and once, he said, in Dresden he introduced a nice young man to her at a party, and as she was looking very pretty, he hoped she might effect something; but she held down her head, and only said "yes" and "no" and the nice young man (Herbert Browning, a son of the Poet) after trying hard to draw her out, withdrew, thinking, probably that she had not an idea in her head. Julian thinks that she has a great many, and judging from her letters, that is my opinion. But you know no one can talk when it is obviously expected and planned for. Julian told me this when he was here with Minnie last September. I hope Julian himself has a little of that faculty of pushing his way of which his Father was [utterly] destitute. He has a very good opinion of himself, and he has always been accustomed to society, so that while he will see the propriety and becomingness of a modest deportment I trust he will make his abilities available for his advancement in something of the way he might have learned in Butler's office. I observed that he seemed to have quite outgrown his Mother's influence, as far as his opinions are concerned.

I have been reading the Diary of a "Besieged Resident in Paris", the correspondent of the London Daily News. He thinks Mr. Washburne, our Minister, exactly what a Diplomatist should be, and draws a eulogistic comparison between him and the priggish and conceited Europeans of the same profession. You know almost every body thought that Grant blundered when he appointed Washburne to that office, especially as he knew [not] a word of French. But for my part, if people, and especially if nations, desire to live in peace, it appears to me much better that they should not understand what each other say. It is possible to put up with people's <u>doings,</u> but their <u>sayings</u> who can endure with patience. The Alabama herself was not so irritating as the things that were said in Parliament, and particularly as the Saturday Review.[149] The besieged Resident says that Mr. W would call upon the authorities in Paris and shake hands in token of good will, and come away, it satisfied them, and took but little time, and committed himself to nothing. Moreover, he was the only Minister who remained at his post, except one or two, who represented States too insignificant to be considered. Then, as we now find the President was right when he withdrew Mr. Motley, who did good service to his country by what he wrote in the beginning of the war, saying every thing that could be said in a manner that he could never improve upon, but who could do nothing in London except exhibit himself as an elegant and cultivated man, thus proving that we had at least one such to show. He was said to be much less known to the middle-class Englishmen than Mr. Adams was. I do not think Mr. Adams has had half the credit that he deserved for maintaining the dignity and respectability of the United States at that period, when he could derive so little support from the condition of affairs at home. It is wonderful that he could be always calm and courteous. To return to the besieged Resident—he says also that the American Surgeons were much more skillful than the French, avoiding amputation and managing broken limbs in such a successful way that the Soldiers almost thought they could put on a leg or arm that had been shot away and make it whole again, and the American Ambulance was so [superior] to any other that it was the hope of every soldier to be carried thither if he were wounded. And the writer says that he himself thought that a man might be worse off than to be lying there with a slight wound, especially because the American girls were the very best of nurses. But I need not tell you all this, for it is very likely not new to you; most of it has been copied into our papers. But I can only write about what I have read, for I neither see nor hear anything[.] Mrs. Cole has concluded to take the Wenham water, which is carried past the house on both roads. She desires me to ask you to come again as you did on Fast Day; she has the highest esteem for you and for Richard, and I believe you are almost the only person whom she ever invites to tea. I wrote to Rebecca about a week ago, when the Laurel was in bloom. You must not let Mrs. Dike know that I wrote to you, because she has good reason to think that she is entitled to a letter from me. But to indite one would be painful to mind and body, for it hurts my hand to use a pen,—Mrs. Cole thinks it will not be well for a year, if it ever is—and it puzzles my brains excessively to find any thing which will not displease her. I do not mind what I say to you. Mrs. Cole thinks you do not read my letters to the end, they are so inordinately long. I shall direct this to you in Salem; you will be sure to receive it in time to come over on the Fourth, which you might not do if it were sent to Boston. If you ever see the Russells do exhort them to come over very soon. I should probably come to Salem to spend a few days in July, and I wish they would come here first.

Your affectionate Cousin
EM Hawthorne[150]

Huntington Library
Number 99: To Una Hawthorne

Montserrat July 24, 1872

My dear Una

For fear I should forget it, the first thing I say must be to caution you against working on Sewing Machines—except for amusement, for fifteen minutes or so. The kind of motion they produce is ruinous to the health. Rebecca and Mrs Cole join in this warning which I intreat you to heed.

Rebecca says she will not write to you until you reply to her letter. There is some excuse for her, because she has literally no spare time. But she does not love you less than if she were an irreproachable correspondent.

Miss Almon called about three weeks ago to tell me that Rose, whom she saw at Cambridge, was going soon to Mrs [Loring's], and then she would drive over to see me. But first Mrs. Lathrop is to make her a visit. Mrs Lathrop is going, I cannot remember where, for a long stay, I presume, because Rose is to have some of her furniture during her absence. Probably you know all about it. I asked Miss Almon how she liked Rose's husband. Her answer was satisfactory. She appears to have the highest opinion of him, and to think them a very happy pair, devoted to each other, and meriting each other's devotion. And she says that Howells, of the Atlantic Monthly, and other literary magazines consider him as a young man of distinguished ability. This also, I suppose you know. But do you know that Mr Emerson's house, in Concord is burned down?[151] I have cut a paragraph containing the tidings from a newspaper. You will be sorry, as all the friends of the family must be. To Mr and Mrs Emerson, at their age, the loss must be irreparable. Rebecca seems to feel as you do about teaching children, whereas to me it appears as wearisome a task as could be undertaken. But I think you happy too in being associated with such a woman as Sister Mary, both cultivated and benevolent. I hope many women are so, but I never saw one who was. People who are bent upon doing good are apt to be fussy, and are very often intolerant of all whose sympathies for suffering manifest themselves in a different way from that which they have chosen; and, because coarseness and want of refinement are lesser evils than some others, they will hardly allow them to be called at all. Aesthetic culture they look upon as forgetfulness of duty, if not as a positive sin. Horace Mann said that no one ought to spend money or thought upon works of art while the world was so full of vice and misery. Such persons bring benevolence into disrepute. But your friend, (do you call her Sister Mary when you speak to her?) Must be of quite a different nature, else you could not love her; and if you can go to her for counsel as well as sympathy, I shall feel less uneasiness about you than I have felt, when I supposed there was no one near you much interested in your welfare. Indeed, I do not fear that Sister Mary will not love you if she has any discernment: but I hope she will not sacrifice you on the altar of beneficence. You must not go into unhealthy places, nor nurse sick people, as charitable ladies do in great cities. It is not your duty to do so: beware of being persuaded that it is. If I could but see with my own eyes what sort of a place you live in, it would be an unspeakable satisfaction. If you were but here, inhaling this delicious air, and content to abide here, it seems to me now that nothing more would be necessary for my happiness.[152]

—⁓—

Phillips Library
Number 100: To Richard Manning

Beverly, January 6th 1873

My Dear Cousin,

You have a good deal of trouble with my numerous correspondents. I regret it, and am grateful to you for the readiness with which you write letters and in other ways [*illegible*] with the demands I make upon your time and patience. That letter from New York from Mr Louis Larson, (whose name I have certainly heard before, where I know not) was only to accept an autograph of my brother's, which I have sent him; he thought I was another daughter. As to "the few thousand dollars" which you suggested might be coming to me, I fear there is no possibility of anything so acceptable.

There is Vanderbilt, whose daughter you know is married to a "far away cousin" of mine—no farther off than second cousin, however—do you think that if I were to write and ask him for an indefinite sum that he would respond liberally. If I were to tell him the precise truth, that I have to live upon about two hundred dollars a year, and <u>that</u> is a slight degree precarious, and that though I know pretty well how to economize, I am utterly destitute of the ability to earn, and that it would be a great pleasure to me to spend money if I had it, do you think he would send me anything worth while? If he were to send me fifty dollars, every body, my own N[ew]. York relatives among the first, would say that it was mean and beggarly in me to make such a request. Instead in reality it would be <u>he</u> who was mean, but if he sent me three or four thousands I should not be in the least ashamed to have every one know it, for it would be pronounced the only sensible thing I ever did. In the meantime, while this accession of wealth is delayed, I must beg you to send me, by mail, $30—

unless someone who could bring it comes over soon. Mrs. Cole thinks it safer to send it by mail than by Mrs Burchstead, who has her wagon full of boys and girls, her grandchildren. My letters are put into Mrs. Israel Cole's box, and she frequently receives large sums from Vermont in this way. That little present from Rose is as you suppose a [*illegible*] rack: you could take it to Mrs Dike's, Mrs Burchstead could bring that with some books that Rebecca is going to leave there for me. I am very glad to hear that Lizzie's health is improving. When she is strong enough, do drive over to see me and bring little Dickie with you. I have great hopes of little Dickie because he has a fondness for books.

EMH

I wrote to your sisters last week. I hope they got the letter[153]

—⁄⁄⁄—

Phillips Library
Number 101: To Robert Manning

Montserrat, [April] 6th—1873

Dear Cousin Robert,

Now that Spring seems actually about to revisit the earth, I trust that you also will remember the existence of that nook of it in which my lot is cast. I write on purpose to ask you to come and take tea—or rather water—with us, and a walk with me. Mrs. Cole expected you on Fast Day, I knew you would not come while the walking was so bad. The snow is almost gone now, and the birds are singing and we should find many green things in the woods. I think it is nearly a year since you were here. You are a favorite of Mrs. Cole's; She says "She does not mind you at all". That means that you will be a welcome visitor, causing no trouble, She awards the same praise to me—and to Una, but to few others. When Rose and her husband came to see me last Autumn, Mrs. Cole was very inhospitable; they were offered no refreshment, and I do not doubt that they were hungry. She does not like Rose, whom she calls proud, a term indicative of great dislike, but I think entirely unmerited in its application to Rose. She says that if Una were in this country she would accommodate her as a boarder whenever she chose to come. But she will not return this summer; and such terrible disasters are continually occurring that I am very glad not to be expecting her. I am afraid that I shall never see her again.

Do you like Middlemarch or do you never read books of that kind? I have been reading, it in Harper's Weekly, but I think all the bright and amusing chapters of it are lost, and those which remain are dull, if such a thing may be said of "the greatest novelist of the time". For my part I think the author is too much of a philosopher; I really do not care much to know what is passing in the minds of her people. She is incomparably inferior to Miss Thackeray. Dorothea (in Middlemarch) is a wearisome young woman; I should strongly object if Mrs. Cole proposed to take such a one as a boarder. As her sister Celia observed, it must be trying to live with "persons who have notions". Then, when she is so absurd as to marry that old pedant, no reader can be expected to retain any sympathy for her. The feeling that I have for the book is probably not peculiar to me; but as it is a novel that intellectual people seem to feel called upon to admire, no one likes to criticise it unfavorably,—though one writer in a magazine does venture to wish Mrs. Lewes would give the world a novel that would leave a cheerful impression in the mind. We have a Volume of Beecher's <u>Lecture-Talks</u> which is far more entertaining than Middlemarch; he records his experience as a speaker in Liverpool and other places in England—the hissings and the hooting that he encountered. It was evidently an enjoyable persecution. I do not approve of the President's Indian policy. You may [think] that I am not a competent judge—of course I cannot be; but I rely upon the opinions of General Sherman, and Sheridan and others, who say that if the Indians want war, enough of it should be given to them. And is it not absurd to take extraordinary pains to perpetuate a race who, if they renounced their murderous impulses, and sought to be civilized, would still be inferior to white people. I imagine the President requires a great deal of stirring up. Do you think there can be any inertness in his mind, I should like to stick pins in him, to give him some feelings for the tortures inflicted by these savages.

Yours, &.c
EMH[154]

Huntington Library
Number 102: To Una Hawthorne

Montserrat, August 25th [1873]

My dear Una,

I am, as you supposed that I should, be, relieved from much anxiety about you by the change in your plans. I have thought a great deal of the impure air you would have to breathe, in the latter part of this summer, when every one who can possibly do so is leaving London—at least, so I infer from all I can learn of English habits. Then, if an epidemic should break out among the children, what would your condition have been! Such ideas as these used to haunt my dreams. You are so intensely English that perhaps you would not if you could help it, permit me to say that it is a disgrace to England to allow so much poverty to exist that foreigners, (yourself and George Peabody, for instance) should feel called upon to relieve it. A sum of money equal to only one year's income which Parliament has voted to one of the Queen's sons, on his marriage, would endow a magnificent asylum. The Queen, excellent woman as she is, is <u>but</u> a Queen, with no views more expansive or advanced, apparently than her stupid old Grandfather had. Probably she thinks her children pillars of the state. I read the other day in a newspaper that the agricultural laborers on her private domain had petitioned for a small increase of wages, and she refused to grant it. I dare say she acted from principle. She would not encourage the poor in demands that might embarrass the rich.[155] She feels bound to maintain the present order of things, not to substitute a better. I wonder if she ever heard of Joseph Arch:—I hope she will be compelled to hear of him.[156] I wish him success. If you will read newspapers, and think of what you read, I shall not be surprised to see you become a radical, but only a speculative, not a practical one, of course. If you were here now, you would enjoy the weather we are having,—bright, sunny days, and clear and serene nights. If it were warmer it would suit me better, but you would like it just as it is. And people seem to do nothing but go to pic-nics—but I think I told you about that in my last letter. Now they are going to Camp Meeting at Hamilton, the next town to Beverly. If you were here you and I might go. There is much to be seen at such places,— all sorts of people, and amusements of various kinds. There are camp-meeting grounds in every part of the country:—villages of pretty cottages whose owners I have something else to say, but I have forgotten what and will write again very soon. I was delighted to have a letter from Julian. I was very glad to see that notice of Bressant, from the N.Y. Times.[157]

—◆—

Phillips Library
Number 103: To Rebecca Manning

Montserrat, March 16th, 1874

My dear Rebecca,

I received the books on Sunday (the day but one after you sent them), and am very thankful for them. I like the new ones, and do not think them dear;

Robert knows how to make purchases of the kind. I have read <u>Lovel the
Widower</u> to the Coles; it is certainly the poorest of all Thackeray's works; except <u>Catherine,</u> a part of which I have read. Catherine was one of the worst of
women; a murderess and every thing else that is bad; the book is intended as a
satire upon those writers who endeavor to make crime less hideous by giving it
a colouring of romance, I wanted <u>Henry Esmond</u> because it is the only one that
I have not read, and that is not in our Library. I believe I told you that I was
reading Jane Eyre. Mr. Cole, who has an instinct for what is good, likes it better
than any book I have ever read to them. I once read <u>The Mysteries of Udolpho</u>
to them, when Mr. Cole was alive, and he said, very emphatically, "that is no
fool of a book". Miss Austin's <u>Emma</u> he said had too much soft soap in it; but
he liked the Professor, (Miss Bronte's) because all the persons in it use very plain
language, not at all complimentary, to each other. I was glad to have those
Tribune novels, and will return them when I have finished them. Do you know
whether "Young Brown" is published in the Tribune? I have seen some parts of
it, but not the beginning, in the Cornhill Magazine. I have read the first part
of "The Wooing o't in Temple Bar,["] and when I can go to the Library myself,
I suppose I can get the rest.

Are you not surfeited with eulogies upon Charles Sumner? How idle it is to
talk of grief upon such occasions! Do you think a single human being, unless
it may be some exceptionally effusive negro has shed a single tear for him? I
shall feel much deeper regret for Bismark, who was said, in the last newspaper
I saw, to be dangerously ill, if he dies. But I trust he will recover, and live many
long years to war with the Pope, with the present Pope, and two or three of his
successors. I hope there will be a change in the dominant personages at Rome
soon, it is always pleasant (at least to me), to hear that any potentate is de-
throned by death or otherwise. I naturally dislike sovereigns; but in the case of
the Pope, whose death may be followed by the election of somebody to take his
place, I think many newspapers['] readers will feel as I do.[158] It is a good while
since anything auspicious has been announced; I mean any event which ought
to gratify people who desire the welfare of the Public. I feel as if the New
Hampshire election would be a lasting calamity, and I anticipate nothing but
evil when I open a paper.

I have good cause to complain of Mr. G. W. Curtis, on account of something of his writing in Harper, soon after Mrs. Hawthorne died. Every body,
you know, reads Harper; many people derive all their knowledge of literature
from it. And Mr. Curtis has given all such persons to understand that Hawthorne was greatly indebted to his wife; that she was not only extremely culti-

vated and accomplished, but that her position in society before marriage was more elevated than his.[159]

—⁓—

Beinecke Library
Number 104: To Una Hawthorne

April 26th [1876]

After writing the letter of April 11, I happened to see G.P.L's contribution to Scribner—"Poe, Irving, and Hawthorne," and at the same time I received your letter of April 2nd, in which you say that he has been writing "unwarrantably" about Hawthorne. Unwarrantably is too mild a term. It vexed me so much that it was only after writing three half letters to Rose that I was able to express myself with tolerable calmness. I suppose that you refer to the same articles; and I do not wonder that you think it time for Julian to assert his claims. I did not tell Rose that you had written about it to me, but left her to suppose that I was prompted only by my own indignation. The same messenger who carried my letter to the Post Office brought back one from her in which she says that finding, upon legal inquiry that there is some doubt "as to the ownership of some letters in the possession of R. C. Manning," (which George has been allowed to copy) "in which however, she says I have a part interest," she asks my permission to have some of them printed in George's book. She thinks the book will exalt Hawthorne's reputation, and prove to the world that he was not morbid and sentimental, as many people have thought. In short, she thoroughly believes in her husband. I am going to write today and say that if I am not the sole owner of the letters, I have no right to authorize the publication of any part of them, and that she must settle the affair with you and Julian. I told her plainly that George was not the fit person to write Hawthorne's life, and that he would only injure himself by attempting it, because of course Julian would expose the blunders he would make. I hope that Peckham will convince them that the publication will not be safe. George went to N York in February to meet Mr. Horatio Bridge, who had some of your Father's letters. Of those he will have a right to make use. Julian must let him see that he is in earnest. I do not wonder that you have been made miserable by all this; but I hope it will cause only a temporary alienation from Rose. She will return to her old affection for you. By the way she did not tell me that you had written to George, and Peckham has not sent me a copy of your letter; but that is of no consequence; I know the purport of it pretty well. But you see she did not wish me to know how you felt about the affair.

I am glad that you have been at Clewer [a convent], where you always seem to find repose. And I wish I could see that little monkey. I am afraid that you will let him die. Do try to keep him warm and write to me immediately. You must not buy me a new dressing gown. As soon as the weather is warm enough to leave it off, it is to be washed and Jane is going to make it look as well as new.[160]

—⁓—

Phillips Library
Number 105: To Maria Manning

Montserrat, May 9th [1876]

My dear Maria,

I was delighted to receive your letter;—the first you have written to me for many months. I am thinking of going to see you soon; when are you coming here? There are flowers in bloom, and the violets will soon be covering the hills. It is several years since you have seen them; in about a fortnight, or less it will be the best time to come.

I quite agree with you about G. P. Lathrop; Mrs. Cole longs to give him a sound whipping, and I should be inexpressibly gratified to see her do it. Have I told you that Una wrote a few weeks ago to say that he had been writing in the most unwarrantable way about her father, and that she had sent him a letter, of which she had requested Mr. Peckham, their lawyer, to send me a copy? He has not done it, but I can guess at its contents. It seems that George has all Hawthorne's private letters and journals, and, as Una says, he will of course use them in his forthcoming book. She says he has advertised it as Biography, and she is made very miserable by these proceedings of his. It is unsufferable, is it not, to have a person come into a family, and understanding nothing at all of its affairs, turn every thing inside out, as George is doing. Una begged me to write to him, and, "with a few dexterous hints", endeavor to make it apparent how very strange every one would think it if he and not Julian should write her Father's life. As to "dexterous hints", I could not manage them at all, but I wrote to Rose, letting her see plainly that I was very angry at the egregious blunders George has made; and the same messenger who carried my letter to the post-office brought back one from her in which she said that, upon legal inquiry they found there was some doubt as to the ownership of the letters in

Richard's possession, but, as I had, at any rate, a part interest in them, they hoped I would allow them to publish extracts from them, and also from two letters which I had lent her and she had copied. She said that I should be charmed with what George had said,—that he had entirely dispelled the illusion prevalent about her father's temperament—proved to the world that he was not morbid, and had avoided every thing unsuited to be made public; with more in the same strain.

I was so provoked that I wrote instantly to Peckham to say that the letters were mine, and he must let George Lathrop know that he has no right to use them. I thought if the law would take cognizance of the affair it would be possible to stop George—and I hope it will be, but, as usual with me, I had mislaid Peckham's address, and so I had time to consider a little what it was best to do, and, accordingly when I answered Rose's letter I told her that if the letters were not mine I could not authorize publication of any portion of them, but, if she wrote to Julian and Una she would undoubtedly find them disposed to be reasonable. I have not heard from her since. She did not tell me that Una had written to her, nor did I tell her that I [had] heard any thing about it from Una. I did not send my letter to Peckham. I am glad to be relieved of the responsibility of the ownership of those foolish letters, which I ought to have burned long ago. I wish Julian and all of them would remember their father's injunction that none of this should be attempted. I believe all biographies are false, just in proportion as they pretend to be true and deal with facts. Fiction is the proper sphere for the representation of character; there a portrait of anybody may be drawn, avoiding names and dates, and if it is, or is not [a likeness], no harm is done.

I am reading Hamerton's "A Painter's Camp". It is entertaining; also, Palgrave's "Golden Treasury of Song". It would be a very pretty present to any one who had few books, for every thing in it is good, If Rebecca would be so obliging I should like to have her buy me "Vers de Societe". Osgood and Co. advertise a long list of Books at reduced prices. Among them Browning's Poems in 10 volumes. I only want one of them, that containing "Christmas Eve and Easter Day". Do you think Robert would call and see if they could be purchased separately? If he would I should be much obliged. I am afraid I shall never have energy enough to go to Boston. In the winter when Lovering was advertising books by the Cartload, Mrs. Cole proposed that I should send for a barrel full by some of the young men in the neighborhood who go to market every Saturday, and pay them in Books. She was much appalled by Rebecca's suggestion that I might go to the Theatre, "such an old woman" as I am—for she seems to think me quite past the period of enjoyment in seeing or hearing. I am afraid that she herself will never be much better than she is now. She has been so active that life without work is wearisome to her, and she is low spirited. If she can go out she will be more hopeful; and I trust that the weather will soon be good.

You must burn this, for I have not stopped to think what I was writing, and I must seal my letter now, and then I can send it immediately. You must all come this year when violets are in bloom, because another season I may not be here. Whether I am or not depends upon Mrs. [Cole's] health.

yours,

EMH

If you any of you come over before I go to Salem, will you bring what money Richard has of mine, after taking payment for the Books purchased on my account.[161]

—⁂—

Phillips Library
Number 106: To Rebecca Manning

Montserrat, May 19th 1876

My dear Rebecca,

The violets are already in bloom and will be plentiful next week. I hope you will not wait for 'Lection, but come the first pleasant day. if Maria is coming you need not wait for anyone else except Robert. Mrs. Cole will be very glad of some of the sugar corn, but does not care for Triumph.

I want you to write to Miss Elizabeth Peabody about George Lathrop's misdemeanors, if you choose to call them by so mild a name. Tell her how every one who speaks of his publication in Scribner thinks it nothing less than atrocious; I should like to have you say that you have heard it suggested that it was she who gave him an erroneous impression of Hawthorne's life in his own family previous to his marriage; perhaps not of its details, but of its general aspect; but that you cannot believe her capable of such misrepresentation, and wish to give her an opportunity to deny it. She will not be in the least surprised by a letter from you, or indeed from any human being—or from any divine or demoniac being. Once, in her youth, she began a letter from the Apostle Paul, to be published in some controversial magazine. St. Paul in this epistle, was proceeding to show himself as good a Unitarian as if he sat, every Sunday, under the preaching of Dr. Channing by the side of Miss Peabody. I do not know why he left the letter unfinished unless it was because she talked so fast and so long that he lost patience. He must have been confirmed in his disapproval of a "woman's speaking in church". He may have known one exactly like her. But if you write you must compliment her as much as you please, and ask her to use her influence to prevent any further folly being perpetrated in print. You can beg her to consider how much it will injure Rose, as well as her husband, if he persists in making use of materials only intrusted to her for safekeeping. It would injure them both, for Una says that Julian is very angry, and is determined to make it publicly known that Lathrop's conduct is dishonorable; he will tell exactly how George obtained his father's letters and journals. Una is unhappy about it, because Rose will suffer from an exposure of her husband, besides being alienated from her own family. My idea of Rose is that she is not likely to be much grieved, but that she will be as angry as I am, and have reason to be. I am angry enough, and breathe out threatenings, if not slaughter; or rather I should breathe them out if it were possible to accomplish them. Now your letter would stir up Miss Peabody, and perhaps her sister, Mrs. Mann, who has a sense of propriety, and might do something with Rose. At any rate it would help to make a fuss, and I have much faith in a fuss. Let George and Rose see plainly that they will not escape censure, and they may be deterred. All that I could say would be unavailing; but the opinions of

I must send this letter this minute.

—◆—

Beinecke Library
Number 107: To Una Hawthorne

Montserrat, June 15th 1876

My dear Una

I have received your letter of May 28th and am glad that you have been paying a little visit in London, and am amused with your criticism of the pictures you saw. If half a dozen good ones are produced in a year, do you not think that the public should be grateful? Some of those contributed to the Centennial in Philadelphia by English Artists are praised in the highest terms. I wish you were here, that you might go to the great house. If I were not old I should want to go—that is, if I had plenty of money. Richard is gone with Little Dicky, who will scrutinize every thing, if time is allowed him, and will all his life retain a vivid impression what he beholds. Lizzie's health will not permit her to accompany them. She must be an undoubting believer in her own invalidism, for she never goes to any particular resort, as I suppose she might do if she chose, without spending much more money than the water cures and the movement cures in which she gets herself tortured absorb. Is it not hard for a man to live alone half the time; as Richard does, while he is maintaining an expensive wife? I should expect to hear of all sorts of misfortunes if I left a husband and two boys uncared for. Richard walked over to see me about a week ago, and talked, among other things, about GPL, of whom he appears to think favorably; and I [*illegible*] given him some judicious counsel. Richard says that, in future, after an indefinite number of years have passed, every incident of Hawthorne's life will be invaluable to the public, as the most trifling details relating to Shakespeare are to us: therefore he thinks that everyone who knows any thing about him should by all means make a permanent record of [*illegible*]; so that Julian and George will not stand in each other's way. Even with this I do not agree: facts are frequently too trifling to be edifying, besides that they are sure to be misunderstood (unless they are set forth at a wearisome length). All that need to be told about Hawthorne he has himself communicated to the public. Any [attentive] reader of his works will understand him, and no one else ever will. I wish there was no thought of a biography of him. But Richard says the forthcoming work is not to be a biography. He told me the title, but I have forgotten it. All I concern myself much about now, (for I have scolded away the indignation I felt at first) is the anxiety and even distress that the affair occasions you. You have no reason to fear that Rose will be permanently unhappy while she has her husband. "Should all the race of nature die." "And none be left but" their two selves she would be consoled if he did not grieve too much.[162] Not that I think her unfeeling; but her love for him seems to fill her heart. I suppose that Julian's indignation makes it difficult for you to put the subject out of your mind;[163]

—ɯ—

Phillips Library
Number 108: To the Mannings

Montserrat, Saturday [January 1877]

My dear Cousins,

I trust Rebecca did not suffer from walking in the snow; I should be very sorry if she did, because she must have come out of pure kindness to me with no expectation of pleasure, except from the consciousness of doing good, and good she really did, to me, for I live a rather dull life just now. There is no one to converse with, except Daisy and Tiger, who, however are both of them intelligent and cultivated. You would like to see them playing together and, to hear them, you would think there were half a dozen children in the house. They are very fond of each other. When Daisy does not see Tiger, she goes from one room to another and looks in every chair where there is a cushion, and on the lounge and in all other soft places, for he is a lazy thing, and when she finds him, she begins to lick him with her tongue, and fondle him; he puts his paws around her neck, and kisses her, but presently begins to bite her ears, which is more than poor Daisy can endure, and it ends in a rough and tumble fight, almost as enjoyable to us, who watch it, as to themselves. It is barbarous to say that cats are only good to catch mice; what I like in a cat is that it is easy to make her perfectly happy, and, in a household, what else is there of which that can be affirmed? Tiger goes out and rolls in the snow like a little dog; and when he comes up to see me he puts his head on the floor and tumbles over and over. He climbs up on me as If I were a tree, and sits on my shoulder; he greets his other friends in the same manner. I wish Una was fond of animals; she would have a resource which I fear she is likely to want.

I sent the cuttings from the Tribune the day after you were here. There was very little about the show of Fruits, and there were one or two Tribunes which I did not have, but I sent every thing Horticultural that I could find; I suppose you have by this time received the package.

If you have not already bought the February Number of the Atlantic Monthly, I do not care about having it; because there is no way of sending it to me except by the mail, and if I cannot get it from the Library Sammie Cole will buy it for me down in town. I am sorry I troubled you about it. I am going to read Ticknor's Diary, as I suppose you have already done. I observe that that Huxley mentions the Lathrops among the pleasant people whom he met in Cambridge—George and Rose I suppose he means. Una will not be convinced that Rose is not unhappy, she wants to get her away from her Husband, and has written to May Almon to telegraph to her if she can do any thing in that way, and she will come home instantly. It provokes me to see her so absurd, and saddens me too, and yet I cannot help laughing. If her husband treats her ill Rose can say so; nothing is more ruinous to a man socially, than a suspicion of unkindness to his wife.

These last cuttings I saw after I had dispatched the package. They do not look as if they were of value. Write as soon as you can. What do you think of Miss Peabody? I shall write soon. I should be very glad to have Robert come to supper.

(The following is in the same envelope as the preceding. It was perhaps not part of the original letter).[164]

Elizabeth Peabody has written a long letter to Julian in which she tells him that [he] is the cause of Rose's insanity; his "persistent persecution" of her husband has driven her mad. She says insanity is in the Hawthorne family, and was beginning to show itself in Hawthorne himself before he died. Una says that ever since her illness her aunt EPP has been disseminating this idea far and wide.[165] I suppose she has, for in the letter of Lathrop which I showed you he says that a "distressing rumour" to that effect is abroad. Miss Peabody says that she has told Mr. Webster. I should be exceedingly relieved if that match were broken off; I wish they could both see that an habitual invalid ought not to be married; but I should rather the unfitness should manifest itself in him than in her. I do not know what would become of her if he were to leave her. I wish she would join that Sisterhood at Clewer where she loves so well to go. It is a society of refined women, and the religious observances would occupy her in a satisfactory way, while the benevolent efforts they make to relieve the poor would give her just about work enough to do. Do not let anyone know that I say this.

Una says that "knowing as she does, the suppressed sufferings of Rose's life", she looks forward to a sad result. For my part, from all I have seen of Rose; both in her husband's presence and when alone, I think that she esteems herself very happy, and that she really is quite as much as most women; when she is well, I mean, and you know that puerperal insanity has nothing to do with hereditary mental disease. I have told Una that the Doctors say so; but she will not see the difference, nor give Rose time to recover, but insists that her husband's cruelty has "driven her mad". Julian is miserable about it, too, and indignant with Miss Peabody; who certainly has a propensity for doing mischief remarkable in a woman of so much benevolence. All her life, since her eighteenth year has been at intervals, directed to this object, and letter writing has been the way in which she accomplished it. She has sowed dissension between husbands and wives, and between affianced lovers. She told me that Sophia was in extreme peril of insanity, but I shall not tell Una that; though I believe it was true.

I cannot feel that I should be doing right to take your best chamber. If on further consideration, you think you shall want it yourselves, do not hesitate to tell me so. We shall have time to think about it, for Jane has decided to remain here for some months, and perhaps permanently. If Una should urge me to live with her, it would be long before we found a place that would suit us both, for I have heard her say that she wished to live in a city. I would not object to that, if the location was eligible—Beacon Street—for instance, in Boston—but I am too old to move about, which she would always be planning to do. I assure you, however, that if I come to you, I shall make it a point to keep the room I occupy in the nicest order as you have always done.

I have some thoughts of writing to ask Mrs. Loring to write and tell Una that Lathrop has not "driven his wife mad". She has had experience of married life, and Sophia said that the Doctor was not always amiable.[166]

—⁂—

Phillips Library
Number 109: To the Mannings

Montserrat, Wednesday, [Early February 1877]

My dear Cousins,

I inclose Una's last letter, which I wish you to return as soon as possible after reading it. Her two letters before this were written in a cheerful spirit; but this shows a melancholy state of affairs. Whenever Miss Peabody or Mrs. Mann have anything to tell that will render Una miserable, they write it forthwith; agreeable tidings may be delayed. It appears to me just as it does to Una, that Rose has nothing but unhappiness to expect—certainly for the present—and perhaps for a long time; and I fear that her mind may be permanently impaired by the treatment she will receive from the odious mother-in-law, as I believe her to be—for I have heard of her—whom her equally odious son will place as a guard over his wife. When Rose first returned from England she told me that she was not kindly received; but since that Mrs. Lathrop has professed to be very fond of her. Mrs. Lathrop was a Salem woman, and her name was Pratt; then she married a Smith, and for her second husband Dr. Lathrop—not an irreproachable man. Rose also told May Almon that George was cruel to her, and that her eyes were so sore with crying that she could not draw. George used to tell people that his wife's high temper made his life wretched—I hope it did-all this, and more May Almon told Una and Una told Mrs. Cole, not me. Perhaps she supposed it would grieve me too much, and perhaps she thought me too hard-hearted to grieve at all. Certainly I do think a woman may fight a good fight, and defend herself. But Una could not imagine such a thing; and

Mrs. Cole said she would come down to breakfast looking as if she had wept all night. Mrs. Cole was sympathetic, and longed to give George a sound whipping; but she saw the absurdity of a separation, which Mrs. Cabot and May Almon and Una all were bent upon bringing about, if they could. She knew that Rose would be ruined if prevailed upon to leave her husband, and moreover that nothing would tempt her to do it, because she was very fond of him. Mrs. Cole had a great deal of penetration; she looked right into George, while I was quite taken by his plausibility. She and Jane both said there was something in his eyes not good to see. If you ever meet him again, look for it. I propose that next summer, Rebecca and I should go to see Rose; If we are denied access to her we can have a talk with the mother-in-law. If she is not glad to see us, I shall be all the better pleased. But I hope that before next summer, Rose will be free of surveillance, which, even from the most loving eyes, seems to me unbearable. Do you remember that her father says somewhere, (it is in Mr. Field[s]'s book), and he is speaking of a friend who was anxious about his health, "he watched me and watched me, till"—I forget exactly till what, I think that constant restraint is enough to drive anyone mad, unless you can blaze out once in a while; and if poor Rose does that it will instantly be ascribed to delirium.

Did you read the whole of Daniel Deronda? I read only the first few chapters; so I am unable to give an opinion as to the wisdom of the authoress, which is so highly extolled by almost every critic. But I never yet saw a good book which I could not read and relish, even though it does not strengthen me in my judgement to find it confirmed by the Edinburgh Review, it certainly pleases me. That criticism in the Advertiser was very good; the writer only ventured to suggest a few drawbacks upon the excellence of the author, but it is evident that she does not really enjoy her later books, and the deficiencies she points out imply a great deal.

I am reading "What she Came through["] to Jane, and am at the end of all there is in the numbers of the Living Age that you brought me. Can you send me some more, before May, by Wallis and Young's, or, if there are but few numbers, by the mail. Jane is impatient to hear what becomes of Plesaunce, to whose fate I am completely indifferent, because she wears spectacles. How could a novelist send a heroine into the world with weak eyes! I had to see her sitting so absorbed in melancholy thoughts as she did and the reading has done her a great deal of good. Mary, I find, has had more experience of novels than Jane, and appreciates a good one. I wish you would come over again both of you.[167]

Phillips Library
Number 110: To the Mannings

Montserrat, Feb 18th. [1877].

My dear Cousins,

Do write and tell me how little Dicky is, for I am very anxious to know. If he has the fever favorably, and if he recovers without serious injury, you will have reason to be thankful that he has had it. Of course you know how much care will be necessary when he is getting better. Shall you let his Mother know about it if he is in no danger? She cannot possibly come home in time to be of use. Does it not seem rather a pity that the world is so wide, and so diversified in climate? If it were small and all alike, relations and friends might at least be within reach of one another, having no temptation to drift apart. But they would probably hate each other and expend all their energies in mutual destruction.

I dread to hear from poor Una from whom I received a letter at the same time with yours, telling me of her terrible loss.[168] She wrote in the best of spirits, anticipating Mr. Webster's arrival in England in a few months, and they were to be married immediately. She was making her wedding dress herself; it was to be very simple, as they were to travel, and after spending some time in California, to visit different parts of the country. I believe I told you this before. I fear that she will not recover from the blow, though, as you say, it might have been worse if they were married. But she will feel as if she had nothing to live for. Some object in life is essential to her, some strong feeling; she cannot go on from day to day, as I have always done, when there was no reason why I should not, finding interest and a moderate degree of pleasure in what did not at all concern me, personally. Neither is she particularly fond of reading, which was never taught her until the age of seven, and then she was forbidden to practice it. Her mother wished to keep her children in complete mental dependence upon herself. She would read to them, in such books as suited herself, and I do not think they were much the better for it. You see that I ascribe every infelicity and every short-coming to her, and I really do feel that there is a comfort in having an explanation for all untoward circumstances constantly at hand. But for the troubles of Una's life her Mother is actually responsible, because it was the Roman fever that ruined her constitution, and that she owed to her abode at Rome, where her Mother kept her family that she might gratify her own love of art; permanently injuring also her husband's health by the same means; this

Una told me, as well as that other man, about her fathers age, one of their intimate friends, died from the same cause. And you need not tell me that "the two Aunts", as Una terms them, meant kindly by her when they told her of Rose's return home; it was a feeling very unlike kindness that prompted Miss Peabody's letter to Julian, laying all the blame for Rose's illness upon him and Una; after his father's death Julian had to write to Miss Peabody desiring her not to come there, because her conversation distressed his mother; and as soon as he was married, Hawthorne found it well to keep her at a distance from himself, because as he told me, she put herself in a false position towards him. So, you see that they cannot love one another. Neither she nor Mrs. Mann is a Model Aunt, as I am, for, as Julian told Una, I "respect his individuality".—A great compliment, which no other Aunt within my knowledge ever merited. To "respect their individuality" is the only thing it is in my power to do for my nephew and nieces, but I never fail in that. And it would be no wonder if I "were spoiling for a fight", for I have been put to a great deal of trouble this winter by the Peabodys, Every Monday comes, or has come, a wailing letter from Una, about Rose's sufferings, and I have been obliged to put every thing else out of my mind and reply in a sympathetic strain; and what is even harder, to vindicate George, whom I endeavor to prove only a scamp, not at all a savage. In a Newspaper that I have just taken up I observe that, in Delaware, a poor fellow has just been publicly whipped for stealing. Now I wish that George lived in Delaware, and might be tempted to steal (he is not a grain too good) and be detected, and whipped just so, before the eyes of all men.

I must write to Una, and what can I say to comfort her? May Almon has convinced her that Rose is happy with her Baby, and now this new sorrow has come upon her.—Do send me a Postal card about Dicky. I only meant to inquire for him when I began this letter.[169]

—⁓—

Phillips Library
Number III: To the Mannings

Montserrat, April 9ᵗʰ [1877]

My dear Cousins,

I think you will be glad to hear that I am nearly well. I was provoked with Jane for sending for Rebecca when I did not feel able to talk, but she was anxious; and it was extremely kind in you to come. Probably you will think me perverse, for after eating one egg prepared in the proper manner with milk, I chose to take the next one raw,—breaking the big end, putting it to my mouth and swallowing it in that way. It is the way I am used to eating eggs, because they are apt to boil them too hard, since that I have eaten chowder and roast Pork, and anything else except bread, which I cannot bear to touch. The Jellies which Maria sent me were very nice, and were good for me.

I have written to Una, and have received a letter from her. When she writes, I observe that she always seems to adopt my own suggestions. I mean that just what I have said to her in the way of consolation she repeats to me as if it were her own, without remembering that the thoughts are mine. I feel flattered by this for it seems to show me that I should have made a good clergyman, excelling in sympathetic and comforting discourses. I send you her last letters; you will see that she seems to be on the verge of a reconciliation with G. P. Lathrop.

I have some hopes that Jane will stay here, but we cannot tell till after the action. There have been secret proceedings, and gatherings of the farmers in the neighborhood but the most that appears clear is that Dear Zachariah Cole, having a farm of his own that he wished to sell, in order to buy one in Wenham that he liked better, persuaded a man who had thought of buying this, to buy his instead. But the man, Mr. White, a milk man, was never quite satisfied with his bargain, always preferring this house, which is better and newer; therefore, as there was nothing to bind him, he went on the very last evening, when Zachariah Cole had every thing packed, and partly sent off, and explicitly refused to ratify his agreement. So Zachariah is left with his own farm on his hands, and the one that he has just bought besides. For which it is supposed he is hardly able to pay. His wife and children always preferred staying here. His wife told Mr. White that she should have been thankful a fortnight ago when she had a pleasant home, if he had drawn back; but now she [has had] her carpets cut and other things that made it impossible for her to stay. No one seems to blame her. So I hope that we shall be able to stay for the present.

When I first came here I was sick, and Mrs. Cole used to come up, bringing an armful of wood, and sit down upon it and stare at [me] and tell me that I was in a consumption. I disliked everything, especially herself, so much that I felt quite indifferent to whether I were or not. I longed to tell her, but refrained, that when I was buried, I desired to have the coffin put out of the window, to get me out of the house as soon as possible. Since that I have taken a great deal of comfort here, and I learned to like Mrs. Cole, who was as good and kind as possible; and the whole family were thoroughly reliable. But it required a constant effort, for a long time, to understand and accommodate myself to them. She always called me "Miss Whats your name". Whenever she disliked any of my proceedings, she scolded, and very often I replied appropriately, so that we soon learned to appreciate each other, which can never be [done] by the practice of constant civility. Then there was Hannah, the blind woman; if you could have heard all the stories she told me you would have wondered how the ideas of rural simplicity ever could have arisen in the mind of man. It seems to me, even now, that the sun never could have shone with its natural brightness, in the times she talked about. Whatever depravity there may be now, I doubt not there has been an improvement. Yet some of the people, both men and women, were truly excellent; but murder and other gross crimes, could not have been hidden; escaping punishment because there was no influential person to bring them to justice.

Sammie Cole has just been down in town and got some ether, with which he offers to accomplish the execution of Daisy's poor kittens, five of them. I have only seen one of them, Jane brought it up to show to Tiger, who was frightened half out of his wits. He ran and hid. I do not believe either of them were uncommonly pretty. Daisy herself will be heart-broken. If I can prevail upon Tiger to be dutiful and affectionate to his poor mother, I shall be glad, but his only recognition of their existence as yet has been expressed by snarling and spitting whenever he dared to go near enough.

Have you heard lately from Lizzie and Charlie? How does little Dickie feel about Colorado. It will be a shame to take him there.

I was sorry I could not see Robert when he called. He was extremely kind to come, and I do trust that there will come pleasant weather and that it will find me here, as of old.

Do you approve of our new President. It seems to me absurd to find fault with his removal of the troops from South Carolina and Louisiana. Of what use have they ever been? If the Southerners are still unmanageable let the Mississippi have its way. Do you remember a letter from some professor who had fought in the Union Army and who said that the negroes proposed to devote themselves to earning money and to leave politics to white men. How profitable they would find almost any industrial pursuit. Cotton and sugar and rice and so many other valuable productions for which the North has to pay a great price would come so much cheaper to them, and for manufactures they have abundant hands.

It does not tire me at all to write. I hope it will not you to read. You must not read my letters critically. Come and see me as soon as you can.[170]

Phillips Library
Number 112: To the Mannings

Montserrat, Monday [December 1879]

My dear Cousins,

I wished to come to see you last Tuesday, with Mrs. Appleton, who endeavored to find a conveyance for us, but could not, even as far as the Horse-Cars. It is a busy set of men who live here. Alice took me down to the Fair, on Wednesday. I wish you had gone; there were many pretty things to see. Of course it was not like the great Fairs, but perhaps as pleasant for all that was worth looking at was displayed in a small space. There were Books, for children, most of them. I bought one for Jennie Cole, ("Eyebright") because her Mother was so civil as to come and invite me to go with her. I also bought "Stories of the War["], a little Book for Boys, by Edward E. Hale; but I think I shall keep it for myself, because it is a good little history, omitting no battle of importance, and with many anecdotes. One noticeable thing that I could not help buying is a paper weight containing a potato-bug whose legs move all the time—as if he were alive. There were others inclosing horses, flourishing their tales. There was pottery ware, very handsomely painted,—Jars, with no covers, very convenient to hold niceties in a sitting room. I could have spent a good deal of money, if I were not so prudent. There were plenty of useful articles, but I never look at them. I saw Holders; you advised me to buy one, but a Newspaper is just as good, and Jennie is going to make me a Holder for a Christmas Present. Mrs. Appleton wants to buy something pretty, in Salem, so we are going to have an early dinner, look in the Shop-windows, &.c. and then call at your house; we shall not be able to stop long, for she says she must be at home soon after three. Tommie is to come with us; he is pleased with the idea of making you a little visit. Yesterday morning they all rose at Four, as Mr. Appleton was going to work upon the roads, about two miles off; Tommie insisted upon going with him; his Mother said she could hear him talking after they started, though it was so dark she could not see him. They did not return till nearly dark, Tommie keeping upon his feet all the time, I think they are training him very well,—letting him [develop], without much instruction; neither of his parents being intellectual people, who usually teach children to go the way that they should not, as Sophia did, you know; yet it was not intellect that misled her, only the aping of it. When anything annoys Tommie, or when he hurts himself in playing, he roars with all his might; it is funny to see his face inflamed and to see him pound his Mother while she threatens to whip him, and all the time we know all will be serene again in a few moments.—As

I have mentioned Sophia, I might as well tell you that she is the only human being whom I really dislike: though she is dead, that makes no difference; I could have lived with her in apparent peace, but I could not have lived long; the constraint would have killed me.

This moderate weather may not last long, but if Rebecca would come now, we could have a good walk.

I bought a few cards, one for Robert with a Cat that he must take for silver gray; she is watching a sitting hen, with the purpose of eating up her chickens as they are out of the shell. I wish little Dickie would come with you and that you would come immediately. My love to Maria.[171]

—⁂—

Phillips Library
Number 113: To the Mannings

Montserrat, May 17th [1880]

My dear Cousins,

It is the time for you to come and look at the violets. I suppose Lizzie told you how abundant they were. I hope little Dickie and the Boy who is to accompany him will come with you. I shall not come to Salem at present because I hear that the Measles prevail both in Salem, and in the town of Beverly; so I must wait till they have spent their malignity, before I go to the regions now infected.

Mrs. Appleton is going to Salem tomorrow if the weather permits, I have commissioned her to buy some flannel for my Wrap. I must have something warm, for I have suffered with the cold for nearly a week until to-day, for I had my stove removed on one of those pleasant, summer-like days. It is easier to pile on clothes than to make fires. Mrs. Appleton is also going to buy a bed-quilt for me, and a Straw Carpet such as she would get for herself.

I have been reading Kismet, in which I felt interested from hearing the story of its author. But novels rather weary me, even good ones, if I begin at the beginning, and try to read regularly through to the end, as I endeavored to do with Sebastian Strome, which must be good, for several persons, and some of them intelligent and experienced in fiction, others only susceptible, have told me that they admire it extremely. But I am so hard-hearted that as soon as the hero's misfortunes began, my interest ceased. I like to be amused. So I read only a few Chapters—The book is well written; Julian inherits a good style. Some day, when I feel bright and strong, I mean to finish it, but newspapers and magazines suit me much better than novels. I suppose you saw in the newspapers that the author of Daniel Deronda, &.c. has resumed her own name, the only name that she has a right to bear, and married again. She cannot be a woman of an elevated mind, though she may have been before her connection with Mr. Lewes. Do you not think it very unfair and ungenerous in him to claim some of the most effective portions of Deronda as his own? The Mill on the Floss and Adam Bede were good; but I have no opinion about her later books, for I could [not] read them.

Mrs. Appleton is going to be absent about a fortnight, on a visit to some relatives in Maine, in September, and she proposes that I should invite Eunice to stay with me while she is gone. I should like it; do you think Eunice would come? Mrs. Appleton would like to have her come now, she thinks it would be particularly pleasant to me to have her then. And I would like to see you at any time; to have you stay a week if you will. I am disappointed about not coming to Salem at present; but as I cannot even go down in town, I can avoid the expense of getting my bonnet repaired,—saving of some importance, for I want several things to make me comfortable at home. Do come both you and Maria and little Dickie very soon.

This letter is hardly legible. Come as soon as you can and ask Robert to come.[172]

—ɯ—

Phillips Library
Number 114: To the Mannings

Montserrat, June 25 [1880]

Before this fine weather passes away I earnestly entreat you all to come and enjoy a little of it here. Come on the Fourth of July, or on the day that represents it, and bring little Dickie. Robert half promised to come when he was here. We had a delightful ramble in the woods, in search of Laurel, which is scarce, and less beautiful, this year, than usual. Strawberries also, are sour, and not juicy. No berries will be good, unless we have rain.

Did you go to The Willows, to hear Miss Larcom's Poem, and the other Performances? Mrs. Appleton went, and I was invited to go, but I do not care for the Willows, and have the very best poetry within earlier reach. There was such a crowd that Mrs. Appleton could not get into the Hall.

What do you think of our next President as I hope he will be.[173] Western men, when they are good, are excellent; but as to the South, I always thought, during the War, and still think, that while our troops were there they might have been usefully employed in digging away the soil, and thus annihilating States, and State Rights, once for all. Think how many difficulties we might have escaped if peace had returned and left us undisturbed by the Carolinas, Louisiana, Alabama, &.c It is a region of mud, and pestilence moral and material. We could have got cotton enough in India, and other places; it can be raised in many countries. Some such process of annihilation is the only effectual means of removing from our borders a turbulent and deceitful race who will always hate us. The idea was suggested to me by a very judicious remark that I always thought showed great political insight, "that the only remedy for the evils of Ireland [was] to sink the island for an hour under the ocean". But it is too late to think of such a decisive measure now.

I wonder if General Garfield, like other Western men, calls a poem a <u>pome,</u> and a poet a <u>pote,</u> &.c If there were to be a Phonetic reform in the language, and words were to be spelled as they are pronounced, we should have no language left, that is the English language would be destroyed; there would be a multitude of dialects, just as there are in most parts of Europe, we should be even in a worse condition [than] different provinces in Europe; for there, there is a written language which all educated people understand, but such a change would destroy that language; as far as the influence of change went, it would lead us into barbarism. I must send this letter now or not at all.

EMH

Come as soon as you can.[174]

—m—

Phillips Library
Number 115: To the Mannings

Montserrat, Monday [December 1880]

My dear Cousins,

I was very glad to receive Rebecca's letter, but I have mislaid it so I trust there was nothing in it that required an answer; I recollect nothing of the kind.

I think one of those book-shelves at 1.50 will probably be just what I want, but I will not ask you to buy it for me, because we hope (Mrs. Appleton and I) to come to Salem at least before New years Day; we thought of coming last Saturday, but it was too cold. We were going about 10, A.M and while she went to the shops, I intended to make you a call, thinking that Rebecca would go back with me, and go round to see what there was worth looking at. Perhaps, either this week [or] next, we shall accomplish this. Mr. Appleton is going to carry us over, but he wishes to go home before dark, so we shall not be able to accept your kind invitation to tea, as I should like to do.

I hope Maria's cold is better. You complain of the cold weather; I wish you were here in my room; you would be glad to go to the door, for a breath of fresh air, once in a while, but I believe the heat agrees with me, for I have no cold. I have to drink cold water, a pint or so at once. I do not believe that it is hurtful to do so when one is warm, for I have always done it.

Tyger insists upon sitting in my lap while I am writing; he sends his regards to Buff and Buff's mother. There are two half-grown kittens living in the yard, and sleeping where he once did, in a barrel of Rags! He likes to play with them. He has become useful; I put him down cellar every night, to frighten away the rats, which were gnawing Apples, Potatoes, &.c. His mere presence is sufficient to prevent their depredations.

I am beginning to want some money, as my Board will be due this week; I pay regularly every month. If any one is coming over, or if I can as I intended call to see you, it would be safer than to send it in a letter. It is Tiger who has made these ink Blots; he was endeavoring to assist me, and at the same time to hide from Tommie, who is certainly the most troublesome boy I ever saw. If he is left to his own devices for a single moment he is sure to do some mischief. He requires constant thought, I suppose as bright children do. But what becomes of their Mothers when there is more than one in a family? And what becomes of the children whose Mothers have other objects in life,—politics, for instance, Woman's rights, or any outside [usefulness]? I think children should never be left to servants, though very often, perhaps servants are more capable than their employers. Rose seems to manage her boy without much difficulty; but he does not appear to me to be so active as Tommie, all [whose] progenitors have been working people and all whose plays [are] work, such as making shoes, or the like. A man came the other day to see to the Hydrant, before the house, and Tommie went out with his little hoe, and worked as hard as the man did. He talks with every man he sees, and perhaps he is receiving the best of educations, the most suitable to the times; learning to understand common people, as most of the men in high positions, at present, did in early life. But I wish he would learn to read, because that would quiet him.

I wish Robert would come over on Christmas Day; it may be mild and pleasant by that time.

Rose sent me the December numbers of the Atlantic and Scribner, to be returned when I have read them, and the Art Journal to keep, so if you would like to see it, you can have it. She says she means to make the publishers send them to me—to tell them that I am a most wonderful woman, &.c. You will be amused with her letter. When she was here she told me that Mr. Fields cheated her Father and I am inclined to believe that he did, for Gail Hamilton said the same in her <u>Battle of the Books;</u> she said that Mr. Fields acted more dishonestly with Mrs. Hawthorne than with her.[175] Rose says that Mrs. Fields urges her to visit them, but that she shall not go, and she asked me whether I thought she ought to speak to them, when they met. I advised her by all means to speak and be civil to [them], but not to be intimate. What is the good of quarrelling with people, if you can do them no injury? Rose is going, or has been to see Sarah Bernhardt. They have Tickets for Concerts, Lectures, &.c. and I think are living very pleasantly.

Mrs. Grote, the wife of the historian, was a woman of great resolution,—"a masterful woman", among other inconceivable things, whenever she was asked to lend a book she would say, "I'll trouble you for a sovereign", and she kept the sovereign till the Book was returned.

I was infinitely obliged to Richard for writing to Mr. Curtis. It ought to be known that Miss Peabody was not on good terms with Hawthorne.[176]

—⁂—

Phillips Library
Number 116: To the Mannings

Montserrat, Dec 27th 1880

My dear Cousins,

Many thanks for your beautiful Cards. We saw none so beautiful in Salem on Saturday; but we only looked at one shop—Smith's, for we had no time to go round much—for Mr. Appleton was obliged to be at home soon after three. There were several things that I wanted; and I particularly wanted to come to see you, but it was impossible; I saw Mary T. as she is called,[177] and Lucy Larcom and her sister, or rather they saw me, so I am not altered quite so much as I thought, and moreover, they came some distance to overtake me, they must have been glad of the meeting. I have got a beautiful little glass vase for Maria, and a lovely Pitcher for Rebecca, besides a little white kitten, whose price was but a few cents, but who appears to be gamboling about the closet, I hope she will not fall down and break herself to atoms. Rose has sent me a Box for newspaper cuttings—very "sweet" indeed, containing cards for me, Mrs.

Appleton and Tommie; and Hattie and Jennie Cole have given me "sweet" cards, and Mrs. Appleton a pair of felt slippers. We could not find just such Bookshelves as we wanted, so I bought a Corner bracket for her, which will hold all her Books. I should have been delighted to buy more things, but had very little money. My board is due and I want some coal so if you will ask Richard to send me a supply, I shall be grateful to you and to him. I dare say it will reach me safely by the mail. Is not Lizzie anxious about Charlie? I observe that a formidable Volcano is added to the other perils of Colorado. It is close to Colorado Springs, which the newspapers suggest may encounter the fate of Herculaneum & Pompeii. If it should I fancy that few treasures of art worth digging for in future ages will be entombed. Newspaper presses and guns there may be, wonderful things perhaps to the people who then live, whether it be a darker period than our own, when this civilization that relies upon gunpowder and is nourished by printers ink has vanished, or a millennial age, when war and politics are banished forevermore. A dull time that would be; you know the Poet Gray imagined one of the Joys of Paradise might be lying at ease and reading new novels; but what are novels to the daily records of a Presidential election? By the way, I do not like Garfield half so well as Grant, who has always been my hero because, besides his efficiency in war, he has peculiarities. Garfield, like Hayes, seems to be in no way odd or inexplicable not to be distinguished from other estimable and able men, therefore unlikely to be elevated much above them, in any one's mind.

Do you think George Elliot is to be lamented? or that she is only removed, happily for herself, from the possibility of future follies? Rose told me that one of her friends knew George Sand intimately, and thought her one of the purest and best of women. I saw Photographs of Sarah Bernhardt in Salem, and thought her countenance very pleasing. I want to send Eunice and Elizabeth Carlton each a card; do you know how I should direct them?

I wish Robert would bring you over tomorrow Evening while the snow remains. Somebody prophesies eleven feet of snow; that would reach nearly to the top of our windows.

If you do not come you can write, but to come would be better.

EMH

I owe Rebecca for the Living Age—my part of it. Get the money from Richard. Can you send the two cards that I have directed to Eunice and Elizabeth Carlton

Mrs. Appleton and Tommie are much obliged for their cards. I have put some cards for you in a large envelope which I find has no *stick* to it, so I cannot send them now.

—m—

New York Public Library
Number 117: To Rose Hawthorne Lathrop

Montserrat September 8, 1881

My dear Rose

I am delighted to have a letter, especially one that tells me that you are coming home soon. I wish you were here already, for the perils of travelling come to my mind much more vividly than its advantages. However I trust you will neither be swallowed up by the deep, nor blown up by the explosives threatened to all British ships. Mrs. Appleton desires me to ask you to come here and make us a visit immediately, before you go home, with Mr Lathrop, and I need not say that I should be very glad if you would do so. It will be pleasant here in October, and after you go home to Concord, and put every thing in order there, the weather will be cold. But I am forgetting that you will not arrive many days before November. However, whenever you come you will be entirely welcome, and trust you stay longer than when you were home before, for your former visits were no more than calls. When I wrote to you, I forgot to ask you, as I intended, to request Julian to let you see the Miniatures of my Father and Uncle, which I sent him many year[s] ago. He has moved about so much, and has suffered so many inconveniences that I have been afraid he has lost them. But they ought to be taken care of, for it is not every family that possesses such a memento of its father. Your Grandfather was a very fine looking man. So I have been told, for I do not remember him.

You must not suppose that we are living in anarchy.[178] According to appearances, England is in greater danger of that than America. Even if the President dies, and the Vice-President comes into power, perhaps he would be as good a ruler as Mr. Gladstone, though immensely his inferior in intellect. Gladstone can write and talk, but to govern is a different thing. At present, things go on very quietly here. The only people disposed to be lawless are a few who are overzealous for justice, and would, if [they could] get hold of the assassin, lynch him. I wish they could, and so does every woman whom I have heard speak of it. But to allow such a proceeding would be inconsistent with the dignity of government. He must be tried, and if it were possible that he should be acquitted, and liberated, nothing could save him. There seems to be no suspicion of any accomplices. The first thing that is recorded as being said by any decent person, was by a Lady at a Fashionable resort, and it was that "she did not care for the President, but if he died it would be so bad for the doctors." A Southern Lady, who tells of it, rebuked her in very strong terms. The Southern people feel as strongly about the affair as anybody at the North. They have prayers in their churches, and it looks as if the spirit of rebellion was melting away. If the President lives he will be everywhere popular, and if he dies his funeral will be worthy of the nation. But except myself, I do not believe anybody has yet been heartless enough to allude to a funeral.

Mrs. Appleton wishes very much to have a London Fashion Book. Can you, without too much trouble, get one for her? I suppose Minnie knows where they can be purchased. Mrs Appleton does not like to trouble you, but I think you will be willing to oblige her. I do not doubt that I have forgotten half that [I] meant to say, but I cannot stop to read my letter, for if I do I shall miss the opportunity of sending it. Tell Julian and Minnie that I am always thinking of them, and the children that they must feel as if they know me because I love them all. We shall expect you here as soon as you arrive, and I wish you a short and pleasant passage.

EMH

Can you without much trouble get Mrs Appleton an English Fashion Book. They are very common here—a sheet of patterns of Dresses. But she thinks a London one must be better than ours.[179]

—∞—

Phillips Library
Number 118: To the Mannings

Montserrat, Friday [December 1882]

My dear Cousins,

This is the third letter that I have begun to write to you, and the two first I almost finished, but mislaid them; they are not worth looking for; it is easier to write another. I hope to be able to come to Salem at least before new Year's Day. I want to go to the Shops. While the roads are so bad it is, I suppose, in vain to ask you to come to see me; but as soon as it is possible, Mr. Appleton is going to take us to Salem. I sent you an order on the Saving Bank; if you will be so good as to get the money you can pay yourself for the Living Age, and if you mean to have them bound you had better buy the missing number. I cannot find it. There is one Book I want you to buy for me—Kinley Hollow—price one dollar. You can keep it and read it before you send it to me. I have read the end of Howells' "modern Instance" I intend to read the beginning and middle; I have them both but a Book is not less interesting if you plunge into it in this way. The author can write a very tolerable story, and seems to be a man of good judgement, though never brilliant, but he ought to know better than to even himself an(d) his compeer in Boston with Thackeray and Dickens. The old witticism will suit him very well, they will be read most when Dickens and Thackeray are forgotten—unless indeed they themselves are superseded by others of their own class. Do you mean to read Julian's book, which if it is as good as Sebastian Strome, which is never dull, will be a success. Julian says he is much better paid here than in England. Rose says, but I perhaps I have already told [you] that Julian is going to live in a large house belonging to one of his wife's relatives,—in which a murder was once committed. For the rent he is to pay the Taxes. Should you be willing to live in a Haunted House? That story told by Dean Stanley's "[Inverawe of Ticonderoga]," is admirable.[180] What a pity he did not pick more of the kind. I do not think a good ghost can ever be invented. The first who tells it must believe it. I think people are beginning to (be) credulous again, I have seen several instances of it in Newspapers. One of the officers of the lost Jeannette has appeared to his wife. Perhaps he actually did appear. I do not accuse her of credulity. A young lady has sent me three stories, cut from Newspapers, which she probably believes, though they are not good. *She* is credulous, a Spiritualist.

Let me know when you receive this.[181]

Postscript

The family buried Elizabeth in Salem's Howard Street Cemetery near Louisa and Mrs. Hawthorne. If a marker once showed their names, none remains, but the house that Elizabeth occupied with the Coles and the Appletons still stands. Years after Elizabeth died, her niece Rose Hawthorne Lathrop wrote of her aunt:

I always felt her unmistakable power. She was chock-full of worldly wisdom, though living in the utmost monastic retirement, only allowing herself to browse in two wide regions,—the woods and literature. She knew the latest news from the papers, and the oldest classics alongside them. She was potentially, we thought, rather hazardous, or perverse. But language refuses to explain her . . . I knew that she had sufficient strength of character to upset a kingdom, if she chose; that she could use a scepter of keen sarcasm which made heads roll off on all sides; that there was nothing which her large, lustrous eyes could not see, and nothing they could not conceal. (473–74)

These observations echo what Elizabeth Manning Hawthorne's letters illustrate about their author. A striking, intelligent, highly literate woman from the nineteenth-century United States recorded the home front of the American Civil War; critiqued new works of literature by authors whom history has since judged; and captured the changing seasons in a manner often worthy of her neighbor Thoreau. Formerly used only to know Nathaniel, Elizabeth Manning Hawthorne's correspondence, properly called an oeuvre, now endures as her own legacy.

Notes

1. Address on envelope: Mr Robert Manning/Raymond/Maine. MS torn in six places on recto and verso by wax seal. At breaks in MS, letters are supplied: Heading: *dnesday* emended to [Wednesday]. Sentence 3: *comenced* emended to [commenced]; sentence 5: *h* added and *wo'nt* emended to [He won't].

2. Woodson explains that "down" means "downwind," in the direction that the southwest wind blows, thus, northeast (110).

3. Chebacco is near the Mannings' original hometown of Ipswich, Massachusetts.

4. Henry Whipple was the owner of a store in Salem (Moore, *Salem* 158).

5. Sentence 4: *Do'nt* emended to [Don't]; letters "sed to wri" added for [promised to write] us; sentence 6: "aam planted a" added for [Maam planted a]; sentence 3: *P* emended to [Priscilla].

6. With the War of 1812 at its height, many inhabitants of Salem sought safety in the country from British ships, which menaced coastal towns around Boston harbor.

7. Sentence 9: *Do'nt* emended to [Don't]. Postscript appears on the verso.

8. Rachel Baker was a young woman who preached sermons in her sleep.

9. Bowdoin College Library records identify the addressor of this addendum to Elizabeth's letter as Priscilla Manning Dike. Priscilla married John Dike in 1817. Sentences 6 and 9: *Do'nt* emended to [Don't].

10. Eliza Needham was possibly a daughter of John or Isaac Needham (see Moore, *Salem* 139).

11. Sally Lord was a relative of the children's grandmother, Miriam Lord Manning.

12. Elizabeth is referring to Ruth Manning Rust, the children's great-aunt, sister to their grandfather Richard Manning (Moore, *Salem* 23).

13. Sentence 6: *recieved* emended to [received].

14. A *bombazet* is a scarf made of light wool fabric.

15. Address: Mrs Miriam Manning/Salem. Above address in another hand: Raymond oct^r 28 1816/12 ½; in pencil: 164. [Archer] added for clarity.

16. The families that Elizabeth mentions visiting are her paternal relatives, aunt Rachel Hawthorne Forrester, cousin Nancy Forrester Barstow, and aunt Judith Hawthorne Archer (Moore, *Salem* 24n).

17. Kezia and Sally were relatives of Susan Dingley Manning; [Richard] added for clarity.

18. Caroline Archer was a Hawthorne cousin.

19. By "our arrival" Elizabeth is referring to a trip to Salem she made with March Gay, who lived in Raymond (Pickard 58).

20. The Hawthorne family had again moved to Raymond.

21. Jane Poole was an employee in the Manning-Hawthorne household.

22. Sentence 3: [here] added for clarity and *your* emended to [our]; sentence 4: *Mrs. M* emended to Mrs. [Manning] and [Poole] added for clarity. Postscript appears on the verso.

23. By "Miss Hathorne" Elizabeth was probably referring to one of the unmarried Hathorne aunts, Eunice or Ruth, her father's sisters.

24. Paragraph 3: Elizabeth interlined "send by Mr Gay." Abbreviation *nrs* emended to [numbers].

25. The Reverend Caleb Bradley ran a boarding school at Stroudwater, Maine, where Nathaniel's stay ended in January of the following year.

26. Address: Mrs Priscilla M. Dike/Salem/Williams St. Lower left corner of address: Mr. Eddy. Sentence 1: Elizabeth interlined "so" with a caret. Dated by evolution of Elizabeth's penmanship.

27. By "come to Salem" Elizabeth meant "move."

28. By "my friends" Elizabeth was referring to her family (Erlich 52).

29. Sentences 1 and 13: [Louisa] added for clarity; sentence 15: *Mr. and Mrs. D* emended to Mr. and Mrs. [Dike].

30. Daniel Giddings was the widower of Miriam Lord Manning's late sister, Sarah Lord (Moore, *Salem* 67).

31. Elizabeth is probably referring to Margaret Heussler Felt, married to Jonathan Porter Felt (see Moore, *Salem,* 124).

32. Elizabeth is referring to Lucy Lord Sutton, a cousin of Elizabeth Clarke Manning Hawthorne (Moore, *Salem* 23).

33. Paragraph 3, sentence 1: [Louisa] added for clarity.

34. Dated by the reference to tulips and by the relatively formal mode of address, indicating a fairly new reacquaintance. MS marked "~~1840?~~" and "1838."

35. Paragraph 2, sentence 1: *number* emended to [numbers].

36. Dated by reference to *Foreign Quarterly Review* article, dated April 1839. Paragraph 2, sentence 5: [no] added for clarity.

37. Elizabeth is referring to Sophia's brother, George Peabody, who died November 25, 1839.

38. Dated by reference to George's apparent turn for the worse. Address: Miss E. P. Peabody/Charter St./Miss E. P. Peabody/Charter St./From Elizabeth Hawthorne. Leaves are folded so that address shows on either side.

39. By the title "Journalism in France" Elizabeth is probably referring to "L'Ecole des Journalistes," March 1840. Dated by journal article and by reference to Nathaniel's apparent absence, probably at the Boston Custom House, thus 1839 or 1840. The New York Public Library catalog lists the date as 1841, but Nathaniel spent much of that year at Brook Farm. Paragraph 2, sentence 5: closing quotes added. Paragraph 3, sentence 1: *her* emended to [you].

40. Address: Miss Sophia A Peabody/Boston. In pencil: Ebie/Louisa/E.P.P. (1)/A genealogical letter. Berg owns a copy in a different hand. The Bancroft Library copy bears a postmark.

41. Address: Miss Sophia A. Peabody./Boston,/Mass.

42. Elizabeth is referring to Charles Wentworth Upham, who was an ordained minister and important political figure in Massachusetts.

43. Elizabeth apparently attempted to translate Cervantes's work into English.

44. Dated by association to Nathaniel's letter dated March 11, 1851 (*CE* XVI 402) and by context: *House of Seven Gables* published 1851. MS marked "Aunt Ebe May 24, '52."

45. Dated by reference to Nathaniel Hawthorne's *The Wonder Book,* published in 1851. MS marked "[Louisa Hathorne] [1852]." Added [the Coles' granddaughter] and [muslin] for clarity. Paragraph 1, sentence 2: *You* emended to [Yes]; sentence 16: Elizabeth canceled one letter between "Jane" and "saw." Paragraph 2, sentence 5: Elizabeth interlined "steel."

46. Una and Julian had moved to Rock Ferry, across the Mersey River from Liverpool (*CE* XVII 119).

47. Miss Rawlins Pickman was probably a daughter of Benjamin Pickman Jr. (see Moore, *Salem* 242) and Sophia Peabody Hawthorne's aunt (see Wineapple 160 and Valenti 37).

48. Elizabeth was referring to her visit to Jeremiah Lee Mansion. Built in 1768, the late colonial Georgian mansion was the home of Colonel Jeremiah Lee, a wealthy ship owner and patriot. It is still open for tours today.

49. Manuscript, a transcription, shows the date 1852. The Hawthornes arrived in Liverpool in July 1853 (Miller 398). The letter's content supports a change in date. All paragraphs have been broken for legibility.

50. Elizabeth was referring to Elizabeth "Betsey" Carlton.

51. Louise Lander was a sculptor who socialized with the Hawthornes in Rome (see Wineapple, 302, 312–13, 452n).

52. By "the new book" Elizabeth was referring to Nathaniel Hawthorne's *The Marble Faun,* published in England as *Transformation* by Smith, Elder, and Company and in the United States as *The Marble Faun* by Ticknor and Fields (*CE* XVII 94).

53. Una had malaria from October 1858 to May 1859 (see Miller, 438–41).

54. Elizabeth is again referring to *The Marble Faun.*

55. Elizabeth was probably referring to Isaiah Thornton Williams, attorney and Swedenborgian.

56. The Connecticut River flows south through Massachusetts to its southernmost point, Springfield. "Mount Holyoke" may refer to Holyoke, also near Springfield.

57. Dated by reference to Thoreau, who died May 6, 1862. Sentence 30: *objectable* emended to [objectionable]. MS marked "(Written to Robert Manning)."

58. Dinah Maria Mulock Craik was a British author.

59. *John Halifax, Gentleman* was a highly successful novel written by Dinah Craik, 1856.

60. Dated by reference to "Elsie Venner," published in *Atlantic Monthly*, December 1859, as "The Professor's Story" and reviewed as "Elsie Venner" in *Living Age*, December 1861.

61. *St. Ronan's Well* and *Guy Mannering* were novels written by Walter Scott in 1815 and 1827, respectively.

62. Dated by reference to "Elsie Venner."

63. Dated by reference to Julian's schooling with Frank Sanborn (see Bassan 26–27).

64. Paragraph 1, sentence 12: [In it] added for clarity.

65. Mrs. Burchstead was a neighbor; *Mademoiselle Mori: A Tale of Modern Rome* is a novel by Margaret Roberts.

66. Dated by reference to *Harper's Weekly* for March 15, featuring an article on Ambrose E. Burnside, commander of the Army of the Potomac. Sentence 1: "March is" emended to March [15].

67. "Mistress and Maid: A Household Story" was written by Dinah Maria Mulock Craik and published in book form by Richmond publisher West and Johnston in 1864.

68. *Why Paul Ferroll Killed His Wife* was written by Caroline Clive and published in 1860. Dated by reference to *Mistress and Maid*, published serially in *Living Age*, 1862.

69. Dated by reference to Hawthorne's "Leamington Spa," published in *Atlantic Monthly* in 1862, and to George Eliot's *Romola*, published serially in *Harper's* beginning in 1862.

70. Elizabeth is probably referring to Charles Reade's *Hard Cash*, 1863.

71. Dated by reference to Reade's *Hard Cash*, published serially in *Harper's Weekly*, 1863.

72. William Lowndes Yancey, of Alabama, was a famous orator and secessionist.

73. Elizabeth is referring to William Napier's *History of the War in the Peninsula*, 6 vols., 1828–1840.

74. Bayard Taylor published *Hannah Thurston: A Story of American Life* in 1863.

75. Elizabeth is referring to attending her brother Nathaniel's funeral.

76. Sentence 11: *Holme's* emended to [Holmes']; [to improve] added for clarity.

77. Adelaide Proctor was a nineteenth-century English poet. Dated by publication of "Enoch Arden."

78. Nathaniel had arranged for $180 per year to be sent to Elizabeth from his estate (see Wineapple 372).

79. Dated by reference to Nathaniel's death.

80. Dated by letter Number 51 to Una, following. Paragraph 1, sentence 1: *you* emended to you[r]. Paragraph 2, sentence 1: [without] added for clarity.

81. Samuel Daniel was a Renaissance poet, who wrote his *History of the Civil Wars* in 1604.

82. "The Battle of Agincourt" was written by Elizabethan sonneteer Michael Drayton in 1627.

83. Elizabeth is referring to William Browne.

84. Paragraph 2, sentence 2: [illegible] emended to [removed]; sentence 9: comma added at Agincourt[,] for clarity.

85. British author Wilkie Collins's *Armadale* was serialized in *Harper's* beginning in December 1864; *Dead Secret,* in 1857; *No Name,* in 1862.

86. Magdalen is the name of the protagonist in *No Name.* Lizzie Hexam is the protagonist in Dickens's *Our Mutual Friend.* Gail Hamilton is the pseudonym of Mary Dodge, an acquaintance of Elizabeth's.

87. Dated by publication of *A New Atmosphere.* Paragraph 1, sentence 1: *you* emended to you[r].

88. Abbie was the Coles' granddaughter.

89. *The Sparrowgrass Papers; or Living in the Country* was written by Frederick Cozzens, and published in 1856. It was a series of humorous sketches about the misadventures of a city man who purchases and moves into a rural home.

90. Frances Power Cobbe (1822–1904) was a British feminist and social and political activist.

91. Paragraph 3, sentence 2: words wiped and overwritten.

92. *Living Age* (in its early years titled *Littell's Living Age*) was published from 1844 to 1900. It was an all-reprint magazine that published fiction, essays, and verse from magazines published abroad.

93. Dated by evacuation of Charleston, February 1865, in advance of Union forces led by General Sherman.

94. Paragraph 3, sentence 4: [not] added for clarity; sentence 5: *composing* emended to [confusing]; sentence 6: *Nigelow's* emended to [Ingelow's].

95. Dated by presumption of Nathaniel's recent death. Second letter: "precious . . . EMH" written above heading and salutation, perpendicular to text.

96. Paragraph 2, sentence 3: [as] added for clarity.

97. These are two novels by Dinah Maria Mullock Craik and Anthony Trollope, respectively.

98. Dated by reference to Una's studies.

99. The *New York Weekly Review* announced that Sophia had authorized William Pike to write Nathaniel's biography. Elizabeth enclosed a clipping.

100. Dated by similarity to letter dated February 22, 1867. Address: Miss Una Hawthorne/Concord. Paragraphs 3–5 written on verso.

101. A more common name for the genus Trientalis is "starflower."

102. Elizabeth probably meant "clout," a piece of fabric.

103. Dated by Hawthorne-Higginson engagement. MS marked "(Addressed to Robert Manning, and dated by him May, 1867)."

104. The novel *All for Greed* was written by Baroness Marie Pauline Rose Blaze de Bury; *Phineas Finn* was written by English writer Anthony Trollope.

105. Dated by reference to late cat and to upcoming journey to Germany, made in autumn of 1868 (Loggins 304). Paragraph 2, sentence 3: [living] added. MS marked "(Addressed to MM)."

106. Indeed, the Franco-Prussian War did come about, 1870–1871.

107. Dated by reference to upcoming trip.

108. Sentence 15: [the] added.

109. A "Copperhead" was a northerner sympathizing with the South.

110. Dated by reference to previous letter.

111. By "and nothing else" Elizabeth meant that women wore hats rather than bonnets.

112. Dated by reference to departure for Germany, which Loggins sets at 1868 (304).

113. The words "Sober to toil, and valiant to fight" are a reference to Nathaniel Hawthorne's short story "The Maypole of Merrymount."

114. Dated by reference to Una's broken engagement. Paragraph 1, sentence 9: [who] added for clarity. Paragraph 4, sentence 3: [it] added for clarity.

115. Madame Henriette Sontag was a famous German operatic and concert soprano.

116. The Forresters were relatives on the Hawthorne side.

117. Sidney Smith and Richard Whately were well-respected nineteenth-century Anglican churchmen.

118. Eugenie de Guérin was a nineteenth-century French writer and mystic.

119. Paragraph 1, sentence 2: *Tenessee* emended to [Tennessee].

120. Mary Albertina Amelung, known as "Minnie," was Julian Hawthorne's fiancée.

121. Thomas Winthrop Coit's *Puritanism, or a Churchman's Defence against its Aspersions, by an Appeal to its own History* was published in 1845.

122. Harriet Beecher Stowe's "The True Story of Lady Byron's Life" was published in the *Atlantic Monthly* in September 1869. In this response to a memoir by Lord Byron's mistress, the Countess Guiccioli, Stowe addresses rumors of incest between Byron and his half sister.

123. Charles Sumner was a U.S. Senator and an opponent of slavery.

124. Dated by a previous letter. Paragraph 3, sentences 1, 11, 12, 14: *Bryon* emended to [Byron]; sentences 10, 11: *can't* emended to [cant].

125. Rebecca Dodge Burnham Manning was the wife of Elizabeth's late uncle Robert.

126. Elizabeth refers to a story about Pope Pius IX's alleged jilting of a woman before taking holy orders.

127. The English man of letters Henry Crabb Robinson kept a detailed diary throughout most of his life. His *Diary, Reminiscences, and Correspondence of Henry Crabb Robinson* was published in 1869.

128. Dated by Robert Manning. Paragraph 1, sentence 25: *soother* emended to [soothe]. Paragraph 1, sentence 41: [,] added for clarity. Paragraph 2, sentence 2: *you*

emended to [your]. Paragraph 3, sentence 15: *woman* emended to [women]. Paragraph 5, sentence 2: *his* emended to [he]; Sentence 8: [be] added for clarity. MS marked "(March 6, 1870—: RM)."

129. Hamilton's "Battle of the Books" was published in *Punchinello,* April 16, 1870.

130. Dated by reference to the Hawthornes' visit to the Bennocks, which Miller sets at 1870 (525), and by Hamilton's publication.

131. Elizabeth is referring to "anything more serious" in the war.

132. The emperor referred to is Napoleon III.

133. Dated by onset of the Franco-Prussian War. MS marked "1870."

134. Paragraph 2, sentence 1: *you* emended to [your]. Dated by context.

135. Paragraph 2, sentence 1: *it* emended to [It].

136. William Symmes, a childhood friend of Nathaniel Hawthorne, was said to be a source of the accounts of Nathaniel's youth.

137. The Mannings had four daughters and five sons in 1808, but one of the daughters would have been the children's mother, thus, not an aunt.

138. Dated by James T. Fields. MS marked "This letter is postmarked Salem, December 12th/70. J. T. F."

139. Dated by association with other letters to Fields.

140. Dated by reference to wrist injury. "I wish you all a happy new year" written above heading.

141. Mary Russell Mitford was an English novelist and dramatist.

142. Paragraph 6, sentence 1: [think] added for clarity.

143. Dated by reference to wrist injury and to Elizabeth's sixty-ninth birthday.

144. Paragraph 1, sentence 3: *Mr. Dike* emended to Mr[s]. Dike; sentence 7: *beleive* emended to [believe]. Paragraph 4, sentence 3: *say* emended to [saw].

145. Elizabeth was referring to their mother Sophia's death.

146. Dated by reference to death of Sophia Peabody Hawthorne, February 26, 1871.

147. The typist, either Richard C. Manning or Marylou Brichmore from the Phillips Library, made this parenthetical note. Content suggests that the material intentionally excised appeared on the back of the leaf, not on the front as the typist's note suggests.

148. Dated by reference to wrist injury and to Una and Rose's life apparently without their mother, who died in February of 1871. Paragraph 2, sentence 12: [showed] added for clarity.

149. The *Alabama* was a British-built commerce-raiding ship used by the Confederacy.

150. Dated by Robert Manning. Paragraph 2, sentence 8: *dould* emended to [could]. Paragraph 3, sentence 2: *tis* emended to [this]; sentence 6: *Hawthorne's* emended to [Hawthornes]; sentence 16: *utter by* emended to [utterly]. Paragraph 4, sentence 3: *no* emended to no[t]; sentence 13: *spperior* emended to [superior]; sentence 16: [.] added for clarity. MS marked "(June 30, 1871: RM)."

151. The home of Ralph Waldo Emerson and his wife, Lidian, burned in 1872 but was later rebuilt.

152. Paragraph 3, sentence 1: *Lorings* emended to [Loring's]; sentence 25: "see . . . happiness" written above paragraph one perpendicular to existing text.

153. Postscript appears above salutation.

154. Originally reading January 6th, the heading was changed to April per the content and Robert Manning's note. Paragraph 2, sentence 12: [think] added for clarity. MS marked "(RM marked this April? 6th 1873)."

155. That is, demands that might prove financially unfavorable to the rich.

156. Joseph Arch was a British farm laborer and prominent union organizer who later became a Member of Parliament. He founded the National Agricultural Labourers' Union in 1872.

157. Dated by reference to Julian Hawthorne's 1873 novel, *Bressant.*

158. Pope Pius IX, born Giovanni Maria Mastai-Ferretti, died on February 7, 1878, after having the longest reign of any Pope before him, thirty-one years and seven months. He was succeeded by Pope Leo XIII.

159. Paragraph 1, sentence 11: ["] added for uniformity. Paragraph 2, sentence 7: *newspapers* emended to newspapers['].

160. Dated by previous letter to Una, April 11, 1876. Paragraph 2, sentence 1: [a convent] added for clarity.

161. Dated by reference to the feuding over Nathaniel's letters, which Loggins sets at 1876 (310). Paragraph 3 broken for legibility; sentence 4:*ahd* emended to [had]; sentence 9: *alikeness* emended to [a likeness]. Paragraph 5, sentence 3: *Cole* emended to [Cole's].

162. The words in quotation marks come from Sir Walter Scott's poem "Nora's Vow."

163. Sentence 15: *att attentive* emended to [attentive].

164. The words in parentheses are the typist's note.

165. Elizabeth is referring to Elizabeth Palmer Peabody.

166. Dated by reference to Tiger, born July 1, 1876. Paragraph 5, sentence 1: *his* emended to [he]. MS marked "(1876: RBM—postmarked: Jan. 18)."

167. Dated by Robert Manning. MS marked "(Postmarked: Feb. 8, 1877: RBM)." Paragraph 1, sentence 20: *Field's* emended to Field[s]'s. Paragraph 3, sentence 1: closing quotes added.

168. Webster died at sea, and soon after, Una entered the convent.

169. Dated by date of Albert Webster Jr.'s death, which Bassan sets at 1876 (114). Heading date was 1876. MS marked "(1877: RBM; corrected: RCM)."

170. Dated by Robert Manning. Paragraph 3, sentence 7: [has had] added for clarity. Paragraph 4, sentence 1: *men* emended to [me]; Sentence 7: *dose* emended to [done]. MS marked "(1877: RBM)."

171. Paragraph 1, sentence 8: ["] added for uniformity; sentence 18: develope emended to [develop]. MS marked "(Postmark: Dec. 13)."

172. Dated by marriage of George Eliot and John Cross, May 6, 1880.

173. Elizabeth was referring to James Garfield, who indeed became president in 1881.

174. Dated by Robert Manning and candidacy of Garfield. Paragraph 3, sentence 7: *was was* emended to [was]. Paragraph 4, sentence 2: *that* emended to [than]. MS marked "(1880:RBM)."

175. Hamilton criticized Fields's practice of paying men more than women for their writing.

176. Dated by Robert Manning. Paragraph 2, sentence 3: *of* emended to [or]. Paragraph 5, sentence 7: *usefullness* emended to [usefulness]; sentence 9: *who* emended to [whose]; *re* emended to [are]. Paragraph 7, sentence 6: *the* emended to [them]. MS marked "(Postmark: Dec 22; Dec 1880, RBM)."

177. It's possible that Elizabeth is referring to Mary Wilder White Foote Tileston, a local author (see Moore, *Salem*).

178. Elizabeth is referring to the fact that James Garfield, shot July 2, 1881, lived until September 19 while the nation debated his ability to govern.

179. Paragraph 1, sentence 8: *year* emended to [years]. Paragraph 2, sentence 6: *they they could* emended to [they could]. Paragraph 3, sentence 5: [I] added for clarity.

180. "The Legend of Ticonderoga" is a ghost story.

181. Dated by Robert Manning's note, by reference to New Year's, and by William Dean Howells' *A Modern Instance,* serialized in *The Century* from December 1881 to October 1882. Paragraph 1, sentence 14: [you] added for clarity; sentence 17: *"Inverawe {?} of {?} Ticonderoga"* emended to "[Inverawe of Ticonderoga]." MS Marked "(RBM: Cousin Elisabeth's last letter to us)."

Works Cited

Bassan, Maurice. *Hawthorne's Son: The Life and Literary Career of Julian Hawthorne.* Columbus: Ohio State UP, 1970.

Baym, Nina. "Nathaniel Hawthorne and His Mother: A Biographical Speculation." *American Literature* 54 (1982): 1–27.

Cantwell, Robert. *Nathaniel Hawthorne: The American Years.* New York: Octagon, 1971.

Centenary Edition of the Works of Nathaniel Hawthorne: Volume XV, The Letters, 1813–1843. Ed. Thomas Woodson, L. Neal Smith, and Norman Holmes Pearson. Columbus: Ohio State UP, 1984.

Conway, Moncure D. *The Life of Nathaniel Hawthorne.* London: Walter Scott, 1895.

Decker, William Merrill. *Epistolary Practices: Letter Writing in America before Telecommunications.* Chapel Hill: U of North Carolina P, 1998.

Erlich, Gloria C. *Family Themes in Hawthorne's Fiction: The Tenacious Web.* New Brunswick, NJ: Rutgers UP, 1984.

Hamilton, John C. *The Life of Alexander Hamilton.* New York: Halsted and Voorhees, 1831.

Hartog, Hendrik. "Lawyering, Husbands' Rights, and 'the Unwritten Law' in Nineteenth-Century America." *Journal of American History* 84 (1997): 67–96.

Hawthorne, Edith Garrigues, ed. *The Memoirs of Julian Hawthorne.* New York: Macmillan, 1938.

Hawthorne, Elizabeth Manning. Letters to James T. Fields. November 6, 1865–January 28, 1871. Hawthorne Family Papers. Boston Public Library.

——. Letters to Una Hawthorne. December 9, 1861–June 2, 1870. Hawthorne Family Papers. Bancroft Library, University of California–Berkeley.

——. Letters to Maria Manning, Rebecca Manning, Robert Manning, and Richard Manning. 1864–1883. Hawthorne Family Papers. Peabody Essex Museum, Salem, MA.

——. Letters to Priscilla Manning Dike, Elizabeth Clarke Manning Hawthorne, Mary Manning, Richard Manning, and Robert Manning. Manning-Hawthorne Papers. Bowdoin College Library, Brunswick, ME.

——. Letters to Una Hawthorne. Huntington Library, San Marino, CA.

——. Letters to Julian Hawthorne, Nathaniel Hawthorne, Rose Hawthorne, Una Hawthorne, Miriam Manning Elizabeth Palmer Peabody, and Sophia Peabody. Berg Collection, New York Public Library.

——. Letters to Una Hawthorne. Beinecke Rare Book and Manuscript Library, Yale University, New Haven, CT.

Hawthorne, Julian. "My Aunt Elizabeth Hawthorne: A Character Sketch from the Memoirs of Julian Hawthorne, Presented by Edith Garrigues Hawthorne." Hawthorne Family Papers. Bancroft Library, University of California, Berkeley.

——. *Nathaniel Hawthorne and His Wife.* 2 vols. Boston: Houghton Mifflin, 1884.

Hawthorne, Manning. "Aunt Ebe: Some Letters of Elizabeth M. Hawthorne." *New England Quarterly* 20 (1947): 215–31.

——. "Maria Louisa Hawthorne." *Essex Institute Historical Collections* 75 (1931): 103–34.

Hawthorne, Nathaniel. *The House of the Seven Gables.* With an Afterword by Cathy N. Davidson. New York: Signet, 1990.

——. Hawthorne's First Diary. Ed. Samuel T. Pickard. Boston, 1897.

Howe, M. A. De Wolfe. *Memories of a Hostess.* 1922. New York: Arno, 1974.

Hull, Raymona. "'Aunt Ebe,' Critic of Books and Their Writers." *The Nathaniel Hawthorne Journal 1978*: 17–37.

Lathrop, Rose Hawthorne. *Memories of Hawthorne.* 1897. Boston: AMS Press, 1969.

Loggins, Vernon. *The Hawthornes: The Story of Seven Generations of an American Family.* New York: Columbia UP, 1951.

Miller, Edwin Haviland. *'Salem Is My Dwelling Place': A Life of Nathaniel Hawthorne.* Iowa City: U of Iowa P, 1991.

Moore, Margaret B. "Elizabeth Manning Hawthorne: Nathaniel's Enigmatic Sister." *Nathaniel Hawthorne Journal* 20 (1994): 1–9.

——. *The Salem World of Nathaniel Hawthorne.* Columbia: U of Missouri P, 1998.

Peabody, Elizabeth Palmer. *Letters of Elizabeth Palmer Peabody: American Renaissance Woman.* Ed. Bruce Ronda. Middletown, CT: Wesleyan UP, 1984.

Peter Parley's Universal History on the Basis of Geography. 1837.

Porter, Charles. Introduction. *Yale French Studies* 71 (1986): 1–14.

Stanbrough, Jane. "Elizabeth Manning Hawthorne." *American Women Writers: A Critical Reference Guide from Colonial Times to the Present.* 4 vols. Ed. Lina Mainiero and Langdon Lynne Faust. New York: Ungar, 1979–1982.

Stewart, Randall. *Nathaniel Hawthorne: A Biography.* New Haven, CT: Yale UP, 1948.

Tanselle, G. Thomas. *A Rationale of Textual Criticism.* Philadelphia: U of Pennsylvania P, 1989.

Turner, Arlin. *Hawthorne as Editor: Selections from His Writings in the American Magazine of Useful and Entertaining Knowledge.* University, LA: Louisiana State UP, 1941.

——. *Nathaniel Hawthorne: A Biography.* New York: Oxford UP, 1980.

Valenti, Patricia Dunlavy. *Sophia Peabody Hawthorne: A Life, Volume 1, 1809–1847.* Columbia: U of Missouri P, 2004.

Van Doren, Mark. *Nathaniel Hawthorne.* New York: Sloane, 1949.

Walsh, James. "A Note as to the Authorship of *Peter Parley's Universal History.*" *American Catholic Quarterly* 43 (1918): 519–21.

Wineapple, Brenda. *Hawthorne: A Life.* New York: Knopf, 2003.

Woodberry, George Edward. *Nathaniel Hawthorne.* 1902. Detroit: Gale Research, 1967.

Woodson, Thomas. Introduction. *Centenary Edition of the Works of Nathaniel Hawthorne: Volume XV, The Letters, 1813–1843.* Ed. Thomas Woodson, L. Neal Smith, and Norman Holmes Pearson. Columbus: Ohio State UP, 1984.

Young, Philip. *Hawthorne's Secret: An Untold Tale.* Boston: Godine, 1984.

Manuscript Credits

The following libraries have generously made their Elizabeth Manning Hawthorne materials available for study and granted permission to reproduce them here. Excepted is the Beinecke Library, which did not require that permission be requested.

Hawthorne Family Papers
72/236 Z-Folder 14-Carton 2
Courtesy of The Library
Bancroft Library, University of California, Berkeley

The Yale Collection of American Literature
Beinecke Rare Book and Manuscript Library, Yale University

Boston Public Library
Rare Books Department

Manning Hawthorne Collection [M223]
George J. Mitchell Department of Special Collections and Archives
Bowdoin College Library

These items are reproduced by permission of
The Huntington Library, San Marino, California:
HM 42640, 42652, 42659

New York Public Library
Berg Collection of English and American Literature
Astor, Lenox, and Tilden Foundations

Phillips Library, Peabody-Essex Museum, Salem, Mass.
Reel #1, Microfilm # 212

Index